REAL-TIME BUSINESS SYSTEMS

ROBERT V. HEAD

MANAGER,
ADVANCED BUSINESS SYSTEMS
TOUCHE, ROSS, BAILEY AND SMART
LOS ANGELES

HOLT, RINEHART AND WINSTON, INC.

NEW YORK   CHICAGO   SAN FRANCISCO   TORONTO   LONDON

August, 1965

February, 1966

Library of Congress Catalog Card Number: 64-23741

23529-0114

Printed in the United States of America

To my colleagues from
ERMA, SABRE, and ACCESS

PREFACE

NOT SO MANY years back, when I was directing a somewhat embattled group of programmers in installing the first deposit accounting system to employ magnetic ink (it wasn't called MICR then), several of us made a solemn vow never to become involved in any similar project. Once is enough, we felt, to endure the eighteen-hour days, the midnight calls, and all the other distressing concomitants of a major system effort, particularly when the system is "advanced" from the standpoint of either application or technological innovation. That was two systems ago. In the meantime, the nature of the implementation job has not really changed very much.

It is this apparent immutability of the task of making a commercial data processing system operational which impelled me to attempt this book. It seems to me important to try to convey, by some means other than experience, at least a few of the constructive steps and pitfalls in system development that have become familiar to those who live through them. If I have failed to describe this process, I hope that this is attributable to my inarticulateness rather than to qualities inherent in the system development task. Should the process itself prove incapable of description, this bodes ill for the future of commercial data processing. For we in this field have already begun a great leap forward in system complexity, an advance for which we are in many respects ill prepared.

I have chosen to regard the real-time system as consisting of at least two subsystems: the equipment, or hardware, subsystem and the program, or software, subsystem. Often, there will be more than one logically self-sufficient piece of equipment that can be described as a subsystem; and there may, and usually will, be several logically separated and individually fabricated collections of programs that deserve to be called software subsystems.

Chapter 1 traces the evolution of real-time systems, identifies

vii

major classes of such systems, and differentiates these systems from their non-real-time predecessors. Chapter 2 is concerned mainly with design of the equipment subsystems; and the remainder of the book, with the development of the program subsystems.

Chapters 3 and 4, in combination with Chapter 2, present some general notions about planning and control of the system development effort. Chapters 5 through 8 deal with the specifics of setting up the group of computer professionals and novices needed to produce an operational system, and the final four chapters of the book are devoted to the problems that can be expected to arise during various phases of system development.

I am indebted to the IBM Systems Research Institute for the time I was able to spend there, pondering what has been happening in this volatile data processing field and speculating about what is to come.

R. V. H.

Los Angeles, August 1964

CONTENTS

LIST OF FIGURES

I

INTRODUCTION

WHY REAL-TIME SYSTEMS ARE DIFFERENT | 1

1.1 WHAT ARE REAL-TIME SYSTEMS?

THE DEFINITIONS of "real-time operation" in the glossaries of literature on the digital computer are very similar to the one included in the Glossary of this book: "Paralleling data processing with a physical process in such a fashion that the results of the data processing are immediately useful to the physical operation." Essentially this definition singles out the feedback characteristic of a real-time system as the predominant one by requiring that system results be available in sufficient time to affect the external process. Strictly speaking, according to this definition, production of a monthly payroll by a computer could be viewed as "real time," since "results" in the form of salary checks are available in time to be "immediately useful" to the employees who require compensation for their past month's labor.

If we wish to exclude such commonly accepted and relatively routine data processing operations as payroll preparation, it is necessary to differentiate real-time processing from this kind of cyclical processing, and this is exactly what many analysts do in trying to arrive at a working definition of a real-time system. In payroll processing, timecards for the pay period are accumulated into batches that, at the end of the period, are sorted into employee number sequence and passed against a master file containing each employee's pay rate, social security information, and tax status. The result of this processing is an updated master file and a set of newly prepared salary checks. This processing sequence based on the accumulation and batching of transactions can be contrasted to the operation of a real-time system in which processing of information occurs almost as soon as the need for the processing becomes evident. A real-time airline reservation system employs this approach, in that each request for space and each booking of a passenger is transmitted to the computer for immediate recording, while the passenger is still on the phone talking to the sales agent. In this way, the Seat Inventory Records for the airline's flights are kept current. In fact, it was in an effort to avoid the accumulation and batching of such input that the airlines first became interested in the development of real-time data processing systems.

Unfortunately, however, this attempt at definition by contrasting batch processing to real time, while instructive, would rule out some systems that appear to be genuinely real time to most observers. The Air Force's Semiautomatic Ground Environment (SAGE) System, for example, developed to control a nationwide surveillance network for detection of enemy aircraft, employs a form of "batch" processing to accomplish its critical mission. Incoming data from radar sets, ground observers, picket ships, and other sources are accumulated on a high-speed magnetic drum before being accepted into the main memory of the SAGE computer. Every few seconds the contents of this drum are read into the main computer memory and a new processing cycle is begun. Although this is admittedly a rather special form of batch processing, it is batch processing nevertheless.

To augment our confusion, it must be noted at this point that many non-real-time systems permit the immediate collection of data at the source but defer the processing of the data until batches have been accumulated. In this category are plant data collection systems of the IBM 357 variety, which employ badge and tag readers to scan workers' identification badges and job tickets. Many of these systems punch out into cards at the processor site the information they collect. The punched cards may or may not be entered into the computer for immediate processing, depending upon the urgency of the requirement for an updated file. Thus, at least some of these data collection systems may be described as "nonbatch" (or real time) at the source but "batch" at the central collection point.

Perhaps, then, the amount of elapsed *time to complete a transaction* is really the most important aspect of a real-time system. It takes the monthly payroll system up to thirty days to respond to the input data of hours worked, whereas batch processing in the SAGE system is such that it takes only seconds to react to its input information. Probably the most useful way to look at real-time computer systems, and the point of view adhered to in this book, is that they must satisfy some reasonable criterion of "immediacy" in providing a response, regardless of whether the input is batched in some way or is in fact processed as soon as received.

If one had to be quite arbitrary in arriving at his definition of a real-time system, he might begin by excluding all systems in which a response cycle of a day or more is tolerable and by examining closely those operating on a cycle of less than one day. If he goes on from there to rule out all those systems whose cycles are greater than one hour or so, he will still end up with a rather sizable collection of systems to dignify with the "real-time" appellation.

We shall discover in Chapter 2 that there is a wide range of complexity among presently existing real-time systems and that system availability, in terms of the period over which the system must be "up" to provide a response and of the time it takes to generate a response, is a factor having a great deal to do with this complexity. In any case, let us here accept as an important part of a working definition that there are many degrees in real-time processing and that the longer it takes the system to react or respond to an input the less real time it becomes, for all practical purposes, in evaluating its complexity and difficulty of installation.

A real-time system may be referred to by other names, which emphasize a particular facet of the system and overlap to some extent any definition of real time. Such terms as "online system" and "control system" are in current usage and, like "real-time system," cover wide variances in the degree to which the systems they describe are on-line and in the scope of their control over noncomputer processes and procedures. In most of these cases, analysis will reveal that such systems should be judged according to their responsiveness to their external environment, in the manner we have been discussing.

1.2 EVOLUTION OF REAL-TIME SYSTEMS

The real-time "family tree" contains two main branches, one devoted to scientific computation and the other engaged in commercial, file-oriented data processing. From its earliest days the history of the digital computer has been marked by this cleavage between the scientific and the commercial realms. Real-time systems may be meaningfully thought of as a major evolutionary step for both the scientific and the data processing specialties. As Figure 1.1 shows, the field can be said to be

	SCIENTIFIC	COMMERCIAL
PUNCHED CARD ERA	CARD PROGRAMMED CALCULATOR	ELECTRIC ACCOUNTING MACHINES
COMPUTER ERA	IBM 704/7094 FAMILY	IBM 705/7080 FAMILY
REAL—TIME ERA	REMOTE COMPUTING AND TIME—SHARED SYSTEMS EXAMPLE: MIT SYSTEMS	FILE—ORIENTED DATA PROCESSING SYSTEMS EXAMPLE: SABRE SYSTEM

FIGURE 1.1.   HISTORY OF AUTOMATIC
COMPUTATION.

entering the third "era" of automatic computation and one that is likely to be as radically different from the preceding computer era as was the advent of the stored-program computer itself, which signaled the end of the punched card era. Let us survey briefly the challenges and the accomplishments each of these three major eras provided.

The Punched Card Era

Business applications predominated during the punched card period, despite early efforts to perform scientific calculations with such machines as IBM's card programmed calculator (CPC). The electric accounting machines (EAM) were specialized as to function, and this feature enabled an equipment salesman to propose a modular system consisting of a grouping of these specialized machines in just the right mix to perform the required accounting jobs with the use of punched cards. Figure 1.2 shows a generalized data flow in such an EAM application, with each operation in the sequence, from keypunching of source data into tabulating cards to final report preparation, performed by a separate machine or a group of machines.

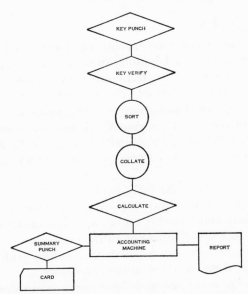

FIGURE 1.2.   EAM SYSTEM DATA FLOW.

The job of the system designer during this era has been aptly described as one of building up a system using the equivalent of a kit of erector-set parts.[1] It was not too difficult to design a system in those days, given a knowledge of volumes and an equipment price list, since the function to be performed by each erector-set part was fairly obvious. And the consequences

1 J. A. Haddad, Remarks at IBM Systems Research Institute, October, 1962.

of a wrong guess were not too severe. System design flaws could almost always be remedied by bringing in another key-punch or two or adding a few more counters to an accounting machine. Not that inadequate system analysis was condoned any more in the punched card era than it is today, or that talented system designers were not sought after. There were poorly designed EAM installations and there were excellent ones. The point is that there was little possibility of developing a system with design inadequacies that could not, once discovered, be fairly readily overcome.

The Computer Era

Because the electric accounting machines could not perform the complex and laborious computations demanded by the accelerated pace of our technology during World War II, the computer era came about. The idea of a stored program, the key concept in digital computer development, is usually attributed to the late John von Neumann, whose interest in automatic calculation led him and his colleagues at Princeton University to design a stored program computer for the United States Army.

From this and similar early work done elsewhere evolved the first commercially available stored program computers, notably Eckert and Mauchly's UNIVAC I and IBM's 700 series in the early 1950's. And at this point the twin branches of scientific computation and commercial data processing both began a rapid, profound, and truly astonishing expansion.

Now, so far as the system designer was concerned, the computer manufacturers were offering not an erector-set kit of modular components but instead a *single* general-purpose computer like that represented in Figure 1.3. And this processor had to be instructed in minute detail, by a program stored inside itself, how to perform the operations previously wired into the plugboard of each special-purpose electric accounting machine. But once these instructions, or program steps, had been written, tested, and entered into the computer's memory, the speed and flexibility of this system far surpassed all previously conceived machines. In a way, this period could more aptly be called the era of the programmer—in tribute to the person who carried out the system design by writing the series of instruction steps which, when assembled, formed the program the computer would follow.

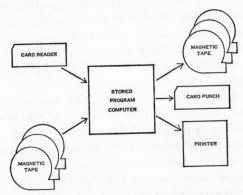

FIGURE 1.3. GENERAL-PURPOSE COMPUTER SYSTEM.

The transition from EAM to stored-program computer was a painful one for many who had to go through it. Users of the new systems often experienced costly delays in installation, during which they discovered that designing a series of programs was not nearly so simple as was the wiring of tabulating equipment. Neither were the consequences of a faulty design so readily remedied. Often the specialists in EAM processing, who had made their living wiring the plugboards and supervising the operators of the tabulating machines, found themselves unable to make the transition to the new era by mastering the programmer's skills.

However, for those organizations which could avoid the shoals of computer system design and installation and for those technicians who could make themselves adept at programming, both the challenges and the rewards were considerable. There were now answers to many questions for which solutions had never before been available in all the thousands of years of development of scientific and mathematical knowledge. And business accounting jobs that had been growing to dangerous dimensions and taking on a complexity not amenable to control by EAM systems could now be brought back under rein. To illustrate, the number of demand deposit accounts in United States banks rose from 27 million to 47 million in the period from 1939 to 1952, and the number of checks written against them from 3.5 billion to almost 8 billion. By 1957 United States citizens were writing checks at the rate of 12 billion a year, and projections indicate that the figure will jump to beyond 22 billion by 1970.[2]

The rapid development of scientific computation is reflected in the evolution, within ten years, of the IBM product line commencing with the model 701 computer, with a memory access time of 12 microseconds and a memory size of 2048 words, through models 704, 709, 7090, and 7094, the last with a memory access speed more than six times as fast as the 701 and a memory size in excess of 32,000 words.[3] A parallel advancement took place in the engineering and production of computers for business applications, which saw a progression from the early IBM 702, with its cathode-ray tube memory, up to the present-day 7080 equipment, with high-capacity, fast-access magnetic core memory.

The Real-Time Era

Although real-time systems have been operating successfully for several years, it would not be amiss to refer to the 1960's as witnessing the true dawn of the real-time era. It has been only within the early 1960's that significant nonmilitary interest in real-time problem solutions, coupled with availability

---

[2] R. S. Aldom, A. B. Purdey, R. T. Schneider, and H. E. Whittingham, Jr., *Automation in Banking*, p. 13. New Brunswick, N. J.: Rutgers University Press, 1963.

[3] A note of caution should be voiced here against overreliance on rated speeds and capacities without paying due heed to the way in which the machines may be programmed or the uses to which they will be put. A computer can win a "horsepower" race and still be uneconomical and unsuitable for many applications. Today, knowledgable users are equally interested in the range and power of the preprogrammed software packages the manufacturer will deliver along with his machine.

of equipment well adapted to real-time processing, has encouraged rapid development of such systems. Before this recent emphasis, one could find military examples of operational real-time systems such as SAGE. Other than this, only the transportation field had encouraged development of early real-time airline reservation systems by Teleregister and Remington Rand during the 1950's. Many of the airlines are, in fact, installing "second generation" real-time systems today.[4]

But only in the very recent past has there been a combination of economically attractive communication tariffs and data processing equipment well suited to real-time applications. Examples of such equipment innovations are:

Computers suitable for real-time needs. Several computers that fulfill the requirements of real-time processing are currently available. These embody a number of useful hardware refinements, including:

- Interrupt feature, which permits the normal processing sequence to be interrupted to give priority to externally generated entries
- Memory protection, which assures that data and programs in the computer memory will not be destroyed by errors in the execution of other unrelated routines
- Program read-in, which facilitates the reading-in from ex-external storage of programs needed to process particular entries but for which the demand is not sufficient to warrant their being retained in main memory at all times

Random-access file storage. This is plentifully available today in several forms—drum, disk, card, film—at several speeds and in many different sizes and cost categories.

Job-oriented terminals. The IBM 1060 banking terminal and 1003 airline reservations agent set are examples of this. In addition, more general input/output capability is available through such devices as the IBM 1050 typewriter terminal as well as standard teletype equipment.

These equipment breakthroughs have come at a time when

---

4 "A Survey of Airline Reservation Systems," *Datamation*, June 1962, pp. 53-54.

many conventional computer systems are straining at their limits. Scientific installations have been experiencing severe delays in getting results back to their users, with what is described as slow "turnaround" time hampering effective use of high-salaried professional personnel and expensive equipment. And on the commercial side, management—having reaped the benefits of applying computers to such clerical operations as payroll, demand deposit accounting, and insurance premium billing—is now beginning to grasp the potentiality of the computer to aid in managerial control, in addition to taking care of the ever-growing burden of record keeping.

In many respects this dual need of the scientific and business communities for more powerful processing approaches is really the outgrowth of the tremendous success of the computer installations activated during the 1950's. For the computers, as tools of science and management, have yielded such significant benefits that they have come to be programmed to the boundaries of their capability, with still further power and capacity always demanded by their beneficiaries. This somewhat self-generated desire for more timely and sophisticated problem solutions has, in combination with newer and more versatile equipment, projected us squarely into the real-time era.

As may be seen from a glance at Figures 2.1 through 2.7 (Chapter 2), we have now come full circle in that the real-time era has equipped the system designer once again with his erector set of varied pieces of equipment that can be combined into a real-time system. But there has been no regression in the difficulty of making the components work smoothly in unison; rather, there has been progression. We have retained the complexities of the stored program computer and added to them by introducing real-time building blocks, each with its own stored program capability.

1.3 CLASSES OF REAL-TIME SYSTEMS

Because there is a substantial dichotomy between real-time systems of the scientific variety and those commonly referred to as commerical or business data processing systems, a few comments should be made here about some of the classes of real-time systems.

The Problem-Solving Scientific System

The problem-solving scientific system is pointed toward improved solutions of problems in the mathematical and the physical sciences. In such problems the emphasis is placed more on the computational speed and ability of the computer than on the speed and capacity of peripheral storage. Further, in the scientific world the computational requirements are not very repetitive. A program may, for instance, be written, tested, and run on a computer to obtain a particular answer to a specialized problem and then not be run again for a week, a month, perhaps never.

Basically, the real-time scientific system strives to do two things for the mathematicians and engineers who are both its programmers and its users.

1) It makes available equipment of the greatest power and speed obtainable. It is preferable to plan, through development of a real-time system, on having a number of users share one large processor on some reasonably equitable basis than to have each using department purchase a relatively small and limited computer for its exclusive use.

2) It reduces the turnaround time for each user. Because so many new programs are constantly being written in a scientific environment and so many "one-shot" problems are generated by the various scientific disciplines that use the computer, it is a formidable job to schedule work through the computing center—especially when all or some of the users are sending in their problems from remote locations. Often the scheduling bottleneck will be found not in the computer itself but in some peripheral device such as an overworked high-speed printer or punched-card-to-magnetic-tape converter.

Turnaround time is the amount of time elapsing between submission of a program to be tested or a problem to be run and the return of the processing results. Since turnaround time should desirably be in minutes or hours and since it must often be measured in days, those concerned with operation of scientific computing centers have developed a real-time approach known variously as "remote computing" or "time sharing" and having as its key objective reduction of turnaround time without sacrifice of the computational ability that a large, centrally available computer offers. Essentially the approach taken is one of bringing the computer to the user by providing him with a terminal that, in some respects, simulates the main computer's console. The user can then, hopefully, reduce his turnaround time by communicating directly with the computer via the terminal rather than through messengers and other human and machine intermediaries at the computing center. And because there will necessarily be many users and many terminals in such a system, the system is said to be time-shared, with a Control Program inside the computer allocating computer time to each user according to some scheduling algorithm that establishes priorities based on such criteria as type of problem, length of time required to run, and amount of time already used up. The IBM 7090 system at Massachusetts Institute of Technology is representative of this kind of approach to real-time scientific computation.[5]

The File-Oriented Data Processing System

The file-oriented data processing system, in contrast to the scientific system, is typified by relatively simple calculations, but these calculations must be performed again and again in the course of processing. The program steps required to post a savings deposit or withdrawal to a depositor's account are certainly not very intricate when compared with the computation required to solve a simultaneous linear equation. But thousands upon thousands of account balances must be posted daily, and each one involves some computing as well as reference to a file. So, in the commercial data processing system burdensome repetitive program steps must be executed, coupled with heavy throughput to file storage.

---

[5] F. J. Corbato, M. Merwin-Daggett, and R. C. Daley, "An Experimental Time-Sharing System," *Proceedings of the Spring Joint Computer Conference,* San Francisco, May 1962.

When reference is made throughout this book to "commercial" or "business" data processing systems, the aim is not to restrict the discussion to applications found only in private business organizations. In civil government as well as in the military establishment, there are vast data processing applications of the "commercial" variety. The check reconciliation procedures of the U. S. Treasury Department certainly qualify for this designation, as does computer maintenance of personnel records for members of the Armed Forces. The federal government is, in fact, the chief user of computers for "commercial" data processing.

The Process Control System

Use of computers to control industrial processes such as petroleum refining and papermaking represents an interesting and fairly well-developed bypath in digital computer technology. The chief goal of such a control system is process optimization in real time. It receives, as input, signals from flow transmitters, pressure transmitters, temperature transmitters, and so on. These provide information about feed composition, pressures, temperatures, and flow rates needed to calculate optimum levels of operation. In an open-loop control system, the computer provides the operator, by typewriter output or other display, with guides to safer and more efficient operation. In a closed-loop system, the computer itself orders the necessary corrections in the process, typing out feedback information for the operator's reference only.

Process control system technology has produced a methodology and a special literature of its own and is, therefore, excluded from the purview of this book. For comparison with other systems, a few salient features of process control systems can, however, be noted.

1) Process control systems have proved operationally feasible. Manufacturers of process control equipment have installed systems in a variety of industries and control environments over the past few years.

2) The central computer in such systems is smaller, as a rule, than in the other systems that have been described.

3) The systems are not file oriented, having little need for auxiliary storage.

4) There is usually provision for analog input and output. Temperature readings, pressure levels, and other information, are sensed by the system and converted to digital form for processing.

5) Programming requirements are rather unique. Unlike the problem-solving scientific system, the programs are not one-shot occurrences. And unlike the file-oriented commercial system, program preparation requires specialists highly trained in computer mathematics and in the nature of the process being controlled.

These characteristics may suggest possible explanations of why process control technology seems to have divorced itself somewhat from both the scientific and the commercial real-time specialties as we have defined them.

The Military Command and Control System

Bearing in mind the basic distinctions between scientific, commercial, and process control systems, it may be seen that "military system" as a classification is really a hybrid one. Such a system will be found to bear a kinship with one or more of the basic types just described, depending upon the kind of problem to which it is applied.

1.4 SCOPE OF THIS BOOK

There is a definite need for real-time systems of great capability in many different organizations. Airlines, railroads, newspapers, savings banks, stock brokerage firms, and insurance companies are but some of the enterprises in which intensive development of real-time systems has already begun. And indeed, there seem to be few barriers to carrying out even the most sophisticated system design today, at least so far as the equipment is concerned.

Unfortunately the process of going from initial system design to operational status does involve some rather substantial difficulties. The mere fact that a system *can,* if properly programmed, exploit today's equipment in a real-time mode of operation does not necessarily mean that the system design will ever become operational. In real-time system development, there is many a slip twixt the system-concept cup and the operational-system lip.

The following chapters will endeavor to develop principles and methods that apply to installation of a real-time system. They will be concerned with both the managerial and the technical problems that arise in connection with this task of *integrating the system into its operational environment.* These problems will be examined within the tacitly understood context of a file-oriented real-time data processing system, although references will occasionally be made to other classes of real-time systems. The primary emphasis will be placed on this class of system because:

1) The interest and background of the author lie within the business field.

2) The scientific system, producing as it does a relatively unplanned mix of one-shot problems, does not present system integration difficulties of the scope exhibited by commercial systems. In a sense the scientific system is a program-as-you-go system, whereas the business system must be programmed and tested *before* any productive work can be performed on it. For this reason a System Integration Team of the kind envisioned in this book would probably not be needed to install a real-time scientific system or, if prudence dictates that such a group be established, it would no doubt be a relatively small one with more manageable organization, control, and communication problems.

In considering the functions to be performed by those responsible for installing the real-time data processing system, due weight will be given to planning for system integration and controlling the effort needed to translate plans into action.

The total real-time system is regarded here as consisting of at least two subsystems: the equipment, or hardware, subsystem and the program, or software, subsystem. As we shall see presently, there will often be more than one logically self-sufficient piece of equipment that can be described as a subsystem; there may, and usually will, be several logically separated and individually fabricated collections of programs that deserve to be called software subsystems. Chapter 2 is concerned mainly with design of the equipment subsystems; the remainder of the book, with the development of the program subsystems.

Chapters 3 and 4, in combination with Chapter 2, present some general notions about planning and control of the system integration effort. Chapters 5 through 8 deal with the specifics of setting up the group of computer professionals and novices needed to accomplish system integration, and the final four chapters of the book are devoted to the problems that can be expected to arise during various phases of system integration.

Reference is made throughout these chapters to the *System Integration Team* and to its leader, or *Controller,* as he will henceforth be called. These name choices were premeditated, and some explanation of them may be illuminating. Both designations serve to differentiate the real-time system integration effort from the normal organizational pattern with the job concepts and performance standards implied by its nomenclature. It is the author's conviction that installation of a real-time system to assume the data processing burden of an organization should be likened to a state of national emergency, during which special forces must be mobilized and extraordinary power vested in the executive. The System Integration Team must therefore possess a unity, an *esprit,* and a sense of mission far beyond that which suffices for other parts of the organization.

In command of this special team is the Controller, vested with the authority to direct every aspect of system integration. This technical executive's paramount responsibility is to exercise control over the following:

- The system configuration, so that changes will be held to a minimum

- The System Integration Team, so that it will be properly staffed, and organized and directed in such a way that no individual who is part of it can unduly disturb the system configuration

- The schedule, so that realistic estimates will be made and meaningful measures of progress obtained

- System standards, so that the System Integration Team will have the benefit of sound technical directions and guidelines.

The author recognizes that such an approach to organization is certainly an idealized and perhaps an exaggerated one. It has been adopted to emphasize the vital importance of control and the compelling need for a group of competent technicians working at intensive pitch and with high morale toward the ultimate success of the real-time system.

1.5 WHAT IS DIFFERENT ABOUT REAL-TIME SYSTEMS?

Granted that one may distinguish real-time systems from those which have come before, and granted further that we may well be turning the corner into a new data processing epoch, it has not yet been established that real-time systems differ enough from others in their implementation aspects to warrant a System Integration Team with its Controller and its tightly disciplined, semimilitary approach, which implies grave problems to be overcome. What are some of these differences and why are they likely to be troublesome?

Real-Time Systems Are Bigger

If one were to call the roll of real-time systems now installed, he would find that such systems as SAGE, Mercury, Ballistic Missile Early Warning (BMEWS), and SABRE rank among the very largest computer systems ever conceived, whether measured by size of program, man-years to develop, or system cost. These systems typically involve machine instructions in the hundreds of thousands, programming man-years in the hundreds, and equipment cost in the tens of millions. It can of course be pointed out with validity that there are also smaller real-time systems, and the argument advanced that future real-time systems will tend to be smaller in scope than those just cited. And it will have to be readily conceded that there have been and will continue to be many smaller real-time systems—and not just those for industrial process control but also business systems modest in scope and cost and applied to a variety of problems. But the overall tendency appears to be toward bigness, and the burden of proof must rest upon those who contend that real-time systems will not, *as a class,* be larger than their non-real-time ancestors.

Two possible reasons for this increase in the size of the real-time system commend themselves:

1) The real-time system usually assumes functions that in earlier systems were performed by human operators. The real-time system has a tendency to be more automatic than the system it replaces so that functions (and costs) previously allocated to humans are now being designed into the real-time system.

2) Real-time systems may, by virtue of their complexity, be applied only to the larger and more difficult problems. One authority, who was associated with the BMEWS effort, has concluded:

A real-time digital system might be so small or so slow as to render its engineering design routine; but for inherent economic reasons, the opposite is usually true: a digital system, being expensive, will not be considered for a given task unless that task is so complex and makes such pressing time demands that hardly any other approach is open.[6]

The solutions being worked out by universities today to overcome the turnaround problem reflect this tendency toward bigness in real-time systems. Many of these institutions prefer to obtain the largest and fastest scientific computer available and provide improved access to it by placing remote

[6] W. A. Hosier, "Pitfalls and Safeguards in Real-Time Digital Systems with Emphasis on Programming," *IRE Transactions on Engineering Management,* EM-8, no. 2, June 1961.

terminals in various departments and classrooms. By so doing, they tacitly reject the alternative solution of eliminating the one large central computer in favor of several small computers, one at each departmental site. The large computer, if it can be made available to all potential users on a prompt and equitable basis, provides greater capability to each of them in solving the larger and more complicated problems.

Real-Time Systems Are More Complex

For reasons that will be explored in the next chapter, both the hardware and the software subsystems of a real-time system exhibit patterns of complexity not explainable by size alone. Just as the logical design and circuit loadings of electronic computers are a great deal more complex than those of the electric accounting machines, and their stored programs more difficult to produce and test than the plugboard wiring of earlier machines, so real-time systems may be compared with previous digital computer systems.

It seems reasonable to expect, for example, that a real-time system employing high-speed communication lines to link remote terminals with a central processor will be more difficult to engineer, install, and maintain than would this same processor when it has only an on-site card reader as a source data input device. Similarly, the program required to poll and respond to these outlying terminals will have much more involved logic than a program written to control only the card reader. This suggests one of the ways in which real-time system design contributes to system complexity.

Real-Time Systems Are Newer

One element that presently distinguishes most real-time systems is their newness. This characteristic has a number of different aspects.

THE APPLICATION MAY BE NEW • The problem to be solved may be new, or at least a computer solution of the problem is new. Many real-time systems are designed to apply in situations that have only recently arisen. The Project Mercury System, which supported the orbital flights of the United States astronauts, is a good example of this, as is BMEWS.

In commercial data processing, the problem itself may be an existing one, but one that did not lend itself to computer solution preceding the real-time era. Savings banks furnish an illustration. Before real-time processing became feasible, human beings and key-driven posting machines maintained the ledger cards and the passbooks, and there was no economically feasible way to introduce a computer into this picture on any sort of batch processing basis.

The System Integration Team is likely, therefore, to be venturing into problem areas that have not benefited from previous scrutiny by computer analysts and programmers.

THE EQUIPMENT MAY BE NEW • The equipment, or at least some of it, needed to solve the problem may be new or newly modified. Any company that has been the recipient of the first model of a computer, whether real time or otherwise, finds both logical and circuit bugs which, despite the most stringent product testing at the plant, require field engineering changes. These equipment difficulties aggravate the problems of the programming staff, which at this point is usually having trouble enough of its own learning the new instruction repertoire and the logical and arithmetic strengths and weaknesses of the machine from the programmer's vantage point.

Because real-time system development today often involves innovation in selecting the application, the chances are better than normal that the using organization will be receiving the first processor of its kind or one that has been extensively modified by the addition of real-time clocks, real-time channels, and other special features. And at the rate at which equipment manufacturers, in their highly competitive environment, continue to produce improvements in computers and peripheral equipment suitable for real-time usage, most real-time installations can be expected to be somewhere between 5 and 100 percent unique in an equipment sense. This situation is not satisfactory for anyone involved—be he manufacturer or user, salesman or market forecaster, engineer or programmer—but there is nothing to indicate that it is not going to persist for quite a while.

THE PROGRAMMING APPROACH MAY BE NEW • Because of the probability that the application selected and the equipment required will be new, new programming approaches may be needed. It has been the experience in pre-real-time systems that the first application of its kind carries with it enormous programming difficulties. For this reason, applications regarded as somewhat routine today, such as payroll, presented huge problems only ten years ago, when the first efforts to get them on a computer were begun. It is to be expected that, until the equipment development rate slows down and the applications selected for real-time processing exhibit a more comprehensive industry and functional pattern, the problem of newness in developing real-time programming approaches and solutions will also remain.

Real-Time Systems Are More Vital

It is one thing for an airline to apply a computer to passenger revenue accounting by taking all tickets from passengers boarding each day's flights, batching them, and sending them to a data processing center where the dollar amounts and itinerary information are punched into cards, the cards converted to magnetic tape, and master accounting records updated by the computer. It is quite another matter to provide a telephone or counter sales agent with a real-time terminal as his means of finding out whether a given flight is available for sale or whether a particular passenger holds a confirmed reservation.

In the revenue accounting case the consequences of the data processing equipment's being unavailable, while undesirable, are not really severe; a "system down" situation simply means that the revenue accounting records will not be updated for a few hours (or days conceivably) until the computer again becomes available. Not so with the real-time reservation system. The ability of the agent to obtain information about seats for sale touches a vital facet of the airline's revenue-producing operation. The potential customer waiting by his telephone or standing in a queue at the counter must be given his answer with celerity. A seat unsold on a departing flight because the system could not produce up-to-date information represents revenue lost to the airline forever.

Real-time systems are by nature better adapted to the more immediate aspects of an organization's operations than to the historical ones. Outside the field of commercial data processing, the dire consequences of real-time system malfunction become alarmingly clear when one imagines an enemy bomber undetected by SAGE or a missile unheralded by BMEWS.

Potential users of real-time systems should review carefully the implications of committing to computer control major portions of their operations before pushing off in pursuit of the great benefits offered by the real-time system. Sober caution at the beginning may not inhibit—and often should not inhibit —a bold decision to go ahead, but it may lend support to the demands of the Controller for the authority he needs to install the system and do it properly.

Real-Time Systems Are More Disruptive

The user of a real-time system is vulnerable to developmental and operational problems on several fronts. Disruptions and inconveniences, especially during the initial period of operation, may arise from several causes.

EQUIPMENT MALFUNCTIONS • The using organization must be prepared to cope with malfunctions that render the system equipment unavailable. The size of the equipment configuration and the newness of the equipment components indicate the dangers facing the real-time system in this area.

PROGRAM MALFUNCTIONS • The user must, at the beginning of his real-time operation—a period when disruption is most distressing to his customers and employees, be prepared to encounter program malfunctions. These bugs are attributable to either logical or clerical errors made by the person who wrote the program. And since, as we have noted, real-time programs are generally larger and the problems they attack newer, the incidence of such program errors will be greater during installation of a real-time system.

SYSTEM DESIGN INADEQUACIES • A system that, according to its design objectives, should deliver a message to its destination within ten seconds of receipt at the computer may, during or after cutover, be found unable to meet this objective. Hopefully such disappointing performance can be corrected, but the correction may require costly and time-consuming redesign of equipment or major surgery on inefficiently written programs. And regardless of the reason for this marginal performance and regardless of who is to blame (usually responsibility cannot be clearly fixed), the system must either falter along in suboptimum fashion or sit totally unusable until it can be repaired.

1.6 SUMMARY

In attempting to define real-time systems, it is misleading to contrast them with batch processing systems. A more satisfactory definition places emphasis on the amount of elapsed time to complete a transaction.

Real-time systems represent a major evolutionary step in the development of automatic data processing. The field has been marked by three major eras, each with its own unique characteristics and problems:

- The punched card era
- The computer era
- The real-time era

As we proceed into the real-time era of the 1960's, we can discern three basic classes of real-time system: (1) the problem-solving scientific system, designed to reduce turn-around time and to make large-scale computers available to many users on a time-shared basis by means of remote terminals; (2) the file-oriented data processing system, devoted to "commercial" applications involving massive amounts of repetitive processing; and (3) the process control system, a specialized class concerned with monitoring and regulating industrial processes.

This book is concerned primarily with integrating the file-oriented business system into its operational environment. To perform this task, a special organization called the System Integration Team is envisioned, headed by a technical executive called the Controller. A highly disciplined approach to real-time system integration is demanded because of the special nature of real-time systems. As a class, these systems differ from their predecessors in that they are bigger, more complex, newer, more vital, and more disruptive.

In the chapters which follow, real-time systems are regarded as being comprised of at least two, and usually more than two, subsystems: the equipment, or hardware, subsystem and the program, or software, subsystem.

II

GENERAL
    CONSIDERATIONS
IN PLANNING
    AND CONTROL

DEVELOPING THE BASIC SYSTEM CONFIGURATION | 2

2.1 TYPICAL REAL-TIME CONFIGURATIONS

To PROVIDE A framework for further discussion, we shall now examine several typical real-time system configurations, keeping in mind that a real-time system cannot be described adequately by drawing equipment diagrams alone, as these do not reflect the specifications of the program subsystems, which are an integral component of the overall system. These configurations cover both scientific and commercial systems; in most cases they represent systems either in being or in some phase of integration.

Simplex System

A simplex system (Figure 2.1) is one in which there is no standby equipment to take over the data processing job in the event of computer unavailability. Fallback must be to a manual

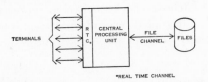

FIGURE 2.1.   SIMPLEX SYSTEM.

system of processing and control whenever the computer is unavailable either on a planned basis for preventive maintenance or on an unplanned basis because of component malfunction.

This configuration has the merit of a very austere equipment subsystem that in turn permits—even encourages—simplicity in the software subsystem. Where an application allows a choice between such an equipment approach and a more elaborate one, substantial savings in equipment and programming costs may be had by choosing the simplex configuration at some sacrifice in system performance standards.

Functional requirements for a message-switching application (directing of messages from a terminal in one location to a distant terminal or terminals) might specify, when first written, that the switching center remain in operation twenty-four hours a day and that no message be delayed more than ten minutes in the process of being switched from one communication line to another. Such stringent requirements categorically rule out the simplex system. If, on the other hand, the system's operation could be restricted to, say, sixteen hours a day and the tolerable message delay requirement relaxed by stating that 90 percent of the messages must be switched within ten minutes during this sixteen-hour period and that all "priority one" messages will be switched by manual methods during the eight-hour period of system unavailability, the field is open to consider a sufficiently reliable simplex switching system.

The advantages of the simplex system are these:

Lessened equipment rental or purchase cost.

Reduced programming expense through elimination of complicated routines needed in more elaborate systems to accomplish (1) switchover between two or more computers and (2) fallback to a degraded level of operation. The simplex system is completely "down" when the central processor is unavailable.

Disadvantages of the simplex system are these:

Shortened period of system availability, owing to the necessity of shutting down the system periodically to perform maintenance on its sole computer.

Need for more extensive and efficient manual fallback procedures. Because the periods of system unavailability are relatively frequent and because a system-down condition necessitates reversion to entirely manual methods, these will need to be as smooth and as rapid as possible. The general rule is: the more reliable the automatic system, the less reliable the manual standby system need be. It follows that some of the savings mentioned under the advantages have to be reinvested in clerical staff to provide an adequate "insurance policy" of manual backup.

Simplex System with Input/Output Multiplexor

The simplex system with input/output multiplexor (Figure 2.2) resembles the system just described except for the added functional specialization introduced by the input/output multiplexor. This device, exemplified by IBM's 7740 and GE's DATA-NET 30, is a stored program computer in its own right. It is connected, as shown, by means of input and output lines to the remote terminals; and it can also communicate data to and receive data from the central processing unit (CPU) by means of a data channel or interface. This specialization in the equipment is reflected in the programs, with those inside the multiplexor being devoted to such input/output functions as polling, network awareness, message assembly, code conversion, and message routing.

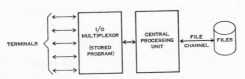

FIGURE 2.2. SIMPLEX SYSTEM WITH INPUT/
OUTPUT MULTIPLEXOR.

In such a configuration there may be considerable variance in the autonomy permitted the multiplexor by virtue of its design and its programmed functions. At one extreme would be a system design in which the multiplexor has "stand alone" capability; that is, it can operate even though the CPU is unavailable. In such circumstances the multiplexor will not normally have access to the system files nor will it possess the memory capacity and computational ability of the CPU. But despite this it may be in a position to continue to perform useful work on receipt of messages from the terminals when the CPU is not available. An example could be found in a system in which the dual functions of message switching and answering inventory status inquiries are being handled. On receipt of a message by the multiplexor, its program would ascertain whether it was dealing with a noninventory message for switching only or an inquiry about inventory status (really a message to the CPU). In the first instance the multiplexor would merely route the message without communicating with the CPU. In the second the status inquiry would be transmitted to the CPU by the multiplexor, and the answer, when prepared by the CPU, would be sent over to the multiplexor to be relayed back to the inquiring terminal. Now, whenever the CPU becomes unavailable, there is no reason why the multiplexor cannot continue to perform its message-switching function, changing its mode of operation only to the extent of notifying those terminals submitting inquiries about inventory status that these requests must be deferred.

At the other extreme would be a multiplexor that is little more than a stored program buffer and cannot stand alone. All inputs must be passed along to the CPU for analysis and action, and communication with the terminals is only at the direction of the CPU.

Regardless of the degree of sophistication built into the multiplexor, it is typically the "junior partner" of the two computers and is largely controlled by the CPU. In many systems, for example, communication between the multiplexor and the CPU takes place only by permission of the CPU. The multiplexor gets the "attention" of the CPU, perhaps by turning on a switch or latch that is periodically interrogated by the CPU. Finding the switch on, the program in the CPU then decides whether it wishes to receive the item that the multiplexor has to send over. On the other hand, when the CPU has some data to send to the multiplexor, it need not request attention but can cause an interrupt of the multiplexor's program and send the data to the multiplexor then and there. There are, of course, many variations in the pattern of control, but the CPU usually predominates.

Among the advantages of an input/output multiplexor configuration are these:

More modular design of both the equipment and program subsystems. This configuration can, for instance, be expanded in capacity by adding extra memory to either the multiplexor or the CPU or both, depending upon where the need arises. Alterations can be made in a multiplexor program to control variables such as the polling sequence without affecting the programs associated with the CPU.

Simplified memory allocation within the CPU. The CPU is no longer burdened with an uncontrollable buildup of entries generated by asynchronous bursts of activity at the terminals. Such queues can be handled inside the memory of the multiplexor instead. (The multiplexor can, of course, cope with this situation, as does the CPU in most nonmultiplexed systems, by refusing to accept more input until queues are worked off. This is done by varying the polling sequence, shutting down communication lines temporarily, and so on.)

Among the disadvantages of this configuration are these:

Increased system cost. It is likely that the cost of the stored program ability of the multiplexor will raise total equipment cost well over that of a simplex system.

More complex reliability considerations. It must now be determined, based on performance figures such as mean time to failure of both computers, what overall system availability will be. If the multiplexor cannot stand alone, then the availability of the system is only as great as that of its least reliable computer. With stand-alone ability in the multiplexor and with a multiplexor that rivals or exceeds the CPU in reliability, system availability may well be greater than in a simplex system. In any case the reliability question is no longer a straightforward one.

Inability to keep programs modular. It often turns out to be more difficult to segregate functions within computers than can be inferred by studying the equipment diagrams. Message-routing characters should clearly be contained in the memory of a multiplexor for twenty outlying locations that receive 95 percent of the messages handled by a particular system. There may, however, be eighty additional locations accounting for the other 5 percent of the messages, and it is very uneconomical to hold the routing characters for these in expensive multiplexor core memory; instead, these infrequently used routing characters should be kept on disk storage and read in only as needed. If the multiplexor in this example does not have its own disk channel, then it must make a request to the CPU for routing information in 5 percent of the cases. And thus the barriers between specialized functions and programs begin to break down. Message routing is now being performed in some measure by both computers.

Programs must be written for two computers. The input/output multiplexor and the CPU, being devoted to different system purposes, may differ in their internal characteristics such as information representation, word length, and self-checking features. They may have different instruction sets and different arithmetic and logical operations. It is quite possible that one machine will be binary and the other decimal. For these reasons, at least some of the programming personnel will find it necessary to spend extra time learning to program two different machines, each with its own programming aids, reference manuals, and special strengths and pitfalls that have to be understood by the programmer.

Increased system test burden. The presence of two intercommunicating computers dictates the need for common understanding on such matters as format of records, meaning of action codes, steps to be taken in overload situations, and passage of control data back and forth. All programs responsible for such intercomputer communication must be tested, and errors inherent in setting up this extra communication step removed. The problem is not too different from the communication "blocks" or changes in understanding that occur as information is conveyed from one human to another. Meaning is blurred by differences in interpretation of human speech or writing. Here, those programming each modular subsystem build similar communication blocks into their programs, which must be detected and removed at system testing time.

Simplex System with Input/Output and File Multiplexors

In the simplex system with input/output and file multiplexors (Figure 2.3) specialization of the computers is carried a step beyond that in the previous section, by the addition of a second multiplexor to control references to file storage. The CPU has thus been stripped, in concept at least, of all specialized functions and programs having to do with communication with the system files as well as with the outside world. Now, when the CPU has need of a record or an additional program, it communicates its request—perhaps in symbolic form by supplying the name of the record or program instead of the actual file address—over an interface to the file multiplexor. This multiplexor queues up the requests and issues the commands to activate the file storage access mechanism.

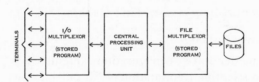

FIGURE 2.3. SIMPLEX SYSTEM WITH INPUT/
OUTPUT AND FILE MULTIPLEXORS.

The advantages and the drawbacks of this configuration are much on the order of those pertaining to use of an input/output multiplexor. Reliability problems and system test problems are, however, compounded by the presence of an additional interconnection.

There is, furthermore, in many of these systems a potentially awkward path to be taken by a request from the input/output multiplexor for control data from the file, such as for exceptional message-routing characters. The request for these characters must be conveyed to the file multiplexor through the CPU, which functions somewhat superfluously as a "middleman" in relaying the file request and then returning the data procured by the file multiplexor as a result of the request.

This sort of possibility may persuade the system designer to modify the configuration by adding an interconnection between the input/output multiplexor and the file multiplexor, so that the CPU may be bypassed in those cases in which it is not required. If this is done and if the two multiplexors are also given stand-alone ability, then it might be possible to operate the system at some degraded level of service even when the CPU is unavailable. The price that has to be paid for this flexibility, however, is in the writing of the programs required to direct the system in various possible operational modes. Additionally, and this will doubtless also have an impact on the programming, there is now a question about "who's in charge here," since the CPU may sometimes be ignored. When *all* communication is via the CPU, the answer is clear—this computer dominates and controls the activities of its multiplexors. If, however, there is the added possibility of skirting the CPU, this unit has a more sophisticated problem of maintaining and controlling the overall processing status of the system.

Master/Slave System

The master/slave configuration (Figure 2.4) is well adapted to scientific computation. In it, all housekeeping and scheduling functions are taken care of by one medium-sized

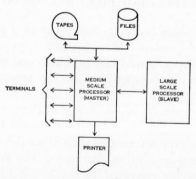

FIGURE 2.4.   MASTER/SLAVE SYSTEM.

computer, the master, leaving the slave computer, a powerful large-scale processor, free to concentrate on problem solution. Jobs to be run are obtained by the master, as are needed inputs such as tables and standard subroutines, and sent across an interconnection to the slave, which, on completion of its computation, returns the result to the master for filing, printing, or transmission to a terminal. Unlike the other configurations we have examined, which sought to divide control and housekeeping tasks among computers along functional lines, the master/slave system vests virtually all nonproductive housekeeping in one place so that the computational ability of a large scientific computer can be exploited to the full.

This system offers the advantage of more computation per dollar, presuming that the extra cost of the medium-scale computer could be justified anyway (as is usually the case). But, of course, to gain this advantage one must write a Control Program to take the place of the more limited monitor program normally used in a scientific computer, whether real-time or not.

This system, like all interconnected systems, presents the problem of unavailability in the event of failure of one of its computer subsystems. The problem can be overcome in the master/slave configuration by giving the slave at least some input/output ability of its own—say magnetic tape read and write ability—to be used when the master is unavailable. This could readily be done by installing an external switch to permit connection of the tape drives to either computer at any given time. Actually, operation of the slave independent of the master in this way may turn out to be the normal mode of operation in some installations. It may, in fact, prove desirable in some installations to restrict permanently the real-time aspects of the system to the master alone, which would batch work from the terminals onto magnetic tape or disk and, by switching these storage devices periodically, load up the slave with jobs it had thus accumulated. In other installations the entire configuration could be developed independent of *any* real-time communication with remote terminals and used only as an efficient work scheduler.

Shared-File System

The shared-file system (Figure 2.5) is another scientific system, somewhat similar in purpose and organization to the master/slave system. Actually the terms are not mutually exclusive, as a master/slave system could be based on the shared-file concept. Here essentially, a medium-scale computer is the controller and the scheduler, receiving job requests from remote terminals and placing them in file storage according to priority sequence in some predetermined location. The large-scale computer, when looking for a job to do, consults this location and, finding work to be done, commences processing. On completion of this processing, the large-scale computer files the results in some other predetermined location, where they are, during the next scan by the medium-scale computer, picked up and conveyed to the requester.

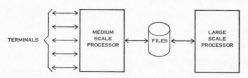

FIGURE 2.5.   SHARED-FILE SYSTEM.

One difficulty that must be worked out in such a system is prevention of the two computers from trying to use the same portion of the file at the same time. This can be accomplished by an engineered interlock of some sort, by a programmed interlock, or by manual means (through which, for example, an operator in a system containing two file modules would assure that neither of them is on line with more than one computer at the same time).

The shared-file system, like the master/slave system, is not necessarily real time at all. This configuration may instead be selected only in order to schedule more efficiently jobs that are hand-carried into the computing center. Potentially great improvement in turnaround time is possible without going to the ultimate length of allowing remote locations to have real-time access to the system by means of terminals.

Duplex or Dual System

In the duplex or the dual configuration (Figure 2.6) there are two combinations of multiplexors and processors, either of which is capable of performing by itself the entire real-time processing application. The additional equipment is present only to achieve the high degree of availability that characterizes this type of system.

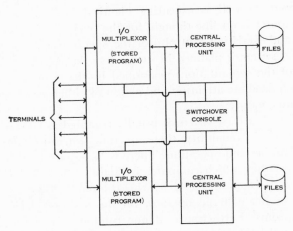

FIGURE 2.6.   DUPLEX OR DUAL SYSTEM.

The word "duplex" usually denotes a configuration in which one processing system stands by to take over from the other on either a scheduled or an emergency basis. The standby equipment is not on-line, however, and has to be switched over, by either console switches or programmed procedures or by a combination of manual and computer action.

The standby equipment may be programmed to perform various off-line applications when it is not undergoing maintenance, perhaps some batch processing needed to support the operation of the real-time system. If the standby processor is used in this way, its off-line programs should be written in a form that permits them to be interrupted with ease; there should be frequent "break points" in these programs so that partial or intermediate results can be saved for later use in the event that standby processing is interrupted by switchover. A special monitor program will probably have to be written for the off-line computer to direct the performance of standby processing and to aid the on-line computer in achieving efficient and rapid switchover.

The dual system differs from the duplex system in that both of its sets of equipment are on line, receiving the same real-time inputs as well as executing identical instructions. Only one computer is on line though, for the purpose of generating output and exercising control over the operation of the system. The dual system is planned in such a way that any variance in results of the computations performed by the twin computers receives immediate attention and action of either an automatic or a manual nature.

Although a dual system is usually regarded as constituting the ultimate in reliability, there are some intrinsic difficulties in its planning and operation. There is, for example, the question of deciding which computer is "right" when results vary. Can this decision be made by the computers themselves or must it be made by an operator on the basis of alarms and error typeouts? Furthermore, if one computer is to check on the other, then the programs of the two will necessarily diverge and their computation steps will no longer be identical. In the dual system there are a number of troublesome questions about what checking will be performed, how the results of checking will be evaluated, and when and in what manner corrective action will be taken.

There are many examples, both scientific and commercial, of systems possessing a double complement of equipment to enhance their availability. The Mercury system[1] offers an ex-

[1] S. I. Gass, W. K. Green, J. E. Hamlin, R. Hoffman, R. D. Peavey, A. Peckar, and M. B. Scott, "Project Mercury Real-Time Computation and Data-Flow System," *Proceedings of the Eastern Joint Computer Conference,* Washington, D.C., December 1961.

ample of equipment engaged in dual processing, and several airline reservation systems[2] are designed to operate in duplex fashion. Apart from the cost of the extra equipment in a duplex or a dual system, special programs need to be written to help assure that system availability is maintained.

There must be switchover programs to perform such functions as the following:

1) Transferring status indicators, internal switches, current polling directories, and other functions, from the memory of one multiplexor or central processor to another, perhaps using file storage as an intercomputer communication medium if there is no direct interconnection between computers.

2) Generating warning messages to users of the system that switchover is to be initiated. This is necessary because the users may have to reenter their inputs if the system is not programmed to save them during switchover. The user may also have to be prepared for a wait of a few moments before service is resumed after switchover and presumably should be told by the computer what is happening in the meantime.

Some of the file-oriented commercial systems have extended the duplex concept to their file storage by requiring that the system records themselves be duplicated in file. Then, if a file module becomes unavailable, the duplicate copies of the records it contains may be accessed when required and the system can continue to operate at a normal level of service. Such a system of duplicated records is extremely inefficient in terms of file throughput, since each record updated must be written back to the file not once but twice.

If the system is one employing these file "carbon copies," still further programming support is needed to keep the system operating under various possible conditions:

1) Some scheme of file address modification or manipulation has to be built into the program controlling the file access mechanisms in order to be able to retrieve either copy of a given record. This means that the status of each file module

2 M. N. Perry and W. R. Plugge, "American Airlines 'SABRE' Electronic Reservations System," *Proceedings of the Western Joint Computer Conference,* Los Angeles, May 1961.

must be known by the Control Program, and file addresses generated by the various Operational Programs checked against this status table. The goal of this approach is to concentrate all the special checking of status and modification of addresses in one program rather than in each program that may need file records.

2) A file updating routine is needed when a file module that has been down is ready to be restored to service. At this point the file will be out of balance if some copies of the records have been updated, and others have not, during the period the module was unavailable. Consideration of this problem may lead the system designer down the path of *reduplication,* using a magnetic tape or a spare file module to receive the duplicate writes during a period of unavailability of a module. This raises some interesting philosophical and practical questions about how far one should venture in pursuit of reliability.

Multiprocessing System

In a multiprocessing system several separate but interrelated processing operations are being carried on at the same time by two or more computers, each concentrating on a particular processing assignment but able to communicate with the other computers when necessary. A multiprocessing system configuration, in contrast to a dual or a duplex system, does not use one computer solely as standby for another in case of equipment malfunction. Standby facility may exist to a considerable extent in the multiprocessing system, but it is such that reversion to a standby mode results in a lengthening of response time or some other dilution of the level of service.

In the figure, three real-time applications are shown, with input for jobs A and B filtering through one input/output multiplexor and input for job C going through a second multiplexor. The interconnection here is such that, should one multiplexor be taken out of service the one remaining could assume input/output responsibility for all three jobs, though in an admittedly slower and less satisfactory manner. The remaining multiplexor might, for instance, be programmed to accept input pertaining to jobs A and B only, and advise anyone requesting type C service that the request must be deferred temporarily. Thus, at the penalty of downgrading the performance of job C under some circumstances, the need for expensive and normally unused multiplexing capacity for standby has been eliminated.

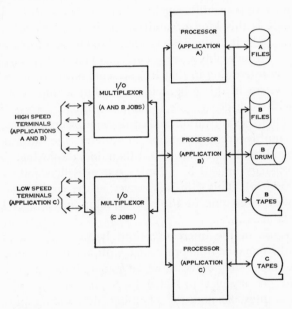

FIGURE 2.7.   MULTIPROCESSING SYSTEM.

Once an input has been processed by the multiplexor, it is distributed to one of three central processors, depending upon the application to which it pertains. And here again, at the level of the CPU, one processor is designated to assume the role normally assigned to another whenever the circumstances so warrant. There may, of course, be limitations to such a fallback pattern, as illustrated in the figure, where processor B could take over jobs A and C plus its own work, whereas processor A lacks the requisite file storage to perform jobs B and C.

Multiprocessing systems are more likely to exhibit a geographic separation of some of their processing equipment than are the other configurations. It would not be unusual to design a multiprocessing system with geographic rather than functional processing diversity by setting up three regional processing centers—say one in Boston, one in Chicago, and one in San Francisco—each geared to service terminals within its own geographic area. When one center goes off the air, another assumes temporary responsibility for handling the work of the disabled region. It is this kind of multiprocessing and standby ability that was built into the SAGE system, though the geographic pattern was considerably more complex. (The SAGE configuration is doubly interesting in that it represents not only a multiprocessing system in this geographic sense but a duplex system as well, with each geographic sector containing a processing center that houses a fully duplexed equipment configuration.)

A multiprocessing system holds out the advantage of standby reliability at a lower cost than does duplexing, since the spare capacity unused in a duplex system is here put to useful real-time work. This gain is, however, at the sacrifice of quality of service when one of the system components does become unavailable.

Because of the interconnections between the communication subsytem and the processing equipment and among the various processing units, reliability analysis to determine the level of performance provided for each application becomes quite complex. So does the planning, developing, and testing of the Control Programs to be lodged in each computer. For instance, these programs, on receipt of the proper signal or command, must be able to adjust processing priorities for various jobs and expand or contract the range of their functional or geographic cognizance. One input/output multiplexor doing the work of two would need to know what the action codes were for each input it might receive so that action code B, let us say, could under some conditions elicit a "processing deferred" response. Such a straightforward operational change as this, however, may require modification in real time of an Action Code Analysis Table consulted by the multiplexor on receipt of each input. This and other tables and parameters like it have to be altered when the multiplexor takes over control from its mate and again when control is relinquished. Similarly in the CPU, available memory storage lists, priority tables, and Operational Programs must be modified when a degraded level of service is initiated, and remodified when it is terminated.

2.2 POINT OF VIEW IN SYSTEM DESIGN

Before a real-time system design like one of those just described can be decided on as a proposed equipment configuration with a projected software subsystem to accompany it, the applications destined for the system must be analyzed in depth to determine what functional requirements the system must adhere to. An organization will expend substantial effort in conducting communication traffic surveys, sampling file volumes, determining activity rates against files, and measuring the performance of employees who will be subject to control by the real-time system, such as telephone sales agents in an airline system and tellers in a banking system. One key objective of the study is to determine whether "holding time"—that time spent in answering one phone call or serving one depositor—can be significantly reduced by an automatic system. Changes in the quality or methodology of job performance in the environment of a real-time system can have a direct effect on manning requirements, location of terminals, and modes of using the terminals.

The organization making a real-time feasibility study must decide whether to go it alone in obtaining and analyzing system facts and statistics and transforming them into functional requirements to be let out for bids by equipment manufacturers. Exclusion of the equipment manufacturer from the system study can produce some potentially harmful consequences. Avoidance of these may be a sufficiently important consideration to allay any concern about the outsiders' objectivity. For one thing, system analysis for a real-time application may be extremely complex, and the potential user should consider taking advantage of the technical skill and experience that the computer manufacturer can bring to bear during the study. Further, the analysis may indicate a need for modifications to announced equipment or other special engineering, and it is difficult to get a realistic idea of the feasibility or cost of such engineering without close liaison with the equipment supplier. For these reasons many companies interested in evaluating a real-time system choose one manufacturer and enter into a joint-study agreement with him, thus initiating a combined attack on system problems at an early stage.

An approach sometimes used is to obtain preliminary proposals from several potential equipment suppliers and select one of them on the basis of his demonstrated ability to conduct an effective study in cooperation with the prospective user. Under this approach the interested manufacturers try to demonstrate their ability to perform the study and supply the kind of system that the study may result in. If the study turns out well, the joint-study agreement can be supplanted by a letter of intent to acquire a system and later by a contract.

In any case, a judiciously planned approach to the system analysis must be developed and a professionally qualified system study and design group constituted. This group should be given an open communication channel to a level of upper management capable of reaching a decision at the appropriate time about whether to continue the system development once feasibility has been proved and cost figures generated. There have been unfortunate instances in which a study group works for months or even years in relative isolation only to discover, on presentation of their exhaustively detailed report, that the financial vice-president regards the whole venture as an expensive caprice and is in an excellent position to block the investment necessary to obtain the system.

Once the desired relationships with equipment vendors have been established and the system study and design group given a charter and sufficient organizational leverage to conduct an effective analysis, management should ensure that the group is staffed in a way that will result in a technically sound system design. To achieve the desired staffing pattern, the system study and design group should encompass a broad diversity of special skills.

Application Analysts

Application analysts should be men with extensive experience in the applications being investigated for the real-time system. The application analyst should have the ability to anticipate what changes can be made in company policy and procedures to adapt them to an automatic system, and what aspects of the present system cannot be compromised for any reason. When decisions on proposed policy and procedure changes are required as the basis for system design decisions, the application analyst should be empowered either to make the judgment or to get a prompt decision from the affected operating department. Because of his intimate knowledge of the special needs of the application, the application analyst should write the functional requirements for the guidance of the system designers and the System Integration Team.

Engineers

Engineering skills are obviously important in the development of a system that includes newly designed or extensively modified equipment. When engineers employed by an equipment manufacturer are participating in the system analysis, the potential user should have people from his own organization with engineering backgrounds working along with them.

Communication Specialists

Employees with experience in running a data collection and transmission system can be valuable additions to the study and design group. Any company operating a teletype communication network has accrued experience in circuit layout, line loadings, error correction, and routing techniques that will prove useful in system study and design. The communication specialists may also be able to obtain and interpret operating statistics if the communications department has done any surveying of message volumes and distributions.

Human Factors Analysts

Human factors analysts are needed to study man-machine relationships at all points at which the real-time system is to be made available to human operators. Human factors analysis and work measurement studies are, of course, indispensable when special-purpose terminal equipment is to be designed. Through such analyses it may be vital to discover that a response time of five seconds rather than three is sufficient for satisfactory performance of a clerical duty. It is also critical to establish the degree of permissiveness to be designed into the system, since this has tremendous impact on the complexity of the entry edit programs. Some systems control the operator at the terminal very closely by means of lighted keys that direct him through a predefined sequence of actions.

Mathematicians and Statisticians

Development of special system simulators or use of general-purpose simulators calls for mathematical and statistical training. Some of the analysis may additionally require application of linear programming, queueing theory, and other techniques of operations research.[3] And if large quantities of system operating statistics are obtained, statisticians will be needed to reduce and otherwise "massage" the data.

Cost Analysts and Accountants

Cost accounting backgrounds must be drawn on to translate the work of others in the group into dollars displaced versus dollars expended for each alternative system configuration. Even when the system does not have to be justified on the basis of displaceable cost, as is true of many military applications, the accountant's *viewpoint* is still needed in system design.

Lawyers

Toward the end of the design period, if it begins to look as though the system will some day become an actuality, legal representatives should become active in behalf of the potential user, the equipment manufacturer, and any other contractors or subcontractors. If the lawyers have worked along with the other members of the study group from the beginning, they will be in a much better position to safeguard the parties they represent by ensuring that the contract contains realistic acceptance criteria, penalty clauses, and other necessary provi-

---

[3] M. Rothstein, "American Airlines 'SABRE': The Analyst's Viewpoint," *Proceedings of the 2nd AGIFORS Conference*, Rome, October 1962.

sions. There should also be legal review of functional requirements and other key system documents that specify design objectives, such as allowable response times and printing speeds. Because of their great significance, some of these requirements should be inserted in the contract itself.

Programmers

At this formative design stage the programmers are really the advance guard of a much larger group destined to enter later as part of the System Integration Team. They must make their viewpoint known in order to protect the interests of the System Integration Team by contributing to a well-balanced system design. The role of the programmer in system design is discussed more fully in the following section.

To the extent possible, management should arrange to transfer the experience gained by members of the system study and design group to the System Integration Team, which commences work once the design has been completed and the decision made to install. The Controller, who is destined to lead the System Integration Team, may himself be chosen from among those who made the system study, if any seem to possess the requisite qualities.

2.3 ROLE OF THE PROGRAMMER IN SYSTEM DESIGN

Numerous technical errors that can insinuate themselves into the design of a real-time system must be guarded against through proper selection of the personnel charged with analyzing the application and designing the system. In the past there have been data processing systems designed almost solely by engineers, and others designed—or which seem to have been designed—by a combination of accountants and lawyers. Blind spots in selection of the design personnel are certain to be reflected eventually in the efficiency of the operating system, if indeed a system with faulty design features can be brought up to operational status at all.

Of all the wrong turns that the potential user of a system can take during the period of system design, failure to extend adequate recognition to programming implications is the most common and potentially the most disastrous. There are understandable reasons why programming has, in the pre-real-time era, been a sort of technical stepchild. The nature of real-time systems demands that it be stepchild no more.

Lack of Understanding of the Programmer's Function

Programming is a new specialty, one that did not even exist fifteen years ago and is today still in a state of violent flux. Within the past five or six years the field has been beset by controversy over the efficaciousness of writing programs in procedure-oriented rather than machine-oriented languages. More shall be said about this later; it is mentioned here merely to indicate that even experienced programmers have difficulty in defining the methodology of their work. Because of this and also because programming carries with it some flavor of higher mathematics, the management of a commercial organization tends to regard the programming task as abstruse if not downright incomprehensible. And since many programmers are deplorably uninterested in the larger world of commerce and industry outside their specialized niche, they have not pressed to make themselves better understood by their management.

Whatever the reason, programming is considered by many management people as a sort of necessary evil and its practitioners as a collection of sneaker-clad individualists who must be tolerated for a year or two while the company progresses from system design to installation, and who can then either be absorbed into middle management or lured away by a project at some other company.

Lack of Appreciation of Software Costs

During the punched card era software costs were negligible, consisting largely of the cost of plugboards plus the time taken by the analyst or tab supervisor to wire in the desired operations. In the computer era software costs for both the manufacturer and the user of data processing equipment ballooned rapidly, but the economic justification of a system still revolved around the cost of the equipment, just as it did in punched card days. This state of mind continues to persist, even though computer manufacturers have begun to invest millions in general-purpose programming packages, and users to invest millions in programs tailored to their own systems. Manufacturers are today becoming more sophisticated about the economics of computer installation, augmenting their sales forces with impressive legions of system engineers and programmers for assignment to customer accounts during the programming phase. And the more astute customers now recognize that software development costs of several hundred thousand dollars should be factored into the economic justification of the larger systems.

Nevertheless, there is still a long way to go. An operation like data code conversion is likely to be relegated to the program subsystem rather than to the equipment because, from a cost standpoint, it can be "buried" there. This transference is often the easy rather than the best way out of a system design problem, especially if there are no programmers present to offer their arguments for and against the trade-off. It is relatively easy to determine in advance the cost of the equipment needed for code conversion; it is quite another matter to try to block out and "dollarize" the equivalent program logic. But this is exactly what should be done to support an objective decision. More often than not, though, balanced consideration of equipment versus programming cost is bypassed because (1) it is difficult, (2) it is time-consuming, (3) we have not had to do much of it in the past, and (4) there are no programmers at hand to help do it anyway. And so the system designer proceeds, mortgaging the future by increasing the software burden of the System Integration Team.

Lack of Professional Standards

Once management has become sufficiently enlightened to appreciate the impact of software costs and has begun to communicate with programming people early enough to assure a sound system design, there remains a problem of evaluating the validity of the programmer's judgment. For programming, unlike more senior and high developed disciplines, cannot impose the same guidelines and standards on its practitioners as does, let us say, accounting or electronic engineering. The system designer and his management must, therefore, assure themselves that they are getting sound technical advice about programming and that the person offering it is not so incompetent or inexperienced (or both) that his advice will be more harmful than beneficial.

Even if the programmer member of the system design group is a topflight practicioner of the art, there is still danger in heeding his advice. Many of the better programmers delight in any opportunity to absorb more and more of the system tasks into the programming part of the system. They regard this as a technical challenge and imagine themselves as personally writing an optimum routine, say for code conversion, that will far surpass any other method of solving this problem. Unfortunately, the senior programmer thus engaged is forgetting that it is unlikely that anyone with his talent and experience will end up actually carrying through on a trade-off by writing the program. It will, in all probability, actually be programmed by a brand-new member of the System Integration Team having but six months' experience and endowed with only average programming ability.

These programming misconceptions during the design period tend to result in a system designed in such a way that it can be installed only by extraordinary programming effort involving personal dedication and sacrifice in the form of long and irregular hours over an extended period. It is seldom demanded that equipment engineers approach near-genius level to perform their assigned tasks or risk physical and psychological exhaustion to produce their subsystems. They are required to be competent and to meet professional standards. But the cards are sometimes stacked against the programmers by design features that cause inordinate programming difficulties during system integration. And the programming problems are often compounded by promulgation of a schedule that demands prodigies of a programming staff whose most outstanding quality may be inexperience.

2.4 SIMULATION AS A TOOL OF SYSTEM DESIGN

One of the most powerful analytical techniques available during system study and design is a simulation program that, by its operation, can help to determine design specifications or pinpoint design flaws in a proposed system configuration. The simulator is a program, written to run on an existing computer, that functions as a model of how a proposed system or some parts of it will behave when operational. A simulation program may be specially written for the unique requirements of a particular system study or it may be general purpose, with the user specifying the operational characteristics of the system design that he wishes simulated.[4]

Input to the simulation program might include such system descriptors as these:

- Size and speed of proposed central computer

- Layout and speed of communication lines

- Volume of inquiries and other inputs to the system including information about daily, hourly, and seasonal peaks

- Indication of the processing required for each input, covering such parameters as processing priorities, file references needed to answer each inquiry, and similar information about the conduct of the processing

Typical output produced by the simulation program might confirm that tentative initial selection of the central computer and layout of communication lines are adequate for the input volumes expected. Inadaquacies in the design in terms of overloaded lines, excessive queueing of items awaiting processing, and delays in response time are pinpointed by the simulator. Use of simulation is frequently an iterative process. The output from one simulation run becomes input to a redesign effort by the system design group, which revises the equipment or com-

---

[4] Geoffrey Gordon, "A General Purpose System Simulation Program," *Proceedings of the Eastern Joint Computer Conference,* Washington, D. C., December 1961.

munication components of the system and resubmits this revision for further simulation.

Advantages of Simulation

The advantages of simulation in system analysis are conceptually quite attractive.

The high-speed capability of a computer is exploited to "drive" the inputs to the simulator through a model of the system that performs in much the same way as will the actual system. This laborious task of generating and running thousands of items through the model could not readily be accomplished without computer simulation.

Simulation can be used to confirm or question other techniques of system analysis. Mathematical solutions or "seat-of-pants" judgments about expected system performance can be measured against the simulator output.

Fulfilling the requirements for simulation by securing volume figures, identifying processing steps, and laying out communication networks helps the analyst to take an organized approach to system study and helps insure that no important factors have been overlooked.

In a way, the input requirements of the simulator become a sort of checklist against which the system analyst measures his work of procuring and organizing system facts and parameters needed for an acceptable design.

Disadvantages of Simulation

But what are the disadvantages of simulation, or are there any? As in the case of many other system engineering tools, the fault lies not so much in the technique itself as in its employment.

Simulation is costly. It takes time to collect the input data and recast it in the form required for simulation. To this data collection and analysis expense must be added the cost of the computer time required to execute the simulation program.

The data processing axiom "garbage in, garbage out" assuredly applies to simulation. The simulator will evaluate a system in which all inquiry volumes for a peak hour from a major station are understated by 68 percent with the same fidelity as if these input figures were the soul of accuracy.

Related to the problem of erroneous factual data as input to the simulation program is the problem of estimating certain other aspects of system performance for which past experience and operating statistics furnish no guidelines. An airline reservation agent, for example, may, in a manual environment, record each booking received by writing the name of the passenger and his itinerary on a three-by-five card, which he then places on a conveyor belt to be transmitted to a back room. There a control clerk inserts the card in a tub file for the appropriate flight and date. The system analyst must, in reviewing this situation before consulting the simulator, know not only the number of flight inquiries made per card produced, the number of cards produced, and other information. He must also *anticipate* the manner in which the random access files of a computer system will be organized to contain the information on the card that is now recorded and filed manually. He must estimate with precision that each flight in the itinerary will require n file references for updating the computer-maintained inventory of seats sold on the flights in question. And he must further estimate the number of file references required to record and index each name contained on the reservation card.

Even assuming that the analyst is a highly skilled senior programmer with real-time experience, we can begin to see the problem he faces in developing realistic input for the simulator. He is trying to envision the *details* of a file and record organization that, should the system development effort continue, may take several man-years of work on the part of persons like himself to define and specify.

So, using judgment and intuition, the analyst estimates that each flight on which space is sold will require between four and fifteen disk file references, with five being the normal case and consisting of two reads and three writes. On the other hand, if the space is unavailable, the disk file reference range will extend from zero to twenty-three, with four as the normal case. Similarly with the recording of the passenger's name,

where the analyst assumes that each name will be entered in an
index for each flight in the itinerary and that such indexing
will be at two levels, with one file reference per level and with
an additional reference to file the name record itself. Well and
good. All this becomes part of his input to the simulator. But if
his judgment errs by so much as *one* file reference for a high-
activity item, say six instead of five file accesses for an available
flight, then the entire simulation result will be valueless, despite the myriad of accurate supporting detail about number of
incoming calls per minute, number of characters in a message to
the computer, and similar information.

It is a dismaying paradox that all the *data needed for
simulation are not available until the system to be simulated has
been designed and put into operation.*

The results of computer simulation, providing as they do
detailed figures on percentage utilization of communication
lines and computation facilities, average and maximum queue
lengths, and other data, may take on an aura of authenticity
that they should not have, especially if traffic and other volume
figures are not reliable or if far-reaching assumptions about
program logic and file accesses have had to be made in order to
prepare input for the simulator.

Unfortunately these simulation results, particularly when
scrutinized by persons unfamiliar with the simulation ground
rules and unaware of the assumptions underlying the preparation of input data, look "official." They seem to imply, "That's
the way our system's going to look some day. There will be
a central processor with 80,000 characters of main memory
storage; two modules of disk storage with a channel utilization
of 63.2 percent, as projected ten years into the future; three
high-speed communication lines with a loading for peak-hour
traffic of from 55 to 70 percent, and two low-speed lines with
65 percent peak-hour utilization. This certainly seems like the
system we need. And after all, we're not just guessing about
it. This is the result of five passes through a simulator!"

It is not entirely facetious to suggest that simulator printouts begin with some warning statement about the validity of

the figures they present, in much the same way that other useful but toxic products must be labeled to prevent their misuse.

2.5 BALANCE IN SYSTEM DESIGN

Within each of the basic system configurations exist possibilities for trading-off, that is, of lodging a system function in one subsystem rather than another in order to balance and optimize the system design. The right choices will result in an economical and efficient operational system. There are three major kinds of trade-offs to be considered in real-time system design.

Hardware/Hardware Trade-offs

In hardware/hardware trade-offs the decision involves placing a function in one equipment subsystem instead of another. An inquiry keyed in at a terminal, for example, might be accumulated, character by character, in buffer storage associated with each terminal. Each character of this message would be held until the "end of inquiry" signal, perhaps a question mark, was keyed in. The terminal buffer storage would then ready itself to transmit the inquiry to the processing center the next time it received a polling or "go ahead" signal. But buffer storage is expensive, especially magnetic core storage, and in this case it is used relatively infrequently, since the operator of the terminal is often engaged in other tasks—for example, conversing with customers—and makes inquiries at the rate of only one every two or three minutes.

A trade-off is in order here and could be accomplished by taking the buffer storage away from each individual terminal and pooling it in one unit where it could be shared by several terminals. The designer might find that where each terminal had thirty-two characters of buffer storage, pooled storage for twenty terminals requires only 400 characters.

Admittedly the system will not be quite as efficient this way. Every once in a while an operator will have to wait a few seconds for more pooled storage. But the designer must weigh this disadvantage against the saving in storage cost and in the continuing cost of maintaining numerous individual buffer devices.

Hardware/Software Trade offs

Hardware/software trade-offs are the classic kinds of trade-offs one usually considers during system design—whether to build a function into the equipment or leave it to be carried out by the program. In a system that contains teletype communication facilities, it is necessary to convert from the teletype representation of each character in a message in Baudot code—a five-bit, unchecked code—into the code used internally by the computer, normally a six- or seven-bit self-checking code. Through the addition of more circuit cards to the equipment connecting the teletype subset to the multiplexor or real-time channel, the conversion could be performed automatically with incoming five-bit codes translated and expanded to seven bits. Similarly, on output the seven bits could be reduced to five and the shift characters inserted. Alternatively this conversion could be performed by the computer or multiplexor program that is going to have to examine and edit the data anyway. At the cost of some computer time (and this will be a continuing cost each time the program must operate), the designer can save the expense of the extra circuit cards.

As has been suggested, participation by an expert programmer is needed in making this kind of trade-off. Unfortunately, such decisions are sometimes made by equipment designers who have never written a program but who feel that the writing of a program to perform code conversion is a rather trivial exercise and that the execution time of the program, once written, can easily be borne by the system. But this individual designer, concerned about his particular problem of teletype code conversion, may be only one of several working on different equipment subsystems. And all of them may be industriously making hardware/software trade-offs, the cumulative result of which is extremely burdensome for the System Integration Team to implement and for the computer to execute each time it performs its processing. All too often these hardware/software trade-offs become not trade-offs at all but *faits accompli* with which the programming staff is confronted long after the equipment subsystem has been designed.

Software/Software Trade-Offs

In many real-time systems, the size and complexity of the programs dictate that this part of the system be designed and produced as several more or less independent software subsystems to be lashed together during the period of system test. If system integration is approached in this way, trade-offs among the various program subsystems become possible.

Kinds of real-time programs will be fully discussed in later chapters, but for purposes of illustration let us differentiate here between Control and Operational Programs. A Control Program is basically a housekeeping routine with various specialized parts devoted to keeping the system running. It may perform such chores as communication line polling, establishment of processing priorities, read-in of programs and data from file storage, and switchover. An Operational Program—and there are many in a system—is application-oriented and written to perform such an action as posting a savings withdrawal or flagging an inactive account.

Between these two kinds of programs are substantial "gray areas" where trade-offs can be made. What, for example, should the system do about accumulating an exceptionally long entry coming in from a typewriter terminal? Most inputs in a hypothetical system may be numeric and limited to twenty digits in a fixed format. But occasionally an operator has to resort to the typewriter and types in a variable-length message of up to thirty-five hundred alphanumeric characters. The question then is, which program should be given responsibility for accumulating segments of this long message until the final "end of entry" signal is received? This is, in a sense, a housekeeping requirement and might therefore be viewed as a Control Program function. On the other hand, there may be merit in editing or validating the long entry as portions of it are received, in which case the accumulation should be done by the Operational Program that contains the edit logic. It is a difficult decision, with at least as many far-reaching implications as the other kinds of trade-offs.

Examples of Balance in System Design

The end result of intelligently made trade-offs will be a well-balanced system in which each subsystem performs those system tasks for which it is most logically and economically suited, and the program subsystems are not overburdened with functions that might better have been built into the equipment. Of course, in many instances the equipment subsystems and perhaps even some of the program subsystems are predesigned and pre-engineered, and so certain trade-off opportunities are forfeited. But even in a prefabricated system, wide areas of choice are usually open to the system designer encompassing both equipment and programs.

To illustrate, let us assume that, based on data collected by the system designers and simulated in a careful manner, a tentative airline reservation system configuration has been arrived at—a simplex system like that in Figure 2-1, which includes an "off-the-shelf" computer with file storage and a multiprogrammed software approach. Under such circumstances, what are some possible trade-off and balancing opportunities?

MAIN MEMORY SPACE VERSUS FILE CHANNEL THROUGHPUT • Superficially, an 80,000-position main memory seems sufficient for the Control Program, the commonly used Operational Programs, and input/output queueing positions in an airline reservation system. But file channel utilization is dangerously high; in fact, projections indicate that a second channel must be added to the system within a year after cutover. One major contributor to this heavy channel throughput rate is the servicing of requests for information about the inventory status of flights departing on "today's" date. Each time such an inquiry is received, two file references must be made, the first to obtain an index set up by flight number and the second to procure from the file the Seat Inventory Record for the flight in question. The index is fairly short, requiring but twelve characters for each of 1000 possible flight numbers, or a total of 12,000 characters. The inventory records proper, however, require much more storage, an average of 200 characters per flight, or a total of 200,000 characters for one day's inventory.

Given this problem of channel utilization and the application characteristics just mentioned, the designer should consider placing the index in main memory rather than on disk storage. Thus at a single stroke he would halve the throughput rate to file storage for this type of high-volume inquiry and extend the single channel capability of the system some years into the future. Follow-up reveals that incremental main memory can be provided by the manufacturer in 20,000-position banks and that an additional bank would cost far less than the second file channel and impose fewer problems of reliability. And so the design decision can be made. The additional main memory will be ordered and the index placed within it, leaving 8000 positions remaining for other purposes.

EXECUTION TIME VERSUS MEMORY SPACE • Let us again assume an 80,000-position memory, but this time for an application of sufficient size that not all the required programs can be kept in main memory at all times. To do this would require a prohibitively large memory of more than 400,000 character positions. Instead, only the most frequently used programs are kept in main memory and the others are read in from disk storage as required. But since, as in many real-time systems, the allocation of this main memory is volatile and dynamic, the programs kept on file must be coded in such a way that they can be positioned at any place in main memory that happens to be available at the time the need for a particular program is experienced. One way in which this can be done is to write all instructions in each program relative to zero by "pretending" that the program, when read into main memory, will be located starting at the very first position in the machine, namely position zero. Then at read-in time, the Control Program could examine each instruction contained in the program being read in and adjust its references to agree with the actual location selected for the program, which might, for example, be brought in and placed in successive locations commencing at memory position 7563.

But such instruction modification by the Control Program to perform program read-in uses up computer time, perhaps as many as ten execution cycles for every instruction read in. If this system is required to read in 1000 instructions per second and if an execution cycle is forty microseconds, the system is chewing up more than twenty minutes out of each hour in this one nonproductive housekeeping job. Analysis of the instructions slated to reside on disk reveals that the instruction read-in rate can be cut by almost half if room can be made in main memory for *only 2000* additional instructions. This can be done by adding additional main memory, as in the previous example. But in this case, over ten minutes' worth of valuable processing time has been conserved per hour. And incidentally in this case, as in the preceding one, the file channel throughput rate has been reduced by adding the extra memory bank.

It is through trade-offs such as these that system balance can be achieved, even if the system configuration does not involve newly designed equipment.

2.6 AUSTERITY IN SYSTEM DESIGN

Along with principle of balance in system design must be ranked a second tenet—that of austerity. Only by weighing every decision about adapting an application to real-time processing against this criterion of austerity can the designers hold the problems of system integration within manageable bounds. There is a tendency toward complexity in designing a real-time system that the designers, and particularly the application analysts, have to take into account.

It may be desirable to have an airline system that encompasses not only the reservation sales department but message switching, maintenance scheduling, flight information, aircraft routing, and a variety of other interrelated tasks which in combination truly merit the name "total system." And there may be few equipment limitations to prevent even the most grandiose system concept from becoming operational. But the burdens imposed by an overambitious design on the System Integration Team may be so enormous as to prove insurmountable. There have been major system failures in the pre-real-time period and there have been, as well, many systems that limp along in a suboptimum fashion, under the weight of a too-complex system design. The system design group must therefore be mindful of the factors that contribute to system complexity in order that these may be minimized through development of realistic functional requirements. Numerous questions about system complexity should be posed and answered. The following constitute a representative checklist. The more "yes" answers this checklist engenders, the more complex a system will turn out to be.

System Availability

This set of complexity questions has to do with the extent to which the system must make itself available to its users. Questions about system availability extend to reliability of the equipment, its error-checking ability, and its overall capacity for performing the application processing in a prompt and satisfactory way throughout the period in which processing is required.

- Is a long period of sustained operation required, such as 24 hours a day, 7 days a week, 52 weeks a year?

- Must elaborate error detection and correction features be engineered or programmed into the system?

- Must a method of protecting vital file records be developed so that such records will continue to be available in the event of system malfunction?

- Can a degraded level of service be tolerated in case of partial system unavailability?

- What are the consequences of the system's going down?
  1) Is it easy to revert to a manual or semiautomatic system?
  2) Can operations be resumed immediately when the system becomes available or must there be a special recovery mode to update records, reactivate files, and so on?

System Variability

Under the heading of system variability are grouped questions about the nature of the application being placed on the real-time system. Some applications exhibit little volatility once they are converted, but most will require modification and expansion that should, insofar as possible, be anticipated when the system is designed.

- Is the application unique; that is, is this the first system of its kind or the first one utilizing new equipment or programming solutions?

- Can the application be expected to expand significantly in volume over the projected life of the system?

- Is the application highly susceptible to changes in government regulations, industry standards, company policy, or competitive practices?

- Are there other applications that management may wish to add to the system?

- Can additional equipment, programs or capacity be added to the system in a nondisruptive fashion?

Input/Output Characteristics

The kinds of input/output[5] devices available today vary greatly. General-purpose terminals with numeric and alphanumeric ability, special-purpose terminals, punched card and paper and magnetic tape transmitters, and devices for transmitting analog signals are some general types of real-time input/output equipment. There is even greater variety in the way in which this equipment can be employed in various configurations. For example, in "conversational" modes, an operator makes an entry from a terminal, then awaits the computer response before taking further action. At the opposite extreme is the closed-loop approach in which input is obtained and processed auto-

---

[5] As a matter of convention, most real-time systems people refer to "input" as data generated at a terminal and "output" as data generated by the computer.

matically by the system, largely bypassing the operator in the decision-making process. Many questions have to be answered in determining system complexity in terms of its input/output.

- Are the messages or signals variable in length?

- Are the incoming messages or signals generated asynchronously rather than on some dependable cycle or schedule; that is, are they based on the arrival of customers at a counter or some similarly uncontrollable terminal environment?

- Must the system accept all input as it is generated, or can the receipt of input be controlled by polling?

- If human operators are the source of the input, does the system permit great latitude in the format and syntax of the input submitted?

- Must the input be thoroughly edited and validated by the computer prior to processing?

- Are there stringent response time requirements, if this is the kind of system where each input elicits a response?

- Does the system generate unsolicited output to the terminals; that is, does it produce messages that are not responses to inquiries and that may be of a priority which necessitates interruption of work in progress at a particular terminal?

Communication Characteristics

The communication characteristics questions are closely related to the preceding group of input/output, but focus more on the difficulties of delivering the data from source to processor and back to source again if need be.

- Is the system geographically dispersed, with remote terminals or possibly even interconnected processors remote from each other?

- Are there peaks and cycles in the communication volume that must be smoothed out by queueing data at the central processor or multiplexor?

- Are there differing transmission speeds for various parts of the system?

- Are there differing communication codes?
- Does the system include a large number of terminals?
- Are there several different *kinds* of terminals in the system?

Equipment Subsystem Features

In the category of equipment subsystem features are collected questions pertaining to the complexity of the equipment —more especially the equipment at the central processing site. The fact that multiplexors are employed in a system or that a duplex or other interconnected configuration is proposed certainly should not be felt to constitute an indictment of the system as a poorly designed one. It is necessary, however, to recognize that such a proliferation of equipment is contributing to system complexity.

- Is much of the equipment newly designed for this application?
- Are there extensive modifications required in existing equipment?
- Are there interconnected computers?
- Is there a stored program multiplexor?
- Is this a duplex or a dual system?
- Are there random access storage devices attached to the system?
- Is there more than one type of storage device attached to the system?
- Is a large volume of storage needed by the system?
- Is this a shared-file system?

Software Subsystem Features

The program subsystems must actually be weighed for complexity of two kinds: developmental and operational. Developmental complexity is the result of functional requirements and equipment features that add to the difficulty faced by the System Integration Team in planning, specifying, writing, and testing the program subsystems. Operational complexity has to do with those programming features of a system that, once operational status is achieved, contribute to the cost and difficulty of running the system. Since many if not most programming features must be identified under both of these categories, the following questions do not make a distinction.

- Is the system multiprogrammed; that is, will there be several transactions in varying stages of processing inside the system at any one time?

- Can all programs be kept in computer memory or must some be called in from file storage on demand?

- Are there processing priorities to be controlled by the programs?

- Is fallback to a degraded level of service programmed in whole or in part?

- Is recovery from fallback programmed in whole or in part?

- Must a special programming language be written for the system, or an existing one modified?

- Must the programming staff learn how to program more than one computer?

- Are there many restrictions on program preparation, such as length of program, efficiency of program?

2.7 AIRLINE SYSTEMS AND BANKING SYSTEMS

Airline reservation systems have been the center of attention for many of those interested in real-time systems, with the result that numerous examples of real-time processing approaches are drawn from airline applications. This is somewhat unfortunate, as real-time system design differs substantially from industry to industry. In many ways the airline reservation systems represent one of the most complex applications of computers to real-time usage. In contrasting a system for savings bank accounting with one for airline reservations, for example, one can discern several design simplifications that make the savings bank system considerably less complex.

Continuous operations. Airline system functional requirements often dictate that the computer be available around the clock. This has tremendous programming as well as equipment implications and adds greatly to the complexity of the airline system. The savings bank system typically requires no more than a single-shift period of real-time operation daily.

Duplex system configuration. In its most basic connotation, a duplex system configuration means two of everything—computers, file modules, multiplexing gear—except the terminals. This redundancy is provided in an airline system to assure continued system availability at a substantial increase in system cost. While some duplex configurations have been proposed for banking use, this approach is not normally found necessary.

Programming procedures. Although both the typical airline system and the typical banking system make a distinction between Control and Operational Programs, the airline system is as a rule multiprogrammed. On the other hand the banking system experiences a sufficiently low level of demand for service from its terminals that a method of processing only one entry at a time and making all others wait their turn is sufficient.

Number of terminals. The airline reservation system may encompass hundreds of agent sets. In contrast, the savings bank system is usually designed to serve no more than a few dozen teller terminals.

2.8 SUMMARY

Several real-time system configurations represent typical designs for both scientific and commercial applications. These configurations range from the relatively primitive simplex system to the multiprocessing system, which comprehends several semiautonomous but interconnected processors. In order to develop a sound real-time system configuration, it is necessary to have many viewpoints represented during the period of system study and design, including those of application analysts, engineers, communication specialists, human factors analysts, mathematicians, cost analysts, lawyers, and programmers.

The programmer's role in system design is frequently misunderstood and consequently is often underestimated, with the result that the software subsystem becomes burdened with problems for which a hardware solution might have been preferable.

Simulation may prove useful in system design, but there are serious disadvantages in its use. These should be understood by the system study and design group and by management.

Two fundamental principles in designing real-time systems are balance and austerity. Balance in system design may be achieved through successful trade-offs among hardware/hardware, hardware/software, and software/software subsystems. Austerity may be pursued by developing functional requirements that do not make excessive system performance demands and by constant awareness that there is a tendency toward complexity in real-time systems.

PRELIMINARY TECHNICAL PLANNING | 3

3.1 SCOPE OF PRELIMINARY TECHNICAL PLANNING

It is difficult to draw a clear line of demarcation between the various activities that take place in the early stages of a real-time system project. The previous chapter discussed development of the basic system configuration as comprehending analysis of the application, decision on feasibility, and selection of the equipment, with adequate recognition of programming implications. At the end of the system study and design period, there is a proposed system configuration that typically provides a detailed picture of the necessary equipment and a more general picture of the program subsystems.

At the conclusion of the system design period, the basic tasks remaining for the System Integration Team are these:

- To specify the program subsystems to a level of detail equivalent to that of the equipment subsystems

- To fabricate these program subsystems

- To test the program and equipment subsystems and unify them

- To convert the application to the new system

Preliminary technical planning represents the first step toward accomplishing these tasks.

The transition between system design and preliminary technical planning is rather blurred in some system efforts. Usually though, an arbitrary dividing point or benchmark can be found. One such benchmark is the signing of a contract. Before this is done, considerable effort has usually been devoted to system analysis and to preparation of functional requirements. Typically, a management decision is then forthcoming about whether to develop the system further. It is unlikely that a System Integration Team will be set up to begin active development of software until a decision is reached which provides the basis for contract negotiations with the equipment manufacturer. Management may be willing enough to invest the manpower to conduct a study and produce a tentative system configuration, but it is not likely to authorize production of detailed software specifications until satisfied that this work will not be undertaken in vain. For this reason, preliminary technical planning can be conveniently regarded as not overlapping the system study and design period to any great extent.

In essence, the goal of the technical planning phase is to refine the system definition so that a framework or outline exists to guide the preparation of record and program specifications. Preliminary technical planning is in essence a bridge between development of the basic system configuration and the full-scale system integration effort. It defines the technical bounds of the system and transforms a general system definition into manageable chunks of work for assignment to individuals and groups within the System Integration Team. This planning is, however, carried out only in enough detail to permit the System Integration Team to mount, during the record and program specification phase, an intensive attack on a reasonably well-defined set of machine-oriented problems.

From this description it may be inferred that preliminary technical planning, such as system study and design, calls for relatively few highly skilled technicians who act as "honest brokers" in advancing the system development from the design period into the subsequent phases of system integration. In fact, one of the responsibilities of the technical planner is to outline the phases of system integration that seem best suited to the application. Indeed, the technical planner may be called upon not only to identify the major steps to be taken by the System Integration Team in installing the system, but also to suggest how the project should be organized during each phase to optimize software production.

Admittedly, it is difficult to isolate a technical planning function such as determining the phases of system integration and to distinguish it from the normal managerial tasks to be performed in setting up any new organization. But there does seem to be a collection of planning jobs that require the attention of persons with technical insight. The technical planning staff would be concerned, for example, with breaking down the anticipated programming work load into perhaps four, five, six, a dozen subsystems. Its concern would not normally extend, however, to decisions about the scheduling of this work, selection of those to perform it, or establishment of priorities for one program over another. These decisions are certainly related in a most direct way to technical planning, but generally the technical planner decides only on what has to be done by the System Integration Team. The Controller, as the director of the preliminary technical planning staff, uses the output of this planning staff to aid him in organizing the System Integration Team and in scheduling and directing its efforts. Preliminary technical planning has, therefore, a twofold result. It provides information needed by the Controller to organize and manage the project, and it produces a master technical plan for the guidance of the System Integration Team.

Both preliminary technical planning and the staff function of establishing standards, described in Chapter 8, have a similar objective: guiding the System Integation Team down productive technical avenues to prevent team members from making unwise or redundant technical decisions and duplicating one other's efforts. But technical planning focuses primarily on the substance of the job to be done and system standards primarily on its form. For instance, the basic decisions about the record organization of the system—what records are needed, how they will be accessed, how they will be maintained—are the responsibility of the technical planner. The standard setter, on the other hand, might prescribe that each file record must have an identifier, what this identifier is to be, how it will be checked, and what action will be taken whenever it fails to check.

The technical planning staff must make many decisions about records and programs, such as those having to do with multiprogramming versus sequential programming and with selection of a programming language. On many of these matters of basic record and program definition, significant technical decisions must often be made on the basis of imperfect knowledge. Consequently, a decisiveness stemming from judgment and experience rather than from absorption of objective facts and statistics is the preferred quality in a technical planner.

In preliminary technical planning the Controller serves as the decision-making focal point in order to achieve system definition. Occasionally this may be a tie-breaking function. It is frequently more conducive to overall system development that a problem *be* disposed of than that the solution chosen necessarily and absolutely be the best one.

3.2 DOCUMENTATION OF SYSTEM DESIGN

Having thus identified some of the attributes of preliminary technical planning, let us determine what guidance and information is needed to accomplish this planning. The planning staff must, of course, receive direction from the Controller and from the application analysts and others who participated in the preceding study. Beyond this a major source of information should be found in the documentation produced during the system study.

In developing the basic system configuration, considerable emphasis should be placed on documenting the basis for critical design decisions. This documentation, supplemented by a carry-over of staff members from the design group to the System Integration Team, provides the continuity needed for further development of the system. It should include, in one form or another, the following basic items.

Proposal

Proposals submitted by one or more of the equipment manufacturers, and especially the one selected, may contain a substantial amount of information. Here one normally finds equipment descriptions and specifications. However, proposals vary widely in the degree of detail offered, and some may be quite general, particularly if there is no special equipment to be provided for the system.

Contract

Like the proposal, the contract varies greatly from one system to another in the amount of detail of value to the System Integration Team. Some contracts contain voluminous exhibits that may even go to the extent of specifying the format of reports to be produced, line by line and character by character. If the lawyers feel impelled to counsel in favor of such detail, then a few "escape hatches" should be left open in the contract for the System Integration Team to use when their more penetrating analysis of the system reveals unworkable or undesirable contract provisions. Unachievable design features will have to be altered, no matter what the contract states, and it is better if all parties are conditioned to anticipate this possibility of change.

System Statistics

Traffic surveys, data samples, simulation results, and other statistics will in most systems generate enough performance statistics to fill a few sizable volumes. This supporting information should be passed on to the System Integration Team so that it can be restudied and re-evaluated periodically.

Functional Requirements

Functional requirements exist in written form for most large systems, sometimes as a part of the contract, more often independently. They establish, largely from a machine-independent standpoint, what the system is supposed to do. Such requirements sometimes specify an acceptance test that the system—equipment and programs working in unison—must pass before delivery is completed. In whatever form, written functional requirements should provide the application definition for the System Integration Team.

3.3 PHASES OF SYSTEM INTEGRATION

Chapter 2 was concerned with the conceptual period of system development, referred to as system study and design. After management decides to commit the organization to a real-time system, the technical planning staff must delineate the remaining phases of the system integration effort. Why is this definition so necessary for real-time system integration when it is not customarily a prelude to integration of a non-real-time system into its operational environment? Mainly because the characteristics cited in Chapter 1 as making real-time systems different also dictate that they pass through several well-defined development phases before being tagged "operational." All the aspects of real-time systems—size, complexity, newness, vitality, and disruptability—add up to an integration approach different in degree if not in kind from non-real-time commercial installations.

In the world of non-real-time systems, technical planning often consisted of little more than drawing the balloons and boxes (Figure 3.1) so familiar to batch processing people. These identi-

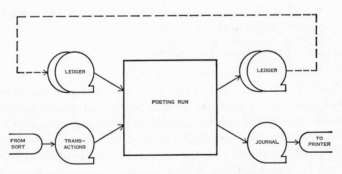

FIGURE 3.1. BATCH PROCESSING PROGRAM.

fied passes of files in sequence on magnetic tape and, when supplemented by record layouts showing how information was represented on magnetic tape and other layouts showing the format of printed reports, they were sufficient to permit the programmers to begin drawing up detailed flow charts of the logic of each passage, or "run," of the magnetic tape. After flow charting came coding and system testing, in which program bugs associated with the transmission of data from one run to the next were detected. These are the same basic developmental steps found in real-time systems, but generally speaking, in the real-time environment there must be more rigorous definition of them.

Preliminary Technical Planning

As has been mentioned, preliminary technical planning is the earliest phase of system integration. It is of relatively short duration and involves relatively few people. The most experienced and able computer specialists obtainable should be assigned to this unstructured and creative work of blocking out the basic features of the software subsystems.

Among the activities to be accomplished by preliminary technical planning are the following:

- Outlining the phases of system integration
- Planning the general record organization
- Planning the general programming approach
- Performing any additional specialized planning needed to control system integration

Record and Program Specification

Record and program specification is really two separate phases, the first devoted to specifying the records of the system, the second to a comparable specification of programs. This phase takes the results of preliminary technical planning and renders them into detailed specifications according to which the programs themselves can be written. Preliminary technical planning can make the job of the specification writer either clear-cut or confusing, depending upon the quality of the system definition that he receives.

Programming

The programming phase encompasses the programming needed to bring the detailed directions contained in the specifications down yet another level—to that of machine instructions.

System Testing

Testing of a real-time system differs intrinsically from test-ing of other systems. In most real-time systems it ranks on a par with the specification and programming phases in terms of du-ration and manpower expended. Usually there are many sub-phases of system testing, *each* of which involves a major commit-ment by the System Integration Team. The technical planning staff must be sensitive to the test implications of their decisions about record organization and program logic.

Conversion and Operation

In order to do a complete planning job and anticipate all major software subsystem requirements, the technical planners must be aware of the special problems that may arise during con-version. Often the conversion approach selected has a direct effect on the way in which system records are designed. There will probably have to be certain items of information in the records and certain logic in the real-time programs for the sole purpose of facilitating conversion.

These are, in brief, the phases of system integration. Each of them will be described in more depth in subsequent chapters; they are mentioned here merely to stress that the planning staff must thoroughly understand the nature of each phase so that technical problems can be anticipated.

Phase-by-phase technical planning has the important inci-dental result of providing the Controller with gross estimates on which he can base his staffing and scheduling plans. Unless the planning staff works within the framework of a phased approach, it cannot furnish the Controller with meaningful estimates on which to base his organization planning and scheduling.

By working closely with his planning staff, the Controller must ensure not only that it is accomplishing its main assign-ment of technical refinement of the basic system configuration but that it is, as well, identifying the problems to be faced by the System Integration Team during each major phase of the project.

It is not too difficult for the planning staff to envision the scope and methodology of the specification phase, as this is a direct extension of its own efforts and may even overlap them. It is much harder to anticipate every individual program that will have to be created and checked out before integration can be completed. In some large systems the technical planning may occur years before testing and conversion is undertaken; therefore these future phases appear hazy and less easy to concentrate on than the more immediate problem of preparing for specification writing. The technical planners must, despite this, discipline themselves to look at the system phase by phase. A record organization plan for disk file storage made without consideration of the method by which manually kept records must some day be converted into disk file form may differ radically from one in which conversion has been taken into account. The Controller must make certain, by properly directing his planning staff, that no one can ever say, "Well, we have a conceptually perfect system of programs and records that meets all the functional requirements. Our only problem now is that we can't figure out a way to get the system cut over without closing the business down for six weeks."

3.4 PLANNING THE SYSTEM RECORDS

One of the chief responsibilities of the planning staff is to generally define and classify all the data formats of the system and develop efficient methods of storing and retrieving information.

Kinds of Records

The planning staff should develop a classification of the system's records to aid the specification writers in detailing these records. This planning should result in a classification much like the following:

File records, which are the substantive records of a system, enabling it to fulfill its functions. A Seat Inventory Record in an airline reservation system and a Deposit Account Record in a banking system fall into this category.

Index records, which are used by programs in the system to obtain other records, primarily file records. There may be several levels of indexes to be read in from file storage and consulted before a file record itself can be retrieved.

Input records, which describe the format and content of each input received from terminals and other input stations.

Output records, which describe the format and content of each output generated by the system.

Linkage records, which are internal system housekeeping records used to transmit intermediate data and results from one program to another.

It should not be inferred that the planning staff will write all the record specifications. On the contrary, they will concentrate on the contents of the most important file records and the relationships between indexes and file records. They may also specify certain key characteristics of input and output records, such as significance of spaces and degree of variability in format, because of the effect this can have on the logic needed in the edit programs. In the case of data transfer, the planning staff may define the way in which registers are to be used to transfer information, the minimum information to be included in a linkage record, and so on. More significantly, they may establish relationships between linkage records and programs.

Organization of System Records

In a file-oriented system, it is essential that optimum methods be established to store and retrieve data. It usually proves desirable that the planning staff itself write the record specifications for the vital records in the system instead of leaving these to be specified later, along with all the other system records. What follows is suggestive of those records deserving such special attention from the technical planners.

FREQUENTLY REQUESTED RECORDS • The more "popular" records must be allocated to file storage in a manner that makes it easy for the programs to obtain them rapidly. Ideally, such frequently requested records should be kept in fast-access main memory, but of course this usually proves impractical because of the high per character cost of such storage. The next best solution is to store such records on a relatively high-speed peripheral device like a magnetic drum. But if drum storage proves too costly for the number of characters of storage involved, the records may end up on a disk file or some other relatively slow storage medium, where the economy of the storage is reflected in the hundreds of milliseconds that each program must wait every time it seeks information.

RECORDS REQUIRING LARGE AMOUNTS OF STORAGE • Records requiring large amounts of storage may or may not be accessed frequently; they usually are not. In an airline reservation system, passenger records may occupy up to 80 percent of the file storage, even though any one individual record is not called for very often—only when the passenger picks up his ticket or boards his flight. Insurance policy records have this same characteristic of massive storage requirements and relatively infrequent demand for any one record.

Significant savings may result by conserving storage space for these records through analysis of functional requirements. The functional requirements for an airline reservation system might provide initially that the system be able to store an itinerary of up to 100 different flights, although not even the most senior application analyst can remember when such a voluminous reservation had to be booked. The technical planner should in this instance design the basic record around the typical case—an itinerary of perhaps three flights. Then, some exception procedure (preferably manual) can be devised to gain the additional characters of storage needed for the small percentage of reservations having exceptionally long itineraries.

EXAMPLES OF RECORD PLANNING • Apart from inculcating realism in the functional requirements, there is an optimization problem in making certain that storage is being conserved through proper record layout. The addition of only a few unneeded fields or redundant characters per record by a maladroit system planner can result in a wastage totaling millions of characters of storage. The more compact the records can be made,

the better chance the technical planner has of getting them—
or a sizable number of them—into fast-access storage. This
makes the technique of "packing" records look very attractive,
especially in a system with binary data representation.

The case of an inquiry about airline seat availability illustrates this. Based on scrutiny of its records, the system is required—if seats are available—to print out on the typewriter of
an agent's terminal set the following response:

HS2 113/13 DEC SFO CHI

This tells the agent that, in response to his request, the computer has "sold" two seats on Flight 113 of the 13th of December, the flight originating at San Francisco (SFO) and terminating at O'Hare (CHI) airport, and has updated its Seat
Inventory Records accordingly. One way in which the system can
provide this response is to store in the Inventory Record for
Flight 113 of December 13th the other information to complete the response, namely, the pair of three-character airport
abbreviations "SFO" and "CHI." Under most methods of character representation, this would require thirty-six bits of storage at six bits per character.

Is there an alternative that is more economical of file storage? Assume that the airline in question serves but forty cities.
Now, six bits alone in binary allows unique representation of
up to sixty-four items of any sort—numbers, letters, airport
codes—so that instead of taking up the full space required
(six characters times six bits per character, or thirty-six bits) one
can merely store two six-bit fields, each of which *represents* the
location of an airport abbreviation contained in a central table.
Thus:

Binary Address Stored in Inventory Record	Airport Code Contained in Table Located at Address Specified by Inventory Record
000000	ATL
000001	CHI
000010	LAX

The bits on the left are what is actually contained in the Inventory Record, the characters on the right are found in the central Airport Table. The central table requires three characters per airport, but that is a relatively small price to pay, since its contents will be used in conjunction with the Inventory Records for *all* flights in the system. If this hypothetical airline operates 100 flights a day and keeps seat inventory for thirty days into the future, this approach of using 6-bit symbols rather than the actual airport representation in each inventory record would save thirty-six bits (six characters per airport pair) less twelve bits (still needed to contain the location of the airport codes in the Airport Table) times 100 records times thirty days, or 72,000 bits of storage. And in exchange, only thirty-six bits per airport code times forty airports, or 1440 bits are relinquished for use in the central Airport Table.

If only record planning were so simple and trade-offs so easy! The technical planner must, before adopting such a compression scheme, ascertain where the central table is to be stored. In main memory? If so, then it must be justified as more important than other tables and programs that may be in competition for this valuable storage space, and this competition must be reconciled with other technical planners working on similar problems. (One of the chief benefits of keeping the technical planning staff small is to facilitate just such reconciliations as this.) If, on consultation with the other planners, it is concluded that the Airport Table cannot be justified for main memory, it must be placed in auxiliary storage, along with the Seat Inventory Records to which it pertains. But doing this means that the throughput rate to file storage for each Inventory Record will be doubled, because now, every time a Seat Inventory Record is brought into main memory for processing, the Airport Table must also be read in to obtain the airport abbreviations for printout to the agent. Thus the conservation of auxiliary storage by including only a six-bit binary representation of the airports served by each flight makes each Seat Inventory Record dependent upon another record—the central Airport Table—which must be brought in from file to decode the condensed binary representation of the airport.

And that is not all. Yet another aspect of this record decision must be considered. It takes instruction execution time to pick up the six bit binary address from the Seat Inventory Record and convert it into an airport abbreviation. Admittedly, not many extra instruction steps; but even a few additional instruction executions become significant if repeated often enough, that is, every time a seat is sold. There is definitely a trade-off here between number of bits of storage saved and amount of computer time required to convert from binary symbol to actual as the result of this compression of data.

A final question remains to be evaluated by the technical planner concerning the adequacy of the central Airport Table in the event of expansion. Under the more straightforward approach of providing sufficient space for the actual airport characters in each Inventory Record and placing no reliance on a table, it makes no difference how many new airports may come to be served by the system. It never takes more than three characters to represent any possible airport and there is room in the record to represent any possible board-point or off-point. Conversely, the binary representation scheme with its table look-up to obtain the airport abbreviation would present an expansion problem. Six bits providing for sixty-four combinations suffices for an airline serving forty airports, but if service should ever expand to more than sixty-four airports, it would take seven rather than six bits in each Inventory Record to keep the scheme workable up to 128 airports. The technical planner must, before making his decision, try to ascertain the probability of such expansion during the life of the system. Realistically, he should in this case probably set aside seven rather than six bits for each airport if he chooses the Airport Table approach.

This illustration suggests that what appears at first to be a fairly clear-cut saving in storage space needed for frequently referenced records may, on analysis, turn out to be costly and even somewhat risky. Record-planning problems of this kind are not confined to airline reservation systems. They present themselves during development of any file-oriented system.

When an inquiry is received by a system, how do the affected computer programs know where the particular record needed to satisfy the inquiry is situated in file? If, in an airline reservation system, control is maintained over 100 flights thirty days into the future, there will be 3000 individual records to choose from in satisfying a request for flight status. There are two basic methods of obtaining a record in a system possessing random access storage: (1) computation of the file address or (2) reference to an index that contains the address. Under the computation method, each record is located in a fixed area in file, and the actual file address required by the access mechanism—perhaps disk surface number, track number, record number—is computable from that portion of the inquiry that contained the flight number and the date. Thus, Flight 113 for the 13th might be transformed by computation into disk surface 18, track 42, and record 6.

This computational approach has two major drawbacks. First it requires computer time to execute the instructions necessary to transform the inquiry into a machine address each time an inquiry is received. Second, it is wasteful of file storage. With a three-digit flight number, storage would have to be set aside for 1000 possible flight numbers, even though the airline might in fact operate only 150 flights numbered anywhere in the range from 1 to 999. Similarly, a record would have to be set up for each flight/date up to thirty, even though no bookings were expected on many of these flights until a few days before their departure.

It may be worth accepting these drawbacks to gain the advantage of minimizing the file accesses to get at needed data. In order to make this approach more attractive in an airline system, the application analyst might be persuaded to modify the functional requirement which states that any three-digit flight number may be used in the system and instead hold these numbers below say 200. This would allow ample room for expansion in a 150-flight system and yet would reduce from 1000 to 200 the range of file records whose addresses must be computable. But such a change, straightforward enough from the technical planner's viewpoint, must be appraised carefully by the application analyst before he gives his assent. Conceivably, these flight numbers have some further significance. Suppose the first digit represents one of five types of aircraft, and the maintenance department has developed a punched card system for overhaul scheduling that takes advantage of this aircraft classification. Furthermore, the industry rule is that flights going in one direction have even numbers and those in the opposite direction odd numbers. Finally, the sales manager objects to any changes from a psychological standpoint, claiming that businessmen who are "air commuters" tend to associate certain flight numbers with a certain class of service at a particular time of day, and he opposes any renumbering of the flights.

The technical planner may at this point decide to consider the alternative—use of an index. Under this approach, flight/ date records can be located anywhere in file, since their location is not directly determined by computation. And because they do not pre-empt any fixed locations, only those records actually needed are set up, with no "dummy" slots for nonexistent flights established merely to facilitate address computation. What might be done in an airline system is this: A Flight Number Index could be set up, with one entry for each flight/date. When a request is received, this index is brought into main memory from auxiliary storage. Suppose that each flight/date index entry takes up six characters for each date thirty days into the future and that, on receipt of a request, say for Flight 113, the 180 characters representing the section of the index devoted to this flight are read in. This index portion might be interpreted as follows:

Flight 113

Dec.	3	40	20	03
Dec.	4	90	20	04
Dec.	5	NO	GO	OD
Dec.	31	40	01	08
Jan.	1	19	30	10

The numbers at the right are the true contents of the Flight Number Index. The dates are used by the Index Analysis Program to select the correct index slot within the Flight 113 section of the index to satisfy various inquiries. A request for December 3 will, on consultation of the index, reveal that the record for this date is stored at disk face 40, track 20, and record 3. If an agent had instead requested December 5, the index would give an indication that this request was invalid, perhaps because the flight does not operate on that date, and the process would be stopped right here. In the normal case, processing continues by picking up the address from the appropriate index slot and then accessing the Seat Inventory Record itself by providing this address to the file access mechanism.

The great merit of the indexing approach—flexibility and economy in allocation of file storage—carries with it a severe penalty: two file references rather than one must be made to get the desired record.

It should not be concluded from these examples that the technical planning phase must accomplish all the analysis underlying every possible trade-off in record design. Most of this will be done during the specification phase. It is important though that the *basic record structure* be optimized before much time is invested in detailed record development. Major record-planning areas must receive attention while the System Integration Team is still relatively small and technical decisions are readily communicable and controllable. Otherwise, inefficiency will creep into the system as specification writers and programmers begin by default to make these important system decisions as an incident to their regular assignments.

Terminal Assembly Area

Certain records in a real-time system may appropriately be designated as "general system records." They must be planned and set up, regardless of the equipment used or the application selected. One such record is a terminal assembly area (TAA) to facilitate determination of terminal status. The need for this type of record can be illustrated by two examples.

1) A time-shared scientific system may provide an option to users of its terminal facilities to request initialization of a program on a low-

priority basis with the results not expected immediately. In this situation the terminal is not operating in a conversational mode, since it may have nothing to print out for a low-priority user for several hours and since the user, moreover, has probably abandoned the terminal after entering his request. Meanwhile the terminal can be made available to a second user with a different problem who enters another low-priority request. Some minutes or hours later the processor, having fulfilled either or both of these requests, must decide whether to print out the results at the terminal or store them somewhere until they are asked for. Since the latter approach is the one usually dictated by this pattern of terminal usage, an area must be set aside for each terminal in the system to hold results that will be asked for by the users at a time they find convenient. This storage area must be subdivided and organized in such a way that varying sizes of jobs, such as assemblies, computational results, and so on, can be filed, and several users of a common terminal identified and serviced.

2) In an airline reservation system it is necessary to accumulate all data pertaining to one passenger until his entire transaction has been completed and the record made ready for final indexing and filing. Final processor action cannot be taken until all the needs of the passenger have been explored, because the passenger may at any stage in the transaction change his mind about some part of his itinerary or about the entire transaction. Because of this possibility the computer must accumulate various pieces of information about the passenger, each separate piece of information the product of one inquiry, until the complete itinerary has been obtained, including:

- Name

- Number in party

- Itinerary (flight number, date, board point, off point, departure time, arrival time for each flight sold)

- Phone number

- Air Travel Card number

All these facts, which may be procured in any sequence, can best be accumulated in a terminal assembly area which, in this system, is designed to function as a repository for intermediate accumulations of data. The agent can, at any time, cancel the whole transaction by ordering the system programs to "blast" or "scrub" the currently accumulated contents of the terminal assembly area.

These examples underline the importance of a set of terminal-address-oriented records to hold information about current status and usage of each terminal. In addition to planning the special features of this type of frequently accessed record, the planning staff should specify the record's fields and make some ground-rule decision about the programs that may use it. Perhaps, for example, decisions should be made that no program other than Program 410X can be allowed to read the terminal assembly area, that Program 411X is the only one permitted to change the contents of the terminal assembly area, and that certain other designated programs can supply these two programs with items for insertion in the area but only in a rigidly prescribed format. In this way a basic system record is defined during preliminary technical planning and its peculiarities and limitations conveyed to the System Integration Team.

3.5 PLANNING THE SYSTEM PROGRAMS

Just as preliminary definition has to be given to the organization of system records, the programming needs of the system must be investigated by the technical planning staff.

Kinds of Programs

Concentrated attention has to be devoted to breaking the programs down into separate groupings or subsystems. Several different kinds of programs usually have to be identified and the boundaries of each established. For some classes of programs a further breakdown within the class must be made because of the heavy contribution of these programs to the work load of the System Integration Team. One possible classification of programs follows.

CONTROL PROGRAM • The Control Program is needed to coordinate and service the other programs in the system and to provide an interface between them and the equipment subsystems. Sometimes called an "executive," a "supervisor," or a "monitor," the Control Program is generally responsible for priority establishment, data acquisition, storage allocation, and related functions essential to the system's operation.

OPERATIONAL PROGRAMS • Operational Programs are application-oriented programs written to perform the user's data processing job within the framework provided by the Control Program. In many systems, there are multiple levels of real-time Operational Programs to be planned, depending upon the system priorities. One priority classification might be made between the following:

1) *Response programs,* which are Operational Programs activated on receipt of an entry from a terminal. They are specified and programmed in such a way that they receive the very highest priority in completing the required processing and in generating a response. Response-type programs are sometimes referred to as "foreground" programs.

2) *Time-available programs,* which, though designed to operate within the real-time environment provided by the Control Program, are activated only when main memory time and space are available and not being used by response programs. These time-available programs, occasionally called "background" programs, are executed in most systems during non-peak hours, when traffic from the terminals is light. In some systems they are planned to perform processing jobs totally unrelated to the real-time work of the system; in others they are scheduled to update real-time files or perform special computations related to action generated by terminal input.

SUPPORT PROGRAMS • Support Programs may be defined broadly as those required to make the system operational and, once it has achieved this status, to keep it running. Some of these are designed to run in real time, others in an off-line mode.

System development programs

- System design programs: simulators, analyzers, and other programs used during system study and design
- Programming programs: assemblers, compilers, and other aids to writing programs
- System testing programs: generators, traces, and similar programs needed to support system testing
- Conversion programs: to convert the files, cut over manual

operations, and perform parallel processing for an initial period

System maintenance programs

- File maintenance programs: to remove and insert records according to the life cycles dictated by the nature of the application
- Fallback and recovery programs: to permit the system to operate at a degraded level of service and to restore it to full capability when all operating subsystems are again available
- *Diagnostic programs:* to insure that equipment is properly tested for marginal conditions and well maintained for the sake of maximum system availability

Allocating Programs among Computers

One way to facilitate program planning is to segregate functions between multiplexor and central data processing unit or among CPU's in those configurations employing multiple computers. It was mentioned in Chapter 2 that functional modularity between multiplexor and CPU may turn out to be more imaginary than real. It is a responsibility of the planning staff to decide what a realistic division of functions is.

Operational Program Breakdown

Operational Programs merit special attention during technical planning because (1) they account for such a large proportion of the effort of the System Integration Team, and (2) they have the greatest impact on use of available computer time, file channel throughput capacity, and main memory storage. When measured by numbers of instructions required, Operational Programs may account for as much as 90 percent of the instructions written for a real-time system. An efficient Control Program should make available for use by these Operational Programs most of the equipment capacity, taking no more than 10 to 15 percent of the computer capacity for its own coordinating functions. Regardless of percentages, the fact is that much of the talent and toil of the System Integration Team will be expended in the production of these application-oriented Operational Programs.

In some of the larger real-time systems, the number of Operational Program steps may exceed 100,000. In such cases it becomes a major responsibility of the technical planning staff to organize this mass of work into smaller pieces that may be specified and programmed more easily. At the risk of oversimplifying the nature of preliminary technical planning, let us state that, given a valid estimate of 100,000 instructions for operational programming, the System Integration Team should not proceed into the specification phase until this overall body of work has been broken down into several subportions. At this level the problem may assume manageable dimensions for the specification writers.

The technical planning staff must transform an input-oriented set of functional requirements into a problem definition meaningful to the specification writers and the programmers. How, pragmatically, should this be done? The most realistic way is to take maximum advantage of the functional requirements as stated. Suppose that in a functionally defined system the two main sources of input are (1) operators at terminals linked to high-speed communication lines and (2) teletype messages feeding in without human intervention over low-speed channels. Suppose also that in this system there are two basic sets of file records, each with its own indexes and collateral records, and that both the terminal and the teletype entries need access to both types of records. One way in which to organize the programming work load for such a system is to outline two distinct sets of input/output programs to receive, edit, and respond to the two types of inquiries, and two sets of file-oriented programs to service messages under control of either set of input programs. Taking this approach, in such a system there would be five interrelated real-time software subsystems to be specified:

Control program. To supervise and coordinate all the others.

High-speed entry. To process all actions from terminals, from receipt to response.

Low-speed message. To handle all teletype messages requiring lower priority service rather than service in the conversational mode employed by the preceding class.

"A" file programs. To retrieve, examine, update, and return to file those records required to process entries from either terminal or teletype.

"B" file programs. To accomplish, for the second set of records, operations similar to those required for set "A." An entirely different group of programs is needed here because the content and format of B records are completely different from those of A records. If, according to the original estimates, this system had "weighed in" at 100,000 instructions, the Control Program might be expected to account for about 10,000, and each of the four Operational Program subsystems, for something over 20,000 each.

When such a gross breakdown is achieved during technical planning, the job of the specification writer is considerably simplified. Groups can be set up to concentrate on these major segments of the problem, and their scope defined within the range of overall system development requirements. The technical planning staff in the preceding hypothetical case accomplished this, after analyzing a set of input-oriented functional requirements, by taking advantage of the existence of two different kinds of input to break out two portions of the problem for further definition. They then applied their knowledge and experience in file organization to split out the two file-oriented program subsystems (something the application analysts would not have been capable of, as it can only be derived from a technical analysis of the functional requirements). Thus the specification writers can, as a result of technical planning, be presented with work assignments of reasonably manageable dimensions. This in turn permits the Controller to organize, estimate, and evaluate more readily the mission of each group within the System Integration Team.

Program Relationships

The planning staff may not be given responsibility for specifying the Control Program; sometimes this program has already been written and has to be accepted by the System Integration Team in more or less the same way as the equipment itself. Even when this is not the case, the Control Program is probably being written by a special group, employed by the equipment manufacturer, which is intimately familiar with all nuances of the equipment and is in the best position to exploit them fully in the Control Program. Generally, the technical planning staff members are more application oriented than the group responsible for developing the Control Program or adapting an existing Control Program. The technical planners are closer to the application, the control programmers closer to the hardware.

Regardless of how the Control Program development is organized, the technical planning staff should:

1) maintain liaison with the Control Program group and suggest modifications where the need has been revealed by the planning process.

2) plan the Operational Programs in such a way that they take a maximum advantage of the features provided by the Control Program.

The Control Program may provide, for example, that all Operational Programs must be broken up into segments of 256 instructions each, with communication from one segment to another achieved by passing along data in the form of intermediate linkage records. This, however, leaves open questions about whether each sequence of Operational Program segments must be self-sufficient, or whether, if sequence A, consisting of twelve segments, happens to be in main memory for the purpose of processing inquiry A and if sequence B happens to be coexisting in memory to process a B-type inquiry, one should plan to take advantage of the fact that some segments are (or could be) common to both inquiries. The answer to this question depends upon a number of rather elusive factors, such as the relative probability of these two programs and all the other sequences coexisting, the estimated degree of commonality, the importance of conserving main memory, and the inhibitions that a shared approach might place on the specification writers and programmers. These questions must be resolved by the planning staff even when they have responsibility only for the Operational Programs and not for the Control Program.

In a time sequence, the Control Program should lead the other programs in preparation, since its specification is essential to the work performed by the technical planning staff. At the time this staff is set up, the functions of the Control Program and the details of the working environment and restrictions it presents should be known.

3.6 MODES OF OPERATION

Unlike the planning discussed thus far, many of the decisions associated with preliminary technical planning are not immediately identifiable with either record or program organization. Certain other fundamental determinations must be made about the way in which the system will operate. These decisions, once made, govern importantly not only the System Integration Team but all who may in some way come into contact with the system once it is operational.

Every real-time system, whether it be simplex or duplex, a one-shift or twenty-four-hour-day operation, has at least two processing modes—real time and off-line. A simplex savings bank system that is on-line one shift a day will have to devote a second shift to such off-line operations as calculation and crediting of interest. In a duplex system, off-line programs need not wait until the system is no longer operating in real time; instead, the standby computer can be used for off-line processing. In the off-line mode, system files may be accessed in much the same manner as in the on-line mode; the off-line programs, however, need not measure up to the same standards of efficiency and brevity that apply to real-time programs. Further, in the off-line mode there is no need for a Control Program, or at most only a simplified version is called for.

These variations in processing conditions are conveniently referred to as processing modes. Each mode requires different programs or modified operation of the regular real-time programs. The planning staff must determine what modes are required to operate the system and evaluate their effect on record organization and program preparation.

Sequential Processing Modes

Modes of operation may be sequential, as in the case of a system for monitoring an astronaut's orbital flight in the manner of Project Mercury. Here, there were such modes as the following:

PRE-LIFTOFF • During the countdown, the system operates in real time but simulates the conditions that may occur on the actual flight and provides predictions and confidence estimates.

LIFTOFF • The system now concentrates on analysis of launch information streaming in from the launching site and telemetered from the spacecraft itself. The objective of this mode is to produce information on which a "go-no go" decision can be based.

ORBIT • While the spacecraft is in orbit, the computing system adapts itself into a mode in which it receives information about velocity, orientation, altitude, and similar conditions that enable it to produce a profile of the orbital flight and provide outputs that predict location and time of re-entry and impact.

RE-ENTRY • In this final mode, the system seeks to equip the decision makers with all necessary supporting data to permit a satisfactory reentry.

From the point of view of the technical planner, the system configuration is being employed in a significantly different manner during each of these sequences. As the system makes the transition from one mode to the next, a different set of Operational Programs must be established in the computer's main memory and a different set of processing priorities and input/output edit routines set up. It is during the technical planning phase that the record and programming requirements of each mode should be laid down.

Parallel Processing Modes

Modes of operation are not always sequential, and in many systems can coexist in time. A typical file-oriented commercial system requires the following modes, all of which could conceivably be in effect at the same time:

TRAINING • Training mode is used to break in new terminal operators. One approach to planning for a training mode is to permit the Operational Programs to go through all normal processing steps triggered by the various types of entries received from a training terminal except that, before conclusion of a program, a "trainee test" is made and if it is discovered that the entry originated at a training set, updated records are *not* returned to file, as they would in the normal case. Instead, they are "blasted" while in main memory. If, for instance, an airline reservation trainee agent had entered a "sell" action, the computer would do everything for this trainee except return to file the modified Seat Inventory Record showing a reduced number of seats available as a result of this make-believe sale.

FALLBACK • In the fallback mode, special treatment is given to entries originating at certain locations or at certain terminals because of a partial system failure. When, for example, a communication-line failure has led to isolation of the San Antonio office from the rest of a system, the processor might compensate by reverting to a prearranged mode of operation in which messages of a certain priority are routed instead to a terminal in Dallas, to be relayed from there by a voice telephone line to San Antonio.

RECOVERY • Following a system-down situation, return to normal operational status cannot occur until certain "catching up" measures are taken. If file records have been removed from system jurisdiction and maintained manually during the period the system is unavailable, these have to be reinstated in the system's file storage. Two basic approaches are available to the planning staff here. The first, and the most attractive technically if not operationally, is to keep the system down (even after all equipment is again available for service) until the files are reinstated. This prolongation of system unavailability, even though equipment is no longer the limiting factor, has definite appeal if the functional requirements can be "bent" to permit it. Otherwise, the alternative of making the system partially available must be pursued. Perhaps not all records got out of date during the down period. If this is the case, then while in a recovery mode normal service will be provided, except when inquiries are directed to file records that have not yet been brought back up to date. This will doubtless be the approach preferred by the application analysts, but it should be pointed out to them that a tremendous bookkeeping burden is placed on programs specified to operate in such a mode.

TESTING • In the testing mode certain programs, and especially the Control Program, are specified to operate, when so required, in a manner designed to protect the system from programs not yet fully tested and to provide the programmer with information about how his newly written program fared in a real-time environment. One fairly obvious difference between the testing mode and the normal mode is that in the testing mode much transitory data should be saved by the Control Program—that is, intermediate results for the programmer to look at—which would otherwise be discarded in the course of completing an action. A testing mode is almost mandatory in those systems in which programs must be added or modified after the first version or model of the system goes into operation.

CONVERSION • If conversion is approached in some modular way—that it, city by city, function by function, file by file—programs designed to accommodate the total system have to run during the conversion period in a partial service mode, testing each entry for its possible effect on the unconverted part of the system. In an airline reservation system, some requests for space might be honored by the system because it has partially assumed the seat inventory control functions; in other cases the receipt of a "sell" action by the computer would trigger the activation of a special interim program to send a teletype request message to those offices, not yet converted, which still control their own seat inventory independent of the computer.

3.7 SUMMARY

Preliminary technical planning follows system study and design and precedes record and program specification. It is the first phase of system integration and, while it is a relatively minor phase in terms of numbers of people involved and man-years of effort expended, it is critical to soundly organized future progress by the System Integration Team. The planning staff usually begins work with (1) a set of equipment specifications, (2) functional requirements that broadly define the application, (3) possibly a Control Program specification, and (4) some broad programming assumptions made during system design. Preliminary technical planning, in seeking to transform these initial requirements and specifications into programmable terms, is necessarily both application and equipment oriented. Among the chief responsibilities of the planning staff are these:

- Outlining the phases of system integration
- Planning the general record organization
- Planning the general programming approach

In the course of planning the software subsystem, the technical planners provide feedback to the system designers when changes in either the application or the hardware are found necessary. This is a continuing responsibility of the System Integration Team, but it is during preliminary technical planning that the most basic defects in either the functional requirements or the equipment should be unearthed and changed.

CONTROLLING SYSTEM INTEGRATION 4

4.1 WHAT KIND OF CONTROL IS NEEDED?

ONCE THE basic system design has been completed and has been augmented by technical planning to provide a description of the software subsystem, the main task of the System Integration Team commences: to progress from initial system design to operational status. It is to guide the team toward the final goal of a productive system that the technical manager, or Controller, is called upon. Chapters 1 and 2 discussed the large size and complex nature of many real-time systems and stressed the influence that they can have on company operations. These characteristics of real-time systems argue for establishment of a strong technical executive to assure that implementation progress is made. Chapter 1 also stated that the System Integration Team and its Controller could, because of the unique nature of real-time systems, be likened to a military force raised to meet some great national emergency. Extraordinary crises call for unusual measures in the life of an administrative organization as well as a nation, and the installation of a real-time system must be ranked among the most demoralizing and potentially traumatic experiences that a company may be forced to undergo.

There are several ways of distinguishing the *kinds* of control, and the underlying authority to control, which the Controller must exercise. Some of these are discussed below.

Control over Personnel • This encompasses authority to staff and organize the System Integration Team in the manner the Controller deems best suited to accomplish system integration. It includes, of course, the right to veto selection of any individual and the right to discharge or reassign members of the System Integration Team.

Control over Schedule • This means first, authority to establish the schedule or at least to exercise a major influence in aiding management to set a realistic schedule. Secondly, it implies authority to secure all human and material resources needed to try to meet the schedule.

Control over Expenditures • This is closely related to the two preceding points in that the System Integration Team must be provided with sufficient financial resources to do an effective job within the schedule time allotted.

These are useful ways of looking at the Controller's responsibility for managing system integration, and they will be explored in subsequent chapters. They are, however, incidental to a more basic control principle around which all managerial functions really revolve. This is the concept of configuration control.

Given the basic system design refined by an intensive period of technical planning, there should come into being a well-balanced and feasible system configuration, accompanied by foreknowledge of the scope and methodology of each phase of system integration. With the configuration of hardware and software thus defined, and with a reasonably realistic schedule, the Controller's job is essentially one of meeting the schedule by creating an environment in which the System Integration Team can work unhampered by changes to the basic system configuration, either hardware or software.

Why should there be such emphasis on configuration control? Are intense pressures likely to be brought to bear to change the application, the equipment, or the programs? The answer is "yes." Pressures are certain to arise in any system integration project. Before examining these pressures for change, however, the interdependent nature of the major system elements should be clearly understood.

4.2 INTERRELATION OF CONFIGURATION CHANGES

The application (as defined by functional requirements), the programs, and the equipment may be viewed as three interdependent elements of the system. They constitute a sort of "eternal triangle," (Figure 4.1) such that a change in any

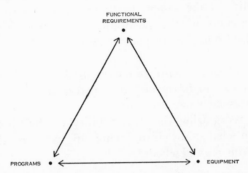

FIGURE 4.1. INTERACTION OF SYSTEM CHANGES.

one of the three system elements is almost certain to affect one, and often both, of the others. A change in the application that adds another class of file records to the system will necessitate the addition of more file storage, and this change in the equipment complement will engender modification of the programs charged with indexing and maintaining the records.

It may be recalled that one salient characteristic of present-day real-time systems, pointed out in Chapter 1, is their newness:

- The application may be one that is being attacked for the first time.
- New or specially modified equipment may be required.
- New programming approaches may be needed.

This means that the problem of configuration control becomes even more acute in systems in which these interrelated elements of uniqueness appear. An application never before placed on a computer, a computer being used for real-time processing for the first time, a multiprogrammed approach being specified for this newly defined application and for this newly engineered equipment all augur the possibility of configuration change. Often in such circumstances the need for change is incontrovertible, leaving the Controller little room for discretion in enforcing configuration control. Frequently, about the most that he can do is recognize in advance the potential vulnerability of the system to change during system integration. Awareness of the possibility of change may at least prompt the Controller to plan more realistically:

1) by allocating more resources to the technical planning phase in order to ferret out and correct at the beginning as many sources of change as possible.

2) by recognizing the susceptibility of the system configuration to change by introducing an extra caution factor into the estimates and schedules.

4.3 PRESSURE FOR CONFIGURATION CHANGE

What are the chief sources of pressure for system change? These must be understood by the Controller if he is to maintain configuration control by discriminating between those changes which are imperative and those which should be resisted, those proposals which must be implemented and those which may be discarded or deferred.

Changes beyond the Control of the Organization

Modification in the rate of deduction of federal income taxes has a direct effect upon every EAM and computer installation engaged in payroll processing. During the installation of a real-time system, such uncontrollable changes can seriously impede system integration. These external changes may come from federal or state laws, from the rulings of regulatory agencies such as the Civil Aeronautics Board or the Interstate Commerce Commission at the federal level, or state banking commissions and similar agencies at the state level.

Another source of outside influence is found in industry

associations or standards boards. It was the American Bankers Association that adopted as a standard the E13B font numerals for magnetic ink character recognition (MICR) that currently appear on checks issued by banks in the United States.

Sometimes these changes may be resisted or at least deferred, even when there is pressure from outside. Effective resistance demands a common front on the part of the company management and the Controller, who jointly decide that for the duration of the system effort the change, however salutory, will not be adopted. Examples of this resistance possibility are found in banking, where the use of MICR is optional with ABA members, and in the airline industry, where a fixed field interline reservation message format is optional as to the sending, even though after a given date all recipients of such messages will be obligated to process them on the same basis as manually prepared messages.

Managerial Pressure for Configuration Change

As the application analysts begin writing functional requirements for approval by management of the affected departments, these operating managers come to grasp more fully the true potential of the real-time system as a managerial tool. During technical planning, specification writing, and the other phases of system integration, there is constant feedback from the System Integration Team to middle and top management in the form of questions about the nature of the application and suggestions for changes and improvements in company policy and procedures. Thus management becomes increasingly well informed about how the system will work and, more significantly, about what the system *could* do for them if additional features were added. Such familiarity fosters suggestions to the System Integration Team as to how the system might further enhance managerial effectiveness.

One of the important initial actions to be taken by the Controller is to organize the System Integration Team in such a way that suggestions for change are channeled through him, so that he, rather than a technical subordinate, becomes the pressure point for requests for change by outsiders. Only in this way can the Controller hope to discern what the suggestions are, let alone evaluate or try to combat them.

An airline reservation system offers abundant opportunity for management to extend the scope of the real-time system to the direct benefit of several operating departments. Once the system has been initially justified to take care of the passenger sales function, others can be added at only a slight incremental equipment cost.[1] The reservation function requires storage in the files of one fundamental set of records—the General Schedule—which describes the pattern of all the airline's flights: days on which they operate, departure and arrival times, cities served, and related information. Now this same General Schedule information, originally set up to serve the reservation application only, can also be used to aid in automation of the following:

Flight information. This requires storage of data about irregular operations due to equipment problems and weather and field conditions. Flight information can be set up and reported in the form of variances to the General Schedule.

Aircraft routing. Based on fixed parameters such as aircraft turnaround and servicing times and mathematical models and formulas, the General Schedule can be used to determine the optimum usage of each aircraft in the fleet, given a particular General Schedule (or perhaps several acceptable versions of a projected General Schedule).

Aircraft maintenance. The General Schedule, as modified by flight information, can provide point-to-point flying times for each flight for use in scheduling maintenance of those aircraft assemblies, subassemblies, and components that must be serviced or overhauled as a function of number of hours flown.

Crew scheduling. Flight crews, like the aircraft in the fleet, must be assigned to fulfill the public service commitment represented by the General Schedule. These crew assignments must be made within the constraint of regulations about hours to

---

[1] R. E. Sprague, *Electronic Business Systems*, p. 92. New York: The Ronald Press, 1962.

be flown within a given period, seniority lists and bidding systems for the more desirable flights, crew qualification for assignment to particular types of aircraft, and similar factors. Much of this application is adaptable to computer processing built around the General Schedule.

Message routing. Even though passenger records, being stored within the central files of the real-time system, no longer have to be communicated by teletype from one board point in the passenger's itinerary to another, a large volume of administrative messages must still flow between each of the locations served by the airline. And since each of these locations already has terminal sets for reservation data input and output, the temptation to add transmission and switching of nonreservation messages is great.

The benefits of adding these applications to the automatic system are extremely alluring. There would be substantial dollar savings if aircraft routing and crew scheduling could be even partially optimized. And the increased operational efficiency through improvement of flight information, aircraft maintenance, and message switching would also be tremendous. These are attractive prospects, but management, in seeking to expand the scope of the system definition (*particularly before the system as originally designed becomes operational*) should be apprised by the Controller of these facts:

1) Some things they wish to do may not be possible, because the demands made on the equipment are excessive.

2) Other extensions of the system may be possible from an equipment standpoint but involve many thousands of dollars in additional programming.

3) Still other proposed applications may lie in a gray area, where a decision as to feasibility must await the kind of exhaustive analysis that was made during the system study of the original application.

4) Even where the equipment is adequate and management is willing to expand the budget of the System Integration Team to enlarge the scope of the system, a direct trade-off cannot be made between staff and schedule. Increasing the size and

complexity of the problem to be solved may have a deleterious effect on the schedule, even though the necessary funds are available to staff for the incremental effort.

The position of the Controller regarding change in the system configuration is fundamentally a negative one. He was hired to produce an operational system from an initial design according to a schedule. His duty, therefore, is to stress to his superiors the consequences of any demands they make for configuration change. In full possession of these facts, management can then decide whether the price is one that can be borne.

Because of the import of decisions about system changes, the Controller should *insist* that he be consulted about all proposed changes. There must be no attempt to modify the configuration by some backdoor approach to a tractable supervisor or programmer on the System Integration Team.

Changes Originating with the System Integration Team

The System Integration Team personnel will, on a somewhat different plane, undergo the same familiarization process with respect to the system as will the members of management. In addition, the system personnel will be directly involved in developing the system records and programs and in coordinating the system at all points where separately fabricated software components must be joined to each other and to the equipment. This gives them a double opportunity to suggest changes in the system configuration.

The Controller must give his subordinates an audience and tolerantly weigh their suggestions, just as he does those originating outside the System Integration Team. But he must suppress unnecessary changes here as ruthlessly as he does those made by outsiders. Understandably, this may turn out to be much more onerous than fending off the outside changes. For would-be innovators who belong to the System Integration Team are more sophisticated in the complexities of system development and are less likely to make the kinds of outlandish or fanciful suggestions that are easy to "field."

4.4 HOW MAY CONFIGURATION CONTROL BE SECURED?

No matter how impregnable his position or how broad his authority, the Controller should rely heavily on logic and persuasion to protect the system configuration from change. This is the most palatable approach to combating change and the one that should first be attempted. Are there any guidelines that might be of value to a Controller in evaluating the need for a proposed configuration change? A few techniques of configuration control may be considered.

Classifying Changes: Necessary Versus Desirable

Some changes must be made no matter what the cost in time and effort, whereas others are to some degree optional and subject to the judgment of those responsible for system integration. It would be reasonable, therefore, to classify all changes according to whether they may be rejected or deferred or whether the System Integration Team is forced to take time out to build them into the system configuration. Many of the proposals originating outside the System Integration Team may be of the deferrable variety, whereas many arising within the group may be necessary, representing the discovery of a logical flaw in the system design or a fault in the technical planning that must, at all costs, be taken care of.

Assigning a Value to Changes

Any process of reviewing proposed changes should have built into it a method for translating the change request into some easily grasped measure of its effect on the system. Number of specifications to be revised or written, number of instructions to be revised or newly coded, number of man-years to be expended, calendar-days' delay in the schedule—all such criteria convey meaningfully the impact of change on the system. The Controller should insert such measurement techniques into the procedure for evaluating proposed changes.

Bureaucratizing Configuration Changes

By endeavoring to quantify the effect of suggested modifications, the Controller is implicitly requiring that whoever proposes a change describe it in sufficient detail to permit him and his staff to analyze it thoroughly. This documentation requirement might be extended somewhat further, to the point where it is made very *difficult* for anyone to prosecute a change successfully because of the elaborate requirements for getting the change reviewed. If one were to seek deliberately to bureaucratize the process of change, he might begin by tightening the documentation standards to require not only that all proposed changes be exhaustively detailed in writing but also that each such write-up then be forwarded through the various organizational levels both within and outside the System Integration Team for an almost interminable series of reviews and approvals, with each reviewing level capable of sending the change back to the originator for further development or explanation.

This may seem a bit too Machiavellian, but the imposition of such barriers to change is a weapon the realistic Controller should not readily forego. It can probably be safely assumed that establishment of such cumbersome review procedures will discourage only the worthless or capricious suggestions, with absolutely necessary changes forcing their way to the surface by dint of their intrinsic logic.

The danger, of course, in this roadblock procedure is that, on encountering an elaborate mechanism to protect the configuration, those interested in modifications will decide to bypass the system authorities and deal directly if unofficially at the System Integration Team working level. In one actual case of this kind, a series of documents titled "Request for Program Change" began to appear with the approval portion (containing space for several names) reading *"To be* Approved by" rather than "Approved by."

4.5 SPECIAL QUALITIES OF THE CONTROLLER

What qualities should be sought in the man who will be given the title and prerogatives of Controller? Though some of the answers to this question border on the obvious, others are quite subtle. The idea of a technical-project manager is by no means new, nor is it unique to real-time data processing systems. In recent years there have been an increasing number of projects of major scope calling for direction from a technically oriented individual.[2]

It is an axiom of non-real-time commercial systems that there is no substitute for living through a programming and conversion effort, thereby getting "hands on" experience at a detailed level. This bromide continues to be valid in the real-time era. Consequently, one should expect to find in the background of the Controller extensive experience in large-scale data processing system projects, though not necessarily of the real-time variety. Such a background implies an ability to direct successfully "under fire" the efforts of system analysts, programmers, and other computer specialists. The Controller should, preferably, have successfully survived two major system development efforts—one as a technical worker and the other as a manager.

Decision-Making Ability

Above all else, the Controller must be a decision maker and, by extension, a risk taker. He must have the courage to avoid postponing unpleasant decisions. Frequently during system integration a problem, if ignored by the Controller and his staff, will go away; or more accurately it will seem to do so. It may disappear for a while, only to return six months or a year later to demand a solution, which, by then, has an enormously adverse effect on the system configuration and the schedule. Some of these decisions have to do with personnel management, others with the equipment or program subsystems, and still others with the functional requirements.

---

2 P. O. Gaddis, "The Project Manager," *Harvard Business Review,* May–June 1959, pp. 89-97.

Let us select an example having to do with equipment in-adequacy. Suppose that technical planning in the area of file records reveals that the size of the standard file record was seriously underestimated in the initial system design, with the result that several additional file storage modules plus an ex-tra file channel will have to be added to the system before the final remote location can be cut over. This miscalculation will prove embarrassing to all those—including the Controller him-self—who participated in the initial study, as it will necessi-tate renegotiation of the contract with the equipment supplier and reapproval by the management committee. There is, how-ever, a slim probability that the estimates of the technical planners will prove too pessimistic and that the judgment of the original design group will be vindicated. The Controller is counseled by friends in management to avoid rocking the boat at this point, as certain individuals on the management com-mittee, who were lukewarm about the system initially, would relish an opportunity to reappraise it critically. If the decision could be deferred for perhaps six months, the attitudes of those on the committee can be expected to improve. Also, the manu-facturer has hinted that he may soon announce a new high-density file currently under development. Despite all this, the Controller, unlike anyone outside the System Integration Team, knows that with each passing day his technical staff will be mak-ing decisions about the organization, format, and addressing of file records based on the existing system configuration; and vir-tually all this work will have to be redone if the configuration is later modified. In this case the schedule and the entire logic of the record structure are seriously imperiled if action is not taken immediately by the Controller, instead of being postponed for what might seem to be good and sufficient reasons. The Controller must bring this matter to a decision, for the costs and dangers of decision postponement are too great. This is especially true when it is realized that, even if the technical planners were partly wrong and the original configuration proves better as system integration proceeds, a marginal equip-ment solution usually has a tendency to worsen over the life of the system.

In another example, a contract is signed with an outside programming organization to supply some of the programs needed for off-line processing. This company is given a set of specifications drawn up by the System Integration Team, and several bench-mark dates for progress reporting are agreed upon. The first date is missed by the group, but a reasonable explanation is offered. Then a second date is missed and is followed by delivery of a piece of substandard work that cannot pass the most elementary requirements of system test. The outside group again offers a seemingly rational explanation for the second delay and for the error-riddled program. Each of these incidents by itself would probably be excusable. But, as the Controller knows well, their cumulative effect is forcing this and other subsystems to fall behind schedule. The president of the contract programming company points out that his personnel have now been fully trained and are in a better position to complete the work than are members of the System Integration Team who would have to be reassigned to fill the gap. Further, if work is terminated now, all the time and effort thus expended will be for naught, because newly assigned personnel would doubtless wish to adopt a different approach to the problem. A decision by the Controller is demanded here. He would be following the line of least resistance to continue to string hopefully along with the outside programming group. But having satisfied himself that this group, based upon past performance, is unlikely to make a better showing in the future, the Controller must precipitate and weather a crisis in contractual and business relationships by getting rid of them.

Ability to Anticipate Problems

The Controller should have prescience, or intuition, so that he may anticipate situations in which impediments may arise during system integration. Conversations with programmers working on file indexing should, for example, give him a feeling (*which even the programmers themselves may not have*) about developmental or operational problems to which their work may be leading. The possibilities of future difficulty in such a technical area as file indexing are virtually boundless, and the Controller should have a propensity for selecting the right ones to be concerned about.

The following are suggestive of the kinds of difficulties that a problem-sensitive Controller might anticipate:

• A design assumption about the increase in the number of beneficiaries for a typical life insurance policy will turn out to be understated by 10 percent within five years after cutover. Based on the indexing scheme for beneficiaries currently specified, disk storage will prove inadequate, and additional fast-access drum or core storage will have to be purchased to keep the system going until it can be reprogrammed, unless this future overload problem becomes known during system integration.

• A file indexing structure for an airline based on a three-digit rather than a four-digit flight number will suffice and will be much simpler if the Controller is able to anticipate a trend toward longer hauls and fewer aircraft.

• If the contract can be renegotiated, certain objectionable features having to do with acceptance testing can be eliminated. Is this a real possibility or must the system be specified around these barriers?

Not all members of the System Integration Team need have prescience. The more the better; but it is almost essential that the Controller possess this quality.

Ability to Motivate the System Integration Team

As the System Integration Team has been likened to a military organization on a war footing, the Controller should have some of the qualities of a war leader. He should be able, by word and example, to motivate the personnel on his team to work harder than can normally be expected. It was stated in Chapter 2 that system integration should not depend for success upon the extraordinary labors of a handful of programmers. Unfortunately, this caution is seldom heeded and pressure situations will doubtless continue to arise.

The Controller cannot himself work a nine-to-five schedule

and reasonably expect his subordinates to work the graveyard shift week in and week out during system testing and conversion. Usually his duties are such that he must be at his desk during business hours; yet it will do wonders for morale if he can in addition spend an hour or two at the processing site on Saturday evening, Sunday afternoon, and occasionally at three or four in the morning if that is the test or conversion schedule.

The Controller should also demonstrate to the System Integration Team that he is endeavoring to buffer them from the demands and depredations of outsiders by exercising effective Configuration Control and by performing other acts, both positive and negative, which give them a conviction that their interests and those of the system are being adequately presented outside the System Integration Team. In this sense the Controller is sometimes thought of as a salesman, alerting management to the accomplishments and problems of the System Integration Team and gaining management's continued support. If management is already "sold," then the Controller's role becomes one of keeping a communication channel open between management and the System Integration Team for the benefit of both.

The members of the System Integration Team are faced with a genuine challenge, by virtue of the arduous problems they must solve. But there is also some glamour arising from the pioneering nature of many real-time systems. And there is, certainly, an unusual sense of achievement to be gained by participating in a project of real-time scope, especially if it is cut over on schedule and operates in a way that justifies the original expectations of the system designers. It is the job of the Controller to strengthen these attitudes and feelings in order to generate a psychological climate and a sense of mission that elicits from every member of the System Integration Team his most dedicated performance.

Ability to Oppose Actions Harmful to the System

W. H. Whyte and others have criticized modern organizations for tending to produce employees and supervisors overly concerned with adjusting to the values of their group and getting along with their fellow employees.

> And why should there be consensus? Must consensus per se be the overriding goal? It is the price of progress that there never can be complete consensus. All creative advances are essentially a departure from agreed-upon ways of looking at things, and to overemphasize the agreed-upon is to further legitimatize the hostility to that creativity upon which we all ultimately depend.[3]

The Controller's job is to impose innovation—as represented by the real-time system—on an organization that is certain to be resistant. To do this he must operate in a manner that from time to time brings him into conflict with representatives of groups on which the system impinges: top management, equipment and software suppliers, line management of the departments, and members of his own staff. The interests of these individuals and groups are seldom identical, and the reconciliation of these interests—through the Controller's decision-making authority—is bound to leave some demands unheeded and some groups unsatisfied.

But, as was implied in the discussion of Configuration Control, the Controller is a kind of lightning rod for the system, protecting it against demands for change emanating from the environment that surrounds it, and endeavoring—by his courage to make decisions, his ability to anticipate trouble, and his qualities of leadership—to press the system development forward in the right direction and on schedule. Certainly it is desirable that he be esteemed by his management and by his peers and subordinates, but this goodwill must be forfeited if it seriously interferes with the well-being of the system. After all it is more essential that he retain the respect and confidence, if not the affection, of his management and staff as he demonstrates progress toward his assigned goal. He must, in short, be mindful of Leo Durocher's maxim that "Nice guys finish last."

---

[3] W. H. Whyte, Jr., *The Organization Man,* p. 65. Garden City, N. Y.: Doubleday–Anchor Books, 1956.

4.6 THE CONTROLLER AS SYSTEM MANAGER

Members of the System Integration Team may come from several organizations—the company installing the system, equipment manufacturers, contract programming groups, consulting firms—indeed, the Controller himself may be an employee of some organization other than the one acquiring the system. This is often the case in military systems work, as represented by such systems as SAGE and BMEWS, where the defense agency participates in the system study and design, then awards one contract for the equipment and another for the programs. Sometimes this award is to the same company—when the equipment supplier can demonstrate that the best interests of the system will be served by a unified approach—but by no means always. It is more common to have several contractors and subcontractors, each responsible for a portion of the system. Where this organizational diversity exists, military experience has demonstrated that a system management function should be formally established to coordinate the total system development for the using organization. In such cases the Controller *is* the overall system manager and is a representative of the company having system management responsibility. His authority then is drawn not directly from the using organization but from the system management contract, which gives him cognizance over all the subsystem suppliers for the purpose of advancing and safeguarding the interests of the using organization.

Nonmilitary users have ventured into the real-time era with no clearly evident pattern of organizing for system integration. Unless the equipment supplier agrees to deliver a total system, there is likely to be organizational diversity without benefit of an overall system manager. Usually, part of the implementation job will be undertaken by the equipment manufacturer and part by the customer. This is an extension of the traditional method employed by equipment manufacturers in dealing with commercial customers by which, although the customer assumes responsibility for programming, the manufacturer, in order to make the equipment sale, is willing to make a commitment of substantial software assistance. Under such a joint venture, the Controller might logically be selected from the staff of either the equipment supplier or the purchaser; in any case he should be someone who owes paramount loyalty to the *system* rather than to the organization that happens to be paying his salary.

If the Controller comes from the staff of the equipment manufacturer, which may have interests that could potentially interfere with or detract from the overriding goal of successful system integration, he should somehow—perhaps by means of a management contract—be made independent of such extraneous interests and influences. If this objectivity cannot be ensured, then the organization acquiring the system should choose the Controller from its own ranks, even though there may be someone in the employ of the equipment supplier who is better qualified technically.

4.7 QUESTIONS FOR THE PROSPECTIVE CONTROLLER

Up to now we have been discussing some of the qualities to be looked for in selecting the Controller. It might be instructive to consider briefly what the prospective Controller should be concerned with when he is approached about taking on such a job. Several questions might merit his attention:

• Is the system, as currently designed, feasible? In other words, has the system study and design group done a good job? Has the group been *permitted* to do a good job by those responsible for committing funds to the project, or has it, for example, been forced to choose a simplex configuration when reliability requires a duplex one?

• Is the proposed schedule realistic and, if not, can it be changed? Have the target dates for equipment delivery dominated the software target dates on the assumption that the programs will be ready? Have plans and estimates for staffing the System Integration Team been made realistically?

• Will the Controller's position be set up in such a way that he will have adequate funds, a reasonably free hand in staffing and administering the System Integration Team, and a clear under-standing of his responsibility for configuration control?

If the answer to any of these questions or others like them is "no" or even "maybe," the prospective Controller would be foolhardy to risk his personal well-being and professional stand-ing by taking the job. Even if the answer were "yes," he might with justification still demand a personal contract, which would enable him to exercise his functions without fear of reprisal. The security assured by a contract would be in the best interest of both the Controller and the organization that he is being asked to serve.

4.8 SUMMARY

Strict control must be exercised over the system configura-tion if the original design objectives are to be preserved and the system installed on schedule. The Controller must resist pressures for configuration change arising from these sources:

- Sources outside the organization
- Management of the using departments
- Members of the System Integration Team

To achieve configuration control, the Controller should em-ploy all available techniques and subterfuges.

Beyond experience and technical knowledge, the Controller should possess a number of special personal qualities, among them ability:

- to make decisions
- to anticipate problems
- to motivate the System Integration Team
- to oppose actions harmful to the system

Where the position of system manager is formally recog-nized, the Controller is the one who should fulfill this role. Be-cause of the risks inherent in functioning as a Controller, cer-tain assurances should be demanded of the organization by candidates for the job.

III

SETTING UP
THE SYSTEM
INTEGRATION
TEAM

ORGANIZATION AND PERSONNEL | 5

5.1 MINIMIZING ORGANIZATIONAL CRISES

IT HAS BEEN stressed that to accomplish preliminary technical planning, there must be recognition of the several phases of a real-time project:

- Preliminary technical planning
- Record and program specification
- Programming
- System testing
- Conversion and operation

In approaching the organization and staffing of the System Integration Team, the same stricture about the need for phased planning applies, as the organizational components of the System Integration Team and its personnel requirements will both vary a good deal from phase to phase. To illustrate, as work on program specifications nears completion, the following changes might be expected:

1) Certain of the application analysts will return to their departments, their role of furnishing functional guidance to the specification writers completed.

2) Several programming groups, consisting of perhaps three to five programmers each, will be set up and the programming work load, which has now been specified, will be allocated equitably among them.

3) Some of the senior record and program specification writers will be reassigned as supervisors of the newly formed programming groups.

4) A number of new programmers will be added to the System Integration Team and assigned to the programming groups.

Unfortunately, such organization and personnel changes are *not* as a rule planned sufficiently far in advance. As another example, those responsible for system integration frequently have only a hazy notion that some day, many months hence, there will have to be a system testing phase and that the System Integration Team is likely to encounter severe impediments before that phase is successfully completed. If a staff position responsible for this system testing were set up at the very beginning—during preliminary technical planning—two salutory effects would ensue:

1) The Controller would gain a progressively clearer picture of the magnitude of system testing and the demands that it will ultimately exert.

2) The Controller would have an opportunity to evaluate candidates for the position of manager of system testing well before the time comes to raise this position to "line" status.

The advantages to the Controller of knowing what his organization and personnel picture will be during each phase of system integration are so readily demonstrable that it is difficult to understand why most organizations go through system integration in an almost continuous state of organizational crisis. It is true, certainly, that not all organizational contingencies can be anticipated in advance. In fact, some fairly major technical problem may arise—such as a change in the CPU selected—that will have profound implications for the work load of the System Integration Team. Even though the inadequacies of any plan covering so complex an effort as system integration are conceded, it still seems preferable to *have* a plan than to attempt simply to "muddle through."

Yet many companies in organizing for system integration set up a System Integration Team, complete with organization charts, position guides, and salary schedules, with the tacit assumption that this organization will weather without change all the phases of system integration. It is naïvely assumed that the organization structure can remain static throughout the effort and still be as valid a tool of system integration during the conversion period as it was much earlier when the emphasis was on record layout and development.

This attitude may be a carryover from the organizational thinking applied in other parts of the company where conditions are more stable and new needs or new technical challenges do not arise so frequently, one following the other with disconcerting rapidity. In fact, many operating departments in a bank or an insurance company take pride in their stability, continuity, and traditions, and so represent the antithesis of the kind of volatile organization that is the System Integration Team.

In any case, there is certain to be trouble if the Controller does not, from the start, regard his System Integration Team in a time scale as four or five separate organizations, one evolving from the other as new kinds of technical activities are initiated. Again consider system testing, which is but one of the major jobs to be performed by the System Integration Team. In the beginning, testing may be the responsibility of only one person, perhaps working only part time on test planning. But toward the end of the project, the entire System Integration Team will have undergone a metamorphosis into one vast system testing "factory," with all but a handful of persons directly or indirectly assigned to system testing. This adaptation of the System Integration Team to the changing requirements of its mission must inevitably take place, regardless of whether the organization is aware of the changes beforehand. The difference between a System Integration Team that undergoes a planned evolution and one that has changes thrust upon it lies in the extent of waste motion, unused skills, and production delays incurred in making an unplanned rather than a planned transition from one phase of the project to another.

In an unplanned environment the System Integration Team will shift and expand from, let us say, a specification group into a coding organization no more rapidly than its management is forced by the weight and logic of circumstances to make the transition. Often the forcing of such change involves a "human sacrifice" in the person of some perceptive senior analyst who sees the need for change. Perhaps he feels that a stepped-up recruiting program is needed to accomplish the massive programming job that looms ahead but is unable to convey to the Controller his concern about these technical staffing requirements. It may be that his only means of dramatizing the issue is resignation or the threat of resignation.

This sacrifice of position or career to overcome "Maginot Line" thinking is assuredly not confined to the military, but very aptly characterizes situations that arise in improperly planned system projects. Usually after a few key people have departed, explaining in detail why they are leaving, the Controller begins to heed their warnings by starting to gear up properly for the next phase. How much better if he could have bowed to the inevitable with more alacrity and without the damaging effects of turnover and low morale within his technical staff.

Management must demand from the Controller intelligent planning of his organization and personnel requirements to avoid the costly and sometimes irreparable lags in system integration resulting from crisis decisions about organization. And the Controller must insure that his System Integration Team is ready to embark upon a new phase at the same time as the system itself is.

5.2 STAFFING THE SYSTEM INTEGRATION TEAM

Having established that organizational elements and the positions within them must be re-evaluated for each phase of system integration—with some jobs disappearing, others changing with respect to their duties and responsibilities, and still other newly identified positions being established—the Controller comes to grips with the problem of obtaining personnel to fill the available positions.

Two related phenomena have characterized the use of computers from the beginning and promise to hold true during the real-time era:

1) The supply of technical computer skills falls far short of the demand. This is true of engineers for digital systems, and especially true of programmers. In the ten or more years of the computer era, demand has far outstripped supply, and industry seers predict no slowing down of this trend.

2) Because programmers have been in such demand, many persons possessing only meager experience and marginal ability have appeared on the employment scene, abetted by placement agencies engaged in the brokerage of technical skills.

These conditions have given pause to company recruiters in the past, in their attempts to staff for the installation of conventional data processing equipment. And when one augments his demands by inserting the "on-line" adjective in the job title, he is competing for talent in one of the scarcest of all computer specialties today. Even with the most handsome salary and benefit offers, he may find his search unrequited.

The Controller, who is doubtless well aware of this recruiting problem or will rapidly become so, must weigh the disadvantages of a campaign of outside recruiting against the possibility of staffing the organization from within. What is he likely to encounter in a search among the using organization's personnel? If it is a large company, with thousands of employees, two personnel categories will merit his attention: employees who have computer systems or programming experience and those who have no experience but demonstrate some aptitude. Let us consider the inexperienced employees first.

Selection of Inexperienced Employees from Within

There may be a sizable number of employees who can be considered for testing, training, and assignment as junior programmers. The prime candidates are usually to be found in departments employing clerical and other junior-level persons to whom the opportunity for training in programming would offer advancement in salary and status. When such employees are carefully selected by means of intensive aptitude testing and interviewing, such selection can contribute to very effective staffing of the System Integration Team. What are some of the considerations to be followed in establishing effective internal selection procedures?

Obtain as wide a base as possible. It would be desirable if several hundred employees could be screened initially to end up with a final selection of perhaps a dozen trainee programmers. Preferably, the application or expression of interest should originate with the employee rather than through a review of files by the personnel department. This assures interest and motivation by those applying that may predict future success if the technical potential is also present. Company newsletters, house organs, and orientation sessions can be exploited to bring the new positions to the attention of prospects.

Concentrate on younger persons. As a rule, younger employees, being more malleable, are more adept at mastering programming skills. And since they will be drawn from junior-level jobs of the more routine and lower paid variety, selection as a member of the System Integration Team offers a tangible opportunity for salary improvement and more rapid career advancement.

Set up realistic qualification requirements. Often the person in charge of selection sets up rather meaningless selection criteria, such as two years of college math. In some business applications such an educational requirement makes sense, but not in the typical commercial data processing installation. Training in mathematics might, in itself, be of value in some exceptional problem areas during system integration and, more importantly, it may furnish an indication of ability to think logically. The recruiter, however, must remember that the project benefits most when the selection base is broadest and that he may be screening out more logical thinkers with his requirement than he is bringing in. More realistically, preliminary screening by administering a general intelligence test and a programming aptitude test coupled with a review of the candidates' work records and performance evaluations is preferable. Personnel who pass these hurdles should then be interviewed either by the Controller himself or by a senior staff member with extensive programming and supervisory experience.

Establish an intensive training program. One purpose of training is to screen the programmer candidates further. Those enrolled for training should be warned that final selection has not yet been completed and that they may be required to return to their old jobs on completion of training. The value of training, not only as an aid in selection but also for its main purpose of imparting the needed technical skills, is heightened if the course covers the specific real-time system to be installed rather than more general training in how to program the computer chosen as the central processor. If the equipment manufacturer is requested to conduct the training, he will usually cooperate by providing an instructor, training materials, computer time for problem solutions, and so on, but his training course will necessarily be geared to teaching people how to program the machine in question without much attention to the particular application on which the trainees will be working. In one course, for example, a group of students spent over a week mastering the floating-point arithmetic ability possessed by the computer, not knowing that in writing their file-oriented programs later on, they would never code a single floating-point instruction.

Some equipment users have overcome such problems by setting up their own training activity within the System Integration Team and developing programming courses specially suited to the real-time application to be programmed, with all examples and illustrations based on actual problems to be solved. Other companies have taken advantage of the equipment manufacturer's course offerings, supplementing these with a special intensive "post graduate" course of a week or two in which real-time control concepts and special-application requirements are stressed.

Set up a trial performance period. If the System Integration Team, following selection procedures such as those mentioned, obtains a group of trainees 10 percent of whom have above-average programming ability, 10 percent simply cannot program at all, and 80 percent are somewhere in between, this will parallel the experience of other real-time users who have gone through a similar process. Because of this situation, it should be company policy that employees who survive the training course and are assigned to the System Integration Team remain in probationary status. The Controller cannot afford to retain the 10 percent who have no programming aptitude, as they will impede integration progress out of all proportion to their numbers by producing coding that has to be redone, and generally requiring an inordinate amount of assistance and supervision. It need not require a particularly ruthless approach on the part of the Controller to rid the System Integration Team of such programmers, as they frequently sense their own inadequacies and accordingly respond to a suggestion for change. Often, these employees can be reassigned to operate consoles or perform similar operational tasks at the processing site and, because of their exposure to programming, do an outstanding job.

In-House Systems Experience

Beyond this survey of inexperienced personnel who constitute a reservoir of potential programming talent, the Controller cannot overlook the existence of previous data processing experience within the company. Many companies venturing into real-time processing have behind them an extensive record of accomplishment in batch processing. When this is true, the Controller must pursue the possibility of transferring experienced people to fill the positions available on the System Integration Team.

The presence of computer experience cannot be greeted as an unmixed benefit, however. Many seasoned veterans find it difficult to make the transition to real-time processing and try to carry over batch processing concepts and standards, with potentially disastrous results. A Control Program, for instance, is *not* the same thing as an input/output control system (iocs) written to supervise the passage of magnetic tape in a batch processing system. To the extent that the Control Program in a real-time system is responsible for supervising input/output, the two are comparable, but that is where the similarity ends. Anyone coming into the System Integration Team with preconceived ideas about the functions of a Control Program, methods of organizing records, and other knowledge acquired in batch processing has to be sufficiently adaptable to adjust his experience to the real-time environment.

If the Controller can select individuals with sufficient mental agility to focus their batch processing backgrounds in a creative way on the problems to be dealt with in the real-time milieu, the System Integration Team can be strengthened immeasurably. For such persons, unlike either the junior programmers selected from within or experienced recruits from the outside, will not be "unknown quantities" and can from the beginning be relied upon by the Controller for technical planning as well as specification and program development.

Though not a law unto itself, the System Integration Team as it is described in this book is at least a separate force in the organization, free of most hierarchical encumbrances, and the Controller should have sufficient authority to obtain personnel from anywhere within the company. Whether he seeks the promising youngster or the experienced computer man, he is necessarily looking for quality—the best. Thus the managers of the other departments will be asked to transfer some of their most outstanding workers to the System Integration Team. All the preachments about the real-time millennium will not serve to pry many good people loose without real authority vested in the Controller and substantiated at a high executive level.

In this respect, the non-real-time data processing department must be no exception. The System Integration Team is divorced in management and mission—and properly so—from existing computer operations. Because of the scarcity of well-trained and able computer programmers, the Controller must be able to exert sufficient leverage to arrange the transfer of key computer people to the System Integration Team.

Outside Recruiting

Since it is usually impossible to staff the System Integration Team adequately with personnel solely from within, the Controller may, for better or for worse, find himself looking to the outside for experienced personnel. Here a few general rules should be noted which have proved valid in conducting outside recruiting for real-time projects.

LIMIT THE SCOPE • Try to limit the number of positions to be filled through outside recruitment. Many companies wisely restrict outside hiring to only a few key persons needed to shore up an otherwise inexperienced staff. Just a handful of experienced persons in supervisory positions and staff jobs such as that of Standards Programmer can provide the leaven needed to transform a group of raw trainees into an effective System Integration Team. The objections usually raised against outside recruitment have considerable validity and present strong justification for holding it to a minimum. Many of these have to do with morale problems among those selected from within, who discover salary differentials between themselves and the newcomers. In addition to this psychological barrier, there is the handicap placed on the Controller in dealing with employees about whose background he has much less knowledge than he would like to have. He knows less not only about their technical ability but also about loyalty, facility at written expression, supervisory ability, and similar personal traits. For these reasons the Controller should limit his outside recruiting to the minimum needed to assure experienced coverage of key positions.

EXTEND THE TIME SPAN • Keep the recruiting effort open over as long a period as possible. It is unfortunate if the staffing schedule is such that group supervisors and senior programmers must be selected on the basis of only a week's talent hunt. Of all the people who might be interested in the positions being offered, only a small fraction of them will happen to read the *New York Times* or the *Wall Street Journal* on the very day that the recruiting publicity appears. The same applies to the technical placement agencies, which can provide only a few candidates for interview if the duration of the search is limited. When the length of the recruitment period is increased, so is the probability that a well-qualified candidate who might be interested will enter the job market.

MAKE COMPETITIVE OFFERS • Be prepared to startle the salary administration department by making offers that will attract high-caliber personnel. The seller's market for programming talent, far from showing any signs of abatement, seems to favor increasingly those programmers who are in the market; this, of course, is particularly true for the relative few who have significant real-time experience. It would be wonderful if these skilled persons happen to fit readily into the existing personnel classification system, but quite probably the Controller will have to obtain exemptions for many of his staff from the wage and salary plans that govern other departments. It is in areas such as this, where there is bound to be resistance from those who feel that such demands represent unwarranted distortions of company personnel policy, that the first real test of strength may come for the Controller. If he is unable to muster sufficient top-management support to set up a professionally competent System Integration Team, he has probably lost the first of many crucial battles with the guardians of the *status quo.*

ACCEPT NON REAL-TIME EXPERIENCE • Give preference to the promising candidate without real-time experience over the marginal candidate with it. A senior man who is a question mark in terms of ability or attitude can, despite his real-time background, severely damage the technical soundness of the project. It would be better to choose a person lacking real-time experience but in whom one can have confidence regarding ability to perform effectively in a technical capacity once he has adjusted his thinking to the real-time environment.

RESERVE SOME OPENINGS • Do not fill all supervisory or upper-level staff jobs with outsiders. Even where all those obtained from within the company do not have programming or systems experience, at least one or two openings should be reserved for promotion of employees who demonstrate outstanding ability during the trial period. This is more than simply a gesture by the Controller to improve morale; if the selection from within has been conducted successfully, at least a few persons so obtained should bring real strength to jobs demanding a high level of technical competence coupled with leadership ability.

DO NOT BE DISCOURAGED • Try not to be easily discouraged over the quality of interviewees, particularly when dealing with technical placement agencies. These firms operate on the premise that the more interviews arranged for their programmer clients, the better the chances of early placement. Their enthusiasm tends sometimes to inhibit adequate preliminary screening of qualifications. On receipt of resumés that are far wide of the mark or after encounters with applicants who clearly do not fit his requirements, the Controller should point out this failure emphatically to the agency. Since the Controller has to pay the fee for anyone hired in this way, he is entitled to be presented with only qualified candidates.

5.3 CONTROL OF SYSTEM INTEGRATION TEAM PERSONNEL

Once the staffing is accomplished and the best obtainable people are selected, trained, and assigned to the various organizational components that comprise the System Integration Team, the Controller must protect his organization, and consequently the system configuration itself, from the damage that can be done by misassigned personnel. Regardless of whether there is much or little real-time experience to draw upon, it is a virtual certainty that some members of the System Integration Team will be placed in jobs for which they are not fitted and from which they must be removed.

It would be fatuous to conclude that once the initial staffing is completed, based on the best organizational judgment at the time and the best people available, the results will invariably be successful, and that the problem of reassigning or dismissing certain persons will not arise. The Controller, in making his beginning assignments, has to take a calculated risk about how an inexperienced person will respond to work on actual problems, regardless of his high rating while in training, and not all these appraisals will be vindicated. Similarly, the heavily qualified and highly recommended outsider may turn out to be a "paper tiger" and may not fulfill the promise suggested by his resumé and personal interview.

Even if the technical merit and performance quality of each person could be confidently predicted, the nature of particular jobs may change radically not only from one phase of the project to another but even within the same phase. It often cannot be predicted exactly what the specific responsibilities of each staff member will be. In one project, record layout may turn out to be the most horrendous barrier; in another, the breakdown of program logic into functional subsystems and hierarchical levels. The scope and content of each *position* frequently cannot be predicted in advance with any more certainty than can the quality of performance of the person assigned.

Some Personnel Problems

Throughout its existence, the System Integration Team will be plagued by personnel problems that can have a serious impact on the system configuration and on the schedule. The occurrence of these problems is difficult to prevent, and when they arise they should not catch the Controller off guard.

SUBSTANDARD PERFORMANCE • Below-standard performance may be encountered at all levels and among persons with varying backgrounds and experience. Sometimes a personnel change for this reason may be initiated by the employee who feels that he is in "over his head." More often, the group supervisor or the Controller must be sufficiently familiar with each person's performance to be able to reach a judgment about its adequacy.

JOB HOPPING • Because programming skills in general and real-time system backgrounds in particular are so highly marketable, some loss of staff through resignations can be expected throughout the system integration effort. This will not be restricted to the more senior persons in the project, although loss at these higher levels is more harmful. Former trainees with only a scant year of experience may find themselves wooed by offers of more money and higher status on other real-time projects. Naturally the loss of a highly valued aide who receives an unmatchable offer elsewhere can deal a damaging blow to the project. In other cases, some of the more marginal employees who might otherwise have to be replaced anyway will decide to leave, usually for a more responsible position with some other real-time project. When these persons leave, the Controller can rejoice at his good fortune while lamenting the fate of his counterpart on the competing project.

To protect the System Integration Team from the effects of sudden and unexpected resignations, the Controller should establish the policy that no punitive action will be taken against any employee who may wish to "look around," and that, in fact, a prerequisite for getting a good recommendation from the Controller is advance notice by an employee of his dissatisfaction or intention to look elsewhere. If an atmosphere of openness and mutual confidence can be established, the Controller gains a twofold advantage: (1) he will have an opportunity to try to persuade the valued employee to remain with the System Integration Team and, (2) at the same time, he can begin to give serious consideration to selecting a replacement.

THE "BURNT-OUT" PROGRAMMER • Many managers have noted the existence of a syndrome among programmers who, having survived a major programming assignment, lose all desire to participate in any further similar projects, even though they are by experience most admirably qualified to carry heavy responsibility in implementing a new system. This has been aptly described as the problem of the "burnt-out" programmer.[1]

Because of the intense and sustained quality of system integration work, psychological and physical wear and tear may force some members to leave the project even before the system is anywhere near operational status. Unfortunately this breaking point is reached by most persons just at that juncture of the project when the Controller can least afford to see them go. The person most knowledgeable about the best method for testing a certain subsystem of records and programs may have to be replaced at the height of testing in this area because it is precisely at this point that his pressure threshold is exceeded.

What the Controller Can Do

What, beyond close surveillance of each person's technical performance and emotional make-up, can the Controller do to insulate the system from the repercussions of personnel dislocations? He must adopt as a principle of personnel manage-

---

[1] Paul S. Herwitz, Remarks at the IBM Systems Research Institute, August 1962.

ment the strategy of not becoming overly dependent upon any one individual. This is far from easy to do, because when a competent person is found—especially one eager to shoulder a heavy burden of responsibility—there is a natural tendency to allow him to work himself into a position on the System Integration Team where his departure would cost weeks or even months of delay.

The Controller must strive to protect the system from the "indispensable" or even semi-indispensable man. A paramount reason for laying great stress on well-developed written specifications and other documents is to get system facts and know-how out of the minds of those cognizant of various facets of the system and into a *written* form readily understandable by others.

Another danger associated with loss of personnel is the possibility that the replacement will, by default, have insufficient ability to follow through competently on the work in progress. A job rotation and understudy system should be developed that will assure sufficient "bench strength" to prevent a programmer with only limited ability and a few months of experience from making major technical decisions about system development simply because he happens to be available at the time a vacancy occurs.

5.4 UTILIZING PERSONNEL FROM OTHER ORGANIZATIONS

In military system development, it is not uncommon for the prospective user of a computer system to demand delivery of a total system, including both the equipment and the program subsystems, which together must meet acceptable performance criteria. To fulfill such requirements, the equipment manufacturer sometimes undertakes to supply the programs as well as the hardware and, in effect, to deliver a "black box" to the customer, who is then concerned with neither the development nor the maintenance of the stored program subsystem. Alternatively, the using organization may contract to obtain the equipment from one company, the program from another, and possibly system management assistance from a third outside concern, which assumes responsibility for supervising the other two. From the viewpoint of the user, the establishment of such contractual relationships makes the implementation problem considerably simpler, since he is contractually assured of a system-in-being.

When one leaves the sphere of military systems, system integration is not nearly so well organized. Delivery of a total system costs (or appears to cost) more, and many companies have trouble enough getting agreement to appropriate sufficient funds for the equipment alone. Consequently the approach toward system justification is frequently in the direction of de-emphasizing, if not altogether burying, software costs. In military projects, there is less need to be so dollar conscious when dealing with a system whose justification lies not in the area of displaceable cost but rather in how well the system will accomplish its defense mission. Furthermore, with many military real-time systems directed at new defense needs, there is not the problem of overcoming the inertia of the traditional way of doing things, which exists in a commercial organization.

But because control of organizational diversity through system management has not heretofore received the same recognition in commercial as it has in military systems does not make the organizational problems disappear. If anything, they are compounded when sound principles of system management are neglected.

When the function of the system manager has not been well defined, the Controller must become a sort of *de facto* system manager if he is to build a cohesive System Integration Team. In doing so, the Controller may at various times utilize persons from numerous organizations.

Let us identify some of the organizations that might be represented on the System Integration Team for a large real-time system and, as a consequence, might come within the purview of the Controller as he seeks to minimize the undesirable influences inherent in organizational diversity.

Personnel from the Using Organization

In the pre-real-time era, personnel from the using organization comprised the most numerous group and the one having basic responsibility for programming with, or course, assistance from the field technical force of the equipment manufacturer. For most present-day commercial real-time system projects, the bulk of the System Integration Team personnel will doubtless continue to be organizationally a part of the company acquiring the system.

Manufacturer's Personnel

Manufacturer's personnel should really be categorized into several subclassifications. In fact a serious coordination problem is sometimes present strictly within the equipment manufacturer's own organization. To begin with, sales personnel will be assigned to the account, perhaps at more than one level. They will be supported by technical personnel of the system analyst or system engineer type. And behind these may be ranked programming personnel committed to work side by side with the customer's programming staff as an integral part of the System Integration Team.

Most equipment manufacturers are organized along functional lines, with the engineering, manufacturing, and marketing divisions each having more or less independent and co-equal organizational status. Because real-time systems usually involve the interests of all three of these organizational components, and possibly a commitment of personnel from each one, there is need for internal coordination of the manufacturer's support of the system, especially when the support personnel are not grouped on a project basis. The System Integration Team represents the ultimate in project organization, and the equipment manufacturer should, if need be, permit people from his functional divisions to be welded into the structure of this team, even when control of the team is not lodged with the manufacturer.

In many projects there are several hardware suppliers, with one vendor providing the central processing equipment and another the terminal equipment, and, of course, one communication common carrier providing the data links. On the ERMA commercial banking project, a large system with a daily processing cycle that exhibited many of the characteristics of real-time processing, there were more than a half-dozen manufacturers, each of whom to a greater or lesser degree supplied sales, technical, and maintenance support to the project:

- Central processing equipment—Company A
    (Prime Contractor)

- Sorter-readers
    Electronics—Company A
    Mechanical—Companies B and C

- Core memory banks—Company D

- Drum memory—Company E

- Tape drives—Companies F and G

- Printers
    Electronics—Company A
    Mechanical—Companies B and H

- Programming—Company A

Although in this case Company A was the prime contractor and the others were in a subcontractor or vendor relationship to Company A, the listing serves to illustrate the degree to which different manufacturers can become involved in supplying major subsystems.

System Management Personnel

It has been noted that in some military projects a system management organization may be designated to oversee the companies supplying the equipment and software subsystems. As commercial real-time systems begin to rival those of the military in scope and complexity, we are likely to see the idea of formal system management contracts extended to such systems. The Controller will then, of course, be the lead man in the system management organization and will build his System Integration Team around a cadre of personnel from the system management company. There is as yet not enough experience with such an approach toward commercial data processing systems to allow confident prognostication about what organizational pattern will prove most successful. It is difficult to see, however, how the equipment manufacturers—especially when new products are involved—can fail to play a significant role in system integration and thus be among the foremost candidates to assume genuine system management responsibility.

It should be stressed that the system management *function* must exist, whether or not it is recognized in contractual fashion. The Controller, no matter what organization he is drawn from, whether operating under a strong charter and with ample resources, or laboring under the weight of inadequate support, remains the logical person to exercise system management responsibility. When the Controller is weak or when the tasks of system integration are spread among many organizations, the fact remains that there is still a *responsibility* for system management. If the responsibility is not focused on one person— the Controller—and on one group—the System Integration Team—it will necessarily be diffused and ineffectively wielded.

An enlightened management will, in the long run, cause fewer dislocations by taking the seemingly radical step of vesting in the Controller and the System Integration Team full system management responsibility than by adhering to the more traditional organizational alignments used to install non-real-time systems. Otherwise, when the using organization begins to experience disruptive delays in the schedule and serious malfunctions in system performance, those topside will realize with regret that they should have established stronger technical leadership from the beginning.

Contract Programming Companies

The past few years have seen a rapid increase in the number of companies offering to produce programs on a contract basis or, alternatively, to provide programmers for work on assignments under the supervision of customer personnel on a daily or weekly fee arrangement. These organizations have come into being in response to the genuine needs of companies installing data processing equipment and are a reflection of two significant attitudes toward today's software:

1) **Recognition** that programming is becoming relatively more important. Ignoring real-time systems entirely, there is a consensus among computer people that a gap exists between the sophisticated data processing machines available today and the user's ability to exploit them fully. When one turns to real-time systems, he finds, not surprisingly, that the gap is even more pronounced.[2]

2) Acceptance of the notion that not just anyone can be taught to program. Although it is still heretical in some programming circles to criticize procedure-oriented languages such as COBOL (Common Business Oriented Language) on the ground that such languages are too difficult for a person of average ability to use efficiently, this point of view is gaining adherents. COBOL was developed originally in the belief that it was both necessary and desirable to divorce programming from the intricacies of the equipment selected, by permitting the program to be stated in plain English (or almost plain English). In this way, according to the partisans of these non-machine-oriented languages, the acute shortage of programmers can be overcome. Experience thus far has not borne out these optimistic expectations, and the growth of contract programming companies consisting of persons with proven programming ability is certain to continue until the merits of procedure-oriented languages are finally established or laid to rest.

Operations Personnel

Once operational status is achieved, a separate company may receive a contract to operate and maintain the data processing center and equipment. This should not interfere very much with the progress of system integration, except that those responsible for operating the equipment will probably need to be represented on the System Integration Team.

Consultants

Consultants can be differentiated from other outsiders, by the scope and the level of their services. An experienced and

---

[2] Robert V. Head, "New Challenge for Programming Systems," *Datamation*, February 1963, pp. 39-41.

well-informed consultant may be invaluable in guiding and protecting the user during the system study and preliminary technical planning. If a consultant becomes involved at this early stage and proves useful, he may be retained advantageously to aid in seeing the project through to completion. Some consulting firms are specialists in such areas as man-machine relationships and human factors, whereas others offer everything from contract programming to active system management as part of their service package. When dealing with outside consultants, the Controller should determine that each person who may be assigned to work with the System Integration Team is well qualified and will be able to devote sufficient time to the project to be of constructive assistance.

5.5 CONSEQUENCES OF ORGANIZATIONAL DIVERSITY

One way in which the problems of multiplicity in organizational backgrounds may be minimized is to establish the organizational cleavage at the group level, not at the individual level. Instead of having, let us say, a high-speed inquiry programming group and a teletype inquiry programming group—both a meld of persons from two or more companies—each of these groups might contain only employees of the same company. Thus the frictions of organizational diversity are raised up one level, so only the supervisors, rather than the programmers, owe allegiance to different companies.

An extension of this idea is to take advantage of the workload breakdown completed during preliminary technical planning by contracting separate portions of the software subsystem to outside groups. In this way part of the system integration job can be performed without ever having to absorb those assigned into the System Integration Team itself. While this has the advantage of removing from the System Integration Team some of the problems of organizational diversity, it places on the Controller and his aides the burden of closely following the work being performed outside their immediate control, as well as specifying this work in sufficient detail to assure that it will be completed satisfactorily.

Such approaches as these provide only a partial solution to the problem of diverse organizations contributing to system integration. Despite the Controller's best efforts, numerous managerial difficulties can arise through organizational multiplicity.

Divergent Loyalties

In attending meetings to resolve technical problems, reviewing program specifications, obtaining work-load estimates, and setting standards, the Controller and his aides must remember that the technical solutions proposed and the opinions advanced may be colored by the organization to which their authors owe loyalty. How can the Controller be certain that a hardware/software trade-off will result in overall system balance and not just in economy in the development of one subsystem at the price of another? He cannot, if his "subordinates," by virtue of their organizational affiliation, are more preoccupied with one subsystem than with another or with the overall system. Under such conditions, the Controller must try as best he can to exploit the technical ability of these persons, at the same time remembering that their view of system integration is, despite the best of intentions, not necessarily his view.

Salary Administration

It is axiomatic among project managers that the key to successful personnel management lies in control over the salaries of the group members. Like all simplifications, this tends to ignore some significant personal and group attributes, such as the professional ethics, *esprit de corps,* and mutuality of interest of those working together. Nevertheless, control of the monetary aspect of employment is an indispensable factor, and he who must direct people without it is grievously handicapped. Anyone who has had to exercise supervision over programmers employed by a company other than his own can attest to the power of the purse as a performance motivator.

We have already mentioned the demoralizing effect of violating the principle of equal pay for equal work by offering higher salaries to attract persons from the outside than are paid to those chosen from within the organization. The same applies to dual organizations where, if a programmer from one company is being paid more than the man sitting at the desk next to him who happens to work for a different company, the Controller has a potential morale problem. Similarly, if one company authorizes compensation for overtime and the other does not, a morale problem can be expected to arise. It seems to do no good whatever to try to conceal these differences. Even when the personnel involved are downrightly conspiratorial in concealing salary information, cleavages have a way of coming up in conversations in car pools or bowling teams (which themselves are usually organized along the same diverse pattern as the System Integration Team itself).

Confidential Material

Differences dictated by diverse organizational loyalties within the System Integration Team also extend to the handling of company confidential material. The equipment manufacturer for his part may be developing some unannounced products for the system, which he wishes to keep under a strict cloak of security and out of the hands of nonemployees. For this reason, it is not uncommon to find segregated routing lists and staff meetings for various members of the System Integration Team. The presence of such restrictions on the dissemination of information serves to emphasize the differences in status of those assigned to the project just as surely as do such things as salary differentials. The Controller must expend extra effort to mold his System Integration Team into a well-knit unit despite the divisive influences of this problem of confidential material.

Intangible Considerations

Apart from the difficulties associated with overt variances in company personnel policies, more subtle differences can affect the performance of the System Integration Team. An illustration may be drawn from an occurrence during one large project in which a company car being driven to the computer center by a customer's programmer was involved in an accident. In the car were several other programmers, one of whom worked for the equipment supplier. This person was injured and required hospitalization, at which point it was discovered that the customer's automobile insurance policy did not extend to coverage of injuries sustained by persons who were not employees of this company, it being company policy not to carry riders in official vehicles. The lawyer for the injured programmer advised her to sue the customer for damages on the ground that negligence on the part of the driver permitted her to ride in the car and thus sustain injuries. This situation created a great deal of acrimony before it was resolved, and caused almost universal regret that an organizational conflict had been allowed to impede progress on the system. Far fetched? Not at all. The Controller, unless he is unusually lucky, will have to obtain legal advice on similar matters more than once in the course of system integration.

5.6 SUMMARY

Organization and personnel planning must be performed for each phase of system integration, as the System Integration Team is actually several different organizations, one evolving from another. In staffing the System Integration Team, the Controller may have to resort to outside recruiting for key personnel, filling the remainder of the positions with personnel carefully selected from within. After staffing is completed, the performance of each member must be followed closely, as it is a virtual certainty that changes and reassignments will be necessary.

Often in real-time system integration there is the problem of organizational diversity within the System Integration Team. Personnel from the following companies may be represented:

- User of the equipment
- Equipment manufacturers
- System management
- Contract programming
- Operations
- Consulting

This diversity creates numerous problems in supervision because of divergent loyalties, nondisclosure constraints, and other intangible considerations.

ESTIMATING AND SCHEDULING 6

6.1 GENERAL CONSIDERATIONS

COMPUTER ENGINEERS are wont to dwell critically on the inability of software specialists to estimate work loads and delivery schedules for program subsystems with the same degree of precision as do the engineers for the equipment subsystems. In rebuttal, the programmers point out that similar delays and problems exist in engineering a major *new* computer or storage module, which might be roughly analogous to developing an extensive new software product. The programmers further contend that while equipment design and engineering may be thought of as a science or at least a highly developed professional discipline, design and fabrication of programs is an art or, at any rate, an intuitive process similar to that involved in creating a painting or composing an étude. This view of programming is not as prevalent as it once was, but it is still encountered with disconcerting frequency in an industry whose sales have grown to the range of three billion dollars yearly. And whatever the reasons, it must be admitted that lack of ability to predict accurately the scope of the system integration effort required to put a real-time system into operation is among the great weaknesses of the field at present.

Before the advent of real-time systems, the integration task for a commercial data processing system, although admittedly difficult and challenging, was generally a good deal less complex than that now demanded by real-time systems. In truth, the programming specialty has never before been similarly extended. In its more than ten years of hectic existence, it has not really had to pay serious heed to the jeremiads of its critics by disciplining its methodology into a more routinized and controlled process.

Consider, in illustration, the development of a demand deposit accounting system in the pre-real-time era. Taking a given equipment capacity, a selection arrived at by use of more or less primitive analytical tools, the programming could be broken down according to a fairly typical pattern. Size of available main memory dictated organization of the processing into several "runs" or "passes," which were, by definition, any collection of related logical and arithmetic steps that could be accommodated in a given-size memory. A sort of the incoming checks and deposit tickets would thus be a run, as would be the editing of statements for output on a high-speed printer. If the original equipment selection turned out to be erroneous, say too many or too few positions of main memory were specified, this would not make a great deal of difference to the programming staff, assuming that the application was otherwise feasible. They might produce fifteen runs or twenty-five runs, rather than the more nearly optimum twenty, to complete the processing sequence, but technical planning and the accompanying estimating procedures were about the same, regardless of the speed or size of the computer—the object was to carve out a workable series of runs of roughly comparable complexity and to estimate the amount of time to write and test the instructions required for each of these runs.

As experience was accrued in major application areas such as deposit accounting, a knowledgeable planner could predict with confidence that for a given computer of a certain size and power, a posting run would, for example, require about 2000 single address instructions and could be regarded as an economical piece of software if it were programmed and tested in twenty man-weeks. In fact, on some commercial applications, experience not only permitted the estimating of programming productivity with great accuracy but, as more became known about how to program various applications, generalized programs (such as GE's BANKPAC for deposit accounting) could be written to take advantage of the similarities in data processing practices within an industry or major application area.

These preprogrammed applications improved even further the ability to estimate by reducing the nonstandard or custom-made portion to a much smaller percentage of the overall software subsystem.

It took a great investment in programming over many years to obtain sufficient experience to arrive at this level of sophistication for any application. In the very early days, during the transition from electric accounting machines to computers, preprogrammed application packages or prior estimating experience was not available to provide a meaningful guideline.

All applications, real time or otherwise, have had during the course of their initial development a difficult time of it in this matter of estimating the scope, complexity, and duration of software production. This uncertainty has prevailed until considerable experience with each new application has been accumulated. Present-generation real-time systems possess not only this handicap of newness but the additional handicap of a more complex software subsystem for which estimates must be derived.

Most rules of thumb that have come down from the non-real-time era are based on the criterion of a certain number of instructions to be programmed within a specified unit of time ranging anywhere between a man-day and a man-year. What is meant by the term "programming" itself varies widely, all the way from the semiclerical task of coding instructions by following an exhaustively detailed flow chart to the job of a programmer-analyst, who takes over a sizable and ill-defined problem and develops it all the way from flow charting through final testing. When such guidelines as 1000 instructions per man-year are proffered as a productivity standard, it is necessary to ascertain whether this includes program planning and testing and, if so, to establish the complexity of such planning and testing as determined by the nature of the problem, and the amount of system analysis previously devoted to the problem. In a scientific application, such as one in meteorology, the analysis would usually require a programmer trained as a meteorologist whose main concern would be to define the bounds of the problem. Compared to this analysis, which from the standpoint of actually coding the computer instructions is "preliminary," the amount of coding time and the length of the program are insignificant. In commercial data processing, time spent in specifying the fields of a file record in a manner best suited to optimum processing is quite likely to overshadow the programming time expenditure. Because of such considerations it is germane to establish the assumptions behind any estimating rules and guidelines that are suggested as a standard.

Fundamental to the derivation of meaningful estimates is the requirement that they be based on as much detailed foreknowledge of the application as can be obtained at the time at which estimates are called for. The more the technical problems can be broken down and considered individually, the more accurate will be the resultant estimates. One of the first steps in generating estimates should, therefore, be to segregate them according to these elements:

- The *organizational components* planned as part of the System Integration Team
- The *phases* of system integration

It is a distressing fact that many data processing projects have in the past recruited dozens of programmers and budgeted hundreds of thousands of dollars for a job for which the only estimate in existence was a gross one of total number of instructions, unrefined as to what this number comprehended, what personnel would be needed for assignment to different portions of the problem, and whether the estimate would be allocated to groups along functional or process lines. In justification of such inadequate attempts at estimating, it is sometimes said that the manpower and the time required will probably be underestimated no matter how painstaking the estimating process, and so no great harm results from making only gross estimates. Persons with this attitude base their argument on the equation that all too frequently exists between misestimating and underestimating. When confronted with this cynical acceptance of ever-rising software costs, one can only retort that a systematic approach will at least enable us to underestimate more accurately.

Operating on the basis of gross estimates is potentially harmful for two reasons:

1) The estimates are virtually certain to be wrong unless the estimator is both immensely astute and remarkably prescient.

2) They fail to provide the Controller with a foundation for allocating functions and personnel during the period of organization planning.

The Controller must not only elicit meaningful estimates but must also actively participate, along with his key planners, in producing estimates for each box on the organization chart and for each anticipated project phase. And he must periodically review and modify the estimates for each organizational component and phase as system integration advances.

6.2 FACTORS TO BE CONSIDERED IN ESTIMATING

Accepting the software estimating picture as it presently is —somewhat bleak—and conceding that programmers, unlike their engineering counterparts, are not subject to a very well defined professional discipline, what are some of the factors that should be taken into account in estimating?

Specialization within the System Integration Team

Whenever possible, estimates for administrative and clerical costs should be separated from those attributable to direct programming effort. Similarly, estimates for staff functions such as system standards should be segregated from those for line functions such as operational programming. Within the line organization, separate estimates for each group performing a more or less self-sufficient and identifiable function should be prepared. One collateral result of preliminary technical planning is breakdown of the total programming burden into logically separate major pieces for which estimates can be more easily derived.

There is significant psychological benefit in making detailed estimates that parallel the organizational structure. To do so involves, or should involve, the judgment of those who will later be responsible for accomplishing the work envisioned by their estimates. A group leader will undoubtedly regard the performance of his programmers against the schedule with considerably more concern if he participated in making the estimate on which the schedule is based. This is reflected in the axiom that *the closer to the problem the estimates originate, the greater is the probability of their accuracy.*

Experience Level of the System Integration Team

Regardless of whether the project is staffed entirely from within or whether extensive outside aid is sought, there will be a period during which those who find themselves in a new organizational environment will not function very effectively. The reduction in productivity implied by this "learning curve" may be expected to reappear during each new phase of the project, as the staffing pattern and personnel assignments change.

If staff selection is mainly from within, time must be allocated for learning the extensive technical skills required for positions like specification writer and programmer. This is not merely the few weeks spent in programming class at the commencement of the effort but a *continuing* period of weeks or months before the individual approaches peak effectiveness. After all, if the Controller were looking for people from the outside, he would unquestionably require a year's programming experience as a minimum. When persons from within are developed, they have much experience to gain before they can be regarded as more than mere apprentices.

If outside personnel are recruited, they must devote time to both learning the application and adjusting themselves to the intangibles of their new surroundings. For this reason some managers resort to outside recruiting only for supervisory and senior technical positions where the emphasis is more on knowledge of the system's equipment than on the details of the application.

Attrition

Some allowance for staff turnover during system integration must be made in the estimates. Several aspects of this phenomenon can have a disruptive effect on the schedule. The loss of time and effort caused by additional training, reworking of problems, and revision of approaches is often appallingly great. Though there are, as was mentioned in Chapter 5, ways of minimizing turnover and softening its impact when it does occur, delays will ensue despite such safeguards.

TECHNICAL INADEQUACY • Whether obtained from within or outside the company, there will be a certain number of persons assigned to technical jobs who simply cannot or will not pull their weight. Unfortunately, this cannot always be discovered during an initial formal training period or apprenticeship. Entirely apart from the personnel problem which this creates, the estimator should anticipate a diminution of staff effectiveness for this reason.

JOB HOPPING • Because real-time systems are technologically advanced, an individual who has accumulated a year or more of solid real-time experience finds himself an attractive prospect on the open job market.

EMOTIONAL PROBLEMS • It would be unusual indeed if no one, for either physical or emotional reasons, is forced to leave the project—usually at a very critical juncture when personal stress is greatest. This can have a devastating effect on the schedule if the loss occurs in a key position.

Organizational Diversity

The presence of personnel from several different companies as part of the System Integration Team has the effect of increasing the amount of time required to complete the project. Although it is difficult to determine exactly why this should be so, it may be due to an understandable proclivity on the part of the Controller and his aides to conduct a detailed review of all specifications and programs produced by employees of other companies. Another reason may be that there is considerable duplication of effort among groups and individuals not having identical chains of command and organizational loyalties. Finally, the efforts of some participating groups may be subject to less control by those having overall responsibility than would be exercised if the System Integration Team were more homogeneous.

Let us consider an example that illustrates these points. Suppose that there is urgent need to expedite work on a considerably sophisticated simulation program needed to help check out individual Operational Programs during the early stages of system testing. A decision is made by the Controller to let a contract for this piece of work, totaling perhaps 5000 instructions, to an outside programming company. Because work is to be performed by outsiders, the need for control in the form of written specifications and progress review meetings is recognized and planned for by the System Integration Team. But since the outsiders know little about the details of the application (and the members of the System Integration Team have little knowledge of the true abilities of these contract programmers), the establishment of specifications and review of performance against specifications at progress meetings turn out to be far more time-consuming than would supervision of a comparable group set up as a part of the System Integration Team.

Suppose further, and this is not an unreasonable supposition, that some delay is encountered in completion of the simulator because of a pronounced lack of ability on the part of one of the contract programmers assigned. If this were the Controller's own man, on his payroll, he would be reassigned immediately, but since he is part of an outside organization the Controller can only protest about the progress being made. This objection may or may not be convincing to the contract organization, which, to extend this example, may simply choose to take some halfway corrective action, such as "talking to" the programmer who is causing the problem. The Controller, in exasperation, then assigns one of his own people to write a "back-up" simulator, considerably less complex than the one originally specified, to be used just in case. And to be sure, the contracted-for simulator turns out to be several weeks late. But so does the back-up simulator, because it was specified and estimated too hurriedly. The end result is that the back-up simulator, though late, is used for two or three weeks (at a reduced level of effectiveness) before the original simulator is released.

What has occurred here? Schedule time was burned up by two misestimates, the first made by the outside company, which failed to reckon with the delaying effects of its incompetent programmer, and the second made by the Controller, as he sought a "crash" solution. Extra manpower was expended (1) in detailed problem specification to guide the outside group, (2) in writing the back-up simulator, and (3) in using the back-up simulator as a less sophisticated substitute for the original. In addition, there was a period during which *no* program testing at all could be done, with a resultant negative impact on the estimates of all programming groups and their respective targets. Admittedly, some of these problems might have occurred in a unified organization, but probably not *all* of them. The salient point is that when making estimates one must be on guard against failing to anticipate the delays inherent in diverse organizational arrangements.

Overtime

The possibility of compensating for overoptimism in estimating through application of overtime is regarded as a protective safety valve by many neophytes at system integration. Unknowingly, they are violating a fundamental software estimating tenet: *Plans and estimates should be pessimistic.* The subjective and imprecise nature of software estimating requires that the initial estimates be quite conservative. Then if, but only if, they prove to be inadequate during system integration should stopgaps be considered. Few who have been through a system integration project would dispute the premise that, given even the most conservative estimates, there is a fair probability that delays will be encountered because some of the estimates were low. Overtime is currency that should not be spent until it absolutely has to be, when a rainy day resulting from underestimating comes along.

Many experienced managers who regard overtime only as a last resort counsel strongly against factoring it into estimates because of its undesirable side effects:

1) It costs a great deal of money. At some point, on a dollar-per-instruction-produced basis, the extra output of an overworked programming staff becomes nil. Long before that point is reached, overtime compensation becomes an uneconomical incentive.

2) It probably cannot be uniformly applied if more than one company is involved. Some companies classify system analysts and programmers as professional or managerial employees, categories for which overtime usually cannot be authorized; others classify these tasks as semiclerical and consequently eligible for overtime pay.

3) It is difficult to discontinue. There is a distinct possibility of featherbedding by those who are put on overtime pay status.

4) It tends to dispel a sense of mission by making people conscious of their hours. If the Controller has succeeded in instilling a sense of urgency, then the more highly motivated people are already logging in long hours without much thought about personal gain. And those who have exhibited no sense of urgency probably will not be much more productive even with generous overtime payments.

The key problem with overtime pay is that, regardless of titles or salary administration plans, one is dealing with creative accomplishment rather than assembly-line work. Essentially, the Controller is trying to schedule and fabricate a software subsystem in assembly-line fashion, but with a group of workers possessing highly individualistic skills and considerable pride and sensitivity about their status and performance.

One Controller recognized these special characteristics of his programming staff and, at the commencement of a sizable system integration project, initiated the following overtime policy:

It is recognized that every programmer will, during the period of system integration, be called upon for extraordinary performance. Sometimes this will require him to work many extra hours a week and often the hours worked will be at irregular times and extend into evenings and weekends. The company is appreciative of this and realizes that, in such a situation, there can be no truly adequate monetary compensation. As something more than a token gesture, however, all personnel will be put on an overtime payment schedule of eight hours a week. In most cases, hours actually worked will far exceed this, but employees will at least have tangible evidence that their efforts are appreciated.

Each employee was then permitted to establish his own hours for carrying out his assigned tasks. The accomplishment of this group under such an arrangement was outstanding, reflecting sustained performance over a period of almost two years.

Another Controller, confronted with a formidable two-month peak work load, felt that extra compensation was warranted but discovered that no overtime pay could be authorized for employees having the salary classification of his programmers. Exhibiting the kind of resourcefulness that commended him as a Controller, this man promptly filled out the necessary forms to "promote" his entire staff with an attendant generous increase in salary. Then, at the end of the six-week period, mustering as much of a straight face as possible, he submitted forms demoting everyone.

These are but two examples of how overtime has been effectively used, in both cases more as a morale builder than as a direct goad to increased production. Overtime should be handled in this way, if it must be resorted to at all in buttressing an underestimated schedule.

Travel

Travel time can be a major ingredient in estimating the work load of the System Integration Team. In the early years of data processing, it was common for members of the using company's programming staff to journey to the computer manufacturer's plant for debugging sessions prior to delivery of equipment. This practice is less prevalent today, mainly because advances in the methodology of program debugging no longer require the programmer to visit the computer site personally each time he wishes to test a program. But there are still valid reasons for sending personnel to the plant or test center before one's own equipment is delivered. For one thing, the turnaround time for test shots is better if the programmer is on the spot, waiting with his program and test data in the back room of the computer center rather than in a distant city from which his cards and tapes would have to be mailed or otherwise transmitted. There is no doubt that improved methods of transmitting digital data over long distances rapidly and cheaply will reduce still further the necessity of the programmer's traveling to use a computer during the initial debugging phases prior to equipment delivery. At present, however, it would be imprudent not to plan for some travel time when making estimates.

Travel also takes on importance for the programmers during system testing and conversion if the real-time system is one that includes terminals geographically remote from the computer site. After the computer is installed at the central site and a certain amount of testing with simulated input is carried out, it becomes necessary to test further both the equipment and the programs by transmitting live data from the remote locations. As this kind of testing begins, travel by the programmers to analyze input and output data and to aid the local staff in trouble shooting can be expected.

Testing and conversion actually imply travel by two distinct groups—programmers and conversion specialists. For the conversion people, who may or may not be organizationally a part of the System Integration Team, travel is a way of life. It is their responsibility to train the operators of the system, hold orientation sessions for supervisors and other employees at the remote sites to explain the operation of the system (and allay fears about automation), and coordinate site preparation and other physical changes needed to accommodate the terminals and peripheral equipment.

Thus, at various phases in the project, travel time may take on special importance for both programming and conversion personnel and must be reflected in the estimates.

Staff Relocation

Allied to travel time is time lost owing to relocation of the System Integration Team in new working quarters. It is probable that, in planning to house the equipment that will comprise the processing center, provision will be made for staff offices at the same location as the equipment. This has been a frequent reason for a personnel move midway through many system projects. A second reason, also common, is a forced move when the System Integration Team expands to the point where its old quarters are no longer adequate. In either case, a move is disruptive to production and some number of man-days per staff member should be included in the estimates for this reason. The effect of a move will, of course, vary markedly depending upon whether the relocation is within the same commuting area or involves a transfer of home as well as office location.

Other Estimating Factors

It should be noted in passing that numerous other time-consuming activities should be recognized in estimating. Formal classroom training, vacations, illness, personal business, and conference attendance must, of course, be allowed for.

6.3 ESTIMATING FOR EACH PHASE OF SYSTEM INTEGRATION

The factors mentioned in Section 6.2 should be applied to each phase of system integration, in order to make the estimates as detailed as possible.

Preliminary Technical Planning

Preliminary technical planning is the most difficult phase for which to derive estimates, since at the beginning relatively little is known about the scope of system integration. Such planning is itself an estimating phase in that it provides the basis for estimating the requirements of the remainder of the project. About all that can be said of this phase is that it should involve relatively few persons as compared to subsequent phases, and should not, in terms of calendar months, represent a significant portion of the total project schedule.

Specification Development

Estimating for specification development is contingent on the standards for specification writing, that is, the "Specification for Specifications" discussed in Chapter 9. By allowing more time and resources for the phases preceding and following this one, a comparatively small amount of effort may be allocated to producing the specifications themselves. For example, the task of preparing a system flow chart with supporting detailed flow charts can be realistically viewed as belonging to either the specification phase or the programming phase. Further, the degree of detail written into the specifications is to some extent dependent upon the ability and experience of the programming supervisors responsible for translating specifications into code. However, if one seeks to capitalize on the skills of these supervisors and save time by making the specifications superficial and skimpy, the time thus gained may be lost again through a prolonged period of program planning at the beginning of the programming phase, during which the supervisors and the programmers spend a great deal of time interpreting and modifying the specifications they have been given.

It is desirable to produce separate estimates for preparation of each type of system specification. Using the terminology employed elsewhere in this book, estimates are needed for preparation of the following:

- Functional requirements
- System flow charts
- Record specifications
- Program specifications

The first of these items is, hopefully, available prior to the specification phase, which should concentrate on the great mass of programming-oriented documentation.

Programming

For estimating purposes, the programming phase should be approached from several different vantage points. First, it must be defined as to its scope and its relationship to the phases preceding and following. There should be agreement as to what sequence of events is comprehended by the term "programming" as applied to this particular project. Programming may, for example, be defined to include the following:

- Flow charting
- Coding
- Unit testing

Possibly each of these may represent a subphase of the project, with specialists in each aspect of programming concentrating on one of them exclusively. More likely, every programmer will perform each of these steps in preparing his assigned programs. In either case, the estimator should seek maximum detail and try to pinpoint estimates according to the weight that should be given to each step in the programming process.

The varied nature of real-time programming necessitates significant variances in the resources allocated to the different software subsystems and in the relative weight given to the steps performed in producing each of these subsystems. Figure 6.1 shows a real-time Control Program which, as measured by total number of instructions, is only 25 percent of the size of a set of Operational Programs but which, because of its greater

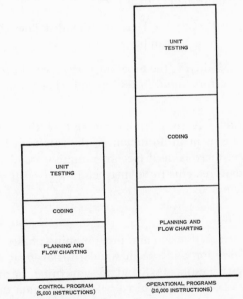

FIGURE 6.1. PROGRAMMING EFFORT EXPENDED.

complexity, requires 50 percent as much effort to produce. Note also that time devoted to coding is a relatively trivial portion of the man-weeks spent in producing this Control Program. Planning and testing are of greater significance here, as compared to the Operational Programs, because of the heightened complexity of real-time control and the greater need for optimization in the Control Program.

It may also prove useful to develop estimates based not so much on the steps that constitute production of a program as on the way in which a programmer allocates his time. Here the categories might include:

PLANNING • Studying and interpreting the specifications, standards, and other rules and restraints that govern his program.

CONSULTING AND COMMUNICATING • Discussing the program with the supervisor, the specification writer, and other programmers working in related areas. (As was mentioned before, if the program is loosely or poorly specified, the amount of time spent here may be inordinately great.)

WRITING THE PROGRAM • Here the detailed flow charting and coding of the program can be categorized.

REVISING • Modifying the program as the result of consultations with others, errors found in testing, and changes in system definition.

DOCUMENTING • A considerable amount of the programmer's time must be spent in documenting the results of his work. As we shall see, there is need for programming standards that set forth the requirements to be met before a given program is accepted as complete.

System Testing

As in the specification and programming phases, the impact of phase definition and system standards has great significance in system testing estimates. Standards governing the amount and complexity of test data required before a program can be certified as bug-free obviously affect the amount of time that programmers and test personnel will be forced to spend in testing at each level. Similarly, a standard governing number of test shots per program and establishing testing priorities by type of program affects the way in which the programming staff utilizes its time.

Turnaround time is often the biggest bottleneck during system testing and the one least subject to managerial control. The Controller must try to resolve the turnaround time quandry by establishing and enforcing efficient testing practices and by anticipating turnaround time delays in estimating for the testing phase.

In illustration, let us consider a System Integration Team in which it is felt that as an efficient testing standard, each programmer should receive, if he so desires, three test shots on the computer daily. Thus, a typical programmer's time might be spent in getting a test shot, analyzing the results, and going back with a suitably modified program or with different test cases for a second shot and then a third during the course of his working day. However, the computer being used is located in a distant test center and the turnaround time is such that each programmer can accomplish on an average only one test shot in a twenty-four-hour period rather than the three that are permissible. Does this mean that the programming effort is only one-third efficient? It may mean exactly that, unless remedial action can be taken. The expedient usually adopted is to assign each programmer three programs, rather than one, to work on concurrently. This has been referred to as "multiprogramming the programmers." It is, unfortunately, not a very efficient solution to the turnaround problem. It may work moderately well where the standard is three test shots and the turnaround time twenty-four hours, but tighten either of these variables and one begins to reach a point of diminishing returns by assigning to each programmer an absurdly large number of jobs to work on in parallel. There is always waste motion and lost time in returning to a specification or flow chart after working on some different problem and, for most programmers, the span of attention is extremely limited.

In the appraising of the testing phase, objective guideposts must be selected to provide a standard for estimating and measuring. One real-time project that had completed testing by each individual programmer took these individually tested units and combined them into "packages" of related programs to be tested together.

Having identified the packages to be tested we then carried out a highly unscientific but, fortunately, fairly effective estimate of the complexity of each package. We called a group of people together, each of whom was highly knowledgeable about a large portion of the system and very well acquainted with the total system. We then took one particular package, with which everyone there was fairly familiar, and arbitrarily assigned it a complexity point value of ten. The complexity point value was simply a weighted number that provided a numerical measure of the difficulty of testing that package and making it work successfully. Having taken one package and given it the arbitrary value of ten, we then went through all the other packages and determined the complexity point value which each should have by comparison with the first 10-point package.[1]

6.4 ESTABLISHING THE SCHEDULE

Once estimates have been produced for the system integration work load, a schedule reflecting these estimates, plus others having to do with the development and testing of the equipment, can be established. The question of who should establish the schedule, and particularly the target dates for cutover, is a vital one. Regrettably, it is one often resolved through the default of those technicians who should be among the most interested parties.

All that has been said thus far implies that firm target dates should not be established until preliminary technical planning has been completed, or at least that any target dates set earlier should be viewed as tentative until the magnitude of the software development is more fully understood. Strangely enough, this rule is not usually followed in practice—perhaps because in batch processing systems there is seldom need for so many de-

---

[1] W. B. Elmore, Remarks at IBM Systems Research Institute, New York, August 1962.

velopmental phases. Starting at contract time, a manager can frequently plunge ahead almost directly into the programming of his batch processing runs with reasonable expectation of having all or part of the application on the air by some predetermined and perhaps arbitrarily selected date. Consequently, many proposals and contracts contain references to calendar dates by which cutover is to be achieved, with such targets usually based on insufficiently careful planning. This may not be disastrous for conventional systems, though such an approach to scheduling goes far toward explaining why so many data processing efforts have encountered delays. In real-time systems, it is imperative that a better job of selecting target dates be done, either by shoving some of the underlying technical planning back into the preproposal period of feasability study, where it probably belongs anyway, or by going ahead with system integration only with full recognition that the cutover target is subject to change as more becomes known about the software subsystems.

Within the constraints imposed by the best estimates available, the preferences of top management necessarily must dictate the pace at which the System Integration Team is to work. Decisions about how the project shall be funded and about how desirable it is from a business and public-relations standpoint to achieve an early cutover must be made by the company officers after drawing on the judgment of their technical specialists. In essence, selection by top management of a major target date, such as cutover of the first office or the first application, should be based on two fundamental criteria:

Technical estimates. How soon the system can be made operational and what the cost is of doing so at a given pace (including the indirect cost of deficient performance of a prematurely converted system)

Business judgment. How badly the system is needed versus the cost of making it operational within a specified period

Management must reconcile these two criteria, which by their nature tend to be contradictory, and make a decision about the target. The more astute the management, the more understanding will be forthcoming that any such decision involves risk. In proceeding along a scheduling path based on the most optimistic technical estimates, management should be aware that there is but minimum confidence that the schedule can be met.

In many projects in which the original schedule turns out to have been unrealistic, the explanation lies not so much in the executive decision-making process as in the lack of technical information on which to base a decision. It is regrettable that technical judgments, especially pertaining to programming, have not heretofore contributed as much as they should have to the scheduling process. With the advent of real-time systems, the spokesmen for the program subsystem must be assigned a more important, if indeed not the dominant, role in estimating and scheduling decisions.

In a batch processing system, even a fairly complex one such as demand deposit accounting, the primary consideration in determining the schedule is usually equipment rather than program availability, even though most programmers would dispute whether this approach is realistic. It is the result of a perfectly understandable predilection for designing data processing systems around hardware rather than around software. The equipment has well-defined specifications; it has a price tag and a delivery schedule, which make the software appear quite nebulous by comparison. As a result, many high-level planners apply a sort of Parkinsonian reasoning process to software: Programs tend to take up the amount of time allocated to them as an incidental result of equipment availability and can be written in time to fit into the equipment delivery schedule.

From top management's viewpoint, the consequences of delay in cutover due to programming difficulties are considerably more costly than in the past. Some of the elements of a real-time system that make delay more costly were mentioned in Chapter 1:

- The equipment cost is greater.
- The size of the programming staff is larger.
- The system is performing (or defaulting in the perform-

ance of) functions having a vital effect on the user's method of doing business.

For dollar reasons alone, it is imperative that management build as many safeguards as possible into the estimates and schedules. Two such safeguards are of special importance.

Obtain Several Estimates

Management should get estimates from different sources to form a basis for comparison. Some obvious sources are:

1) *Potential suppliers of system software.* This includes, but is not necessarily limited to, the equipment manufacturer.

2) *The in-house programming staff.* This group may have an extensive background in estimating for batch-processing applications.

3) *Reputable and experienced consultants.*

Discount Biased Estimates

Management should make certain that the estimates are not biased, or at least it should recognize that bias is reflected in the estimates. Bias may be due to the adviser's organizational affiliation or technical background or both. Some representative biases are those of the following persons:

EQUIPMENT SALESMEN • Hardware salesmen tend to seek early delivery of the equipment, especially if their firm is not delivering the software subsystems as well or is not tied into an acceptance test that encompasses both equipment and programs.

ENGINEERS • Computer and communications engineers tend to agree with the salesmen that once the hardware is developed and put together, there should be no further impediment to use of the system and that the programs certainly should be capable of being written within whatever the installation time span turns out to be. The feeling here is essentially that the equipment development should govern the entire schedule.

PROGRAMMERS • The programming staff is as a rule more pessimistic than the other specialists. Since estimating for software **is** a rather crude exercise, management can expect to get varying estimates all the way from "impossible" to "no problem" and will have to choose from among them. One great fallacy encountered among programmers, against which management should be on guard, is that many outstanding ones tend to view the complexity of a problem from their own vantage point rather than from that of the considerably less talented apprentices and journeymen who will actually write the code. This attitude is akin to that (noted in Chapter 2) of these programmers, who seek more and more functions for placement in the programming subsystem. It is unfortunate that there are not more of these able people, but in their absence optimistic estimates proffered by the gifted few should be diluted.

6.5 SUMMARY

The present-day status of estimating the scope and cost of real-time system integration, whose major components are the specification, production, and testing of computer programs, is unsatisfactory. Some important factors in estimating the work load of the System Integration Team can, however, be isolated. Detailed estimates must be derived for each organizational component and function, and these estimates must, further, be produced for each major phase, and many of the subphases, of system integration. The selection of target dates by management must be based not only on business judgment but equally on the soundest technical judgment available. It is to be hoped that, before many more years go by, one constructive incidental effect of the increasing emphasis on real-time systems will be to force development of better and more objective estimating standards and techniques than have been evolved in the past.

MEASURING PROGRESS | 7

7.1 SCHEDULE DELAYS: A FACT OF LIFE?

BECAUSE THE chief product of the System Integration Team—a set of real-time programs—is such a nebulous one, the possibility of schedule delays is very real. Delays have characterized many data processing efforts in the past. They usually are attributable to two main causes, which have been discussed in earlier chapters but which can appropriately be summarized here.

Faulty Estimates

Estimates made during the early phases of system integration cannot be accepted with confidence if there is no feedback procedure for revising and updating them as more experience becomes available. Re-estimating should follow closely behind the "front lines" of system integration progress so that the current set of estimates always reflects the most realistic appraisal of project status.

Estimates derived without the participation of those responsible for defining the subsystems of records and programs are certain to prove inadequate as a gauge of actuality. One reason why many projects suffer delays is that the programming staff is directed to implement a schedule whose target dates are based not on an appraisal by the programmers of the amount of time required to complete the job but rather on such fundamentally irrelevant considerations as when the equipment can be delivered or when management would like to have the system in operation.

Configuration Changes

Although the necessity of exercising configuration control can hardly be emphasized too much, it should be accepted that system specifications will change despite the most rigorous control. At each phase of system integration, from technical planning through conversion, there will be changes to the system—especially to the software, which is that part of the system still under active development. If the System Integration Team is properly organized and directed, the more far-reaching of these changes in the system configuration will be detected during the earlier phases, particularly during preliminary technical planning. Hopefully, the system flaws that require major configuration revision can be discovered *before* firm estimates have been drawn up or schedule commitments made. In any event, the impact of configuration changes on the schedule should be greater during the initial phases of system integration in a well-planned and technically sound project. A combination of doing the best possible job of estimating and scheduling and rigorously exercising configuration control minimizes the probability of delays and *serious* revisions of the schedule.

A realistically derived schedule and a method of evaluating performance against schedule are essential from the point of view of the Controller and his management, who must be aware of what are realizable goals to set and what the consequences of falling behind in pursuance of these goals will be. The members of the System Integration Team are directly involved in attempting to make progress against the schedule. From a psychological viewpoint, it is important, then, that the schedule be:

• Ambitious enough to offer a challenge to the System Integration Team.
• Realistic enough to be taken seriously by the System Integration Team.

A schedule that is too loose will establish a gait for the System Integration Team that is less than what could reasonably be expected. It is easy to proceed at a desultory pace, and even the most industrious programmers will extend themselves less than they otherwise might when they are working in a sluggish organizational environment.

If, on the other hand, the schedule is such that those at the working level do not feel that the System Integration Team has the slightest chance of meeting it, then the same relaxed attitude may infuse the organization as would prevail if the schedule were too slack. What is needed, therefore, is an *optimum* schedule, one requiring the System Integration Team to work just as rapidly as possible consistent with a sound appraisal of the amount of technical effort that has to be invested at each phase. Management can be more confident that the schedule is optimum when it embodies the estimates of those responsible for performing the technical work of system integration, as they have the most accurate knowledge about the magnitude of the job to be performed.

Because estimating and the setting of target dates must be done by phase, it follows that the schedule for one phase may be less optimum than for another. In certain situations, much less may be known in advance about the hazards of real-time system testing than about the complexities of file record design. Sometimes one phase of the schedule may be developed based on sound technical judgment and another on management fiat. If an arbitrary cutover date, say two years in the future, is selected by management as the goal for having an operational system, and if the scheduling problem is then given to the Controller with this date as a constraint, it is probable that the more immediate phases of system integration, such as preliminary technical planning, will be scheduled with some realism, whereas the more distant phases, such as final system testing, will be slighted. There is little reason to believe that human nature can be improved sufficiently to prevent management's placing goals that it understands (competitive advantage, increase in gross sales, and so on) above goals that it does not (coding of 2000 computer instructions to examine the status of a disk file once a month to detect "lost" records). The technical people, when confronted with an unrealistic deadline, tend to budget enough time to do the job immediately ahead and hope that the realities of the system will assert themselves when the more distant phases are reached. Then, when it begins to look as though the project is running out of time, management will be forced to adopt a more tractable attitude toward the schedule.

If the technical staff, and particularly the Controller, does not *try* to obtain a realistic schedule to begin with, a major responsibility has been abdicated. But when management sets the schedule, it is often against the recommendation of the technical subordinates, who are told: "Yes, we know it's unrealistic, but do the best you can. We have access to the 'big picture' and we have no choice but to be ready to go on-line in eighteen months." The technical people can, at this point, either make an issue of this matter or play a waiting game, accepting the fact that when the system goes into operation *two years* hence, their judgment about the schedule will be vindicated.

7.2 CONCURRENCY IN SYSTEM INTEGRATION

It is axiomatic that a job of the magnitude of integrating a real-time data processing system cannot be performed serially. Whether the estimates call for five man-years or one hundred, many of the necessary programs have to be written in parallel, even though such programs logically follow one another as they are executed in an operational system. In an airline reservation system, development of a Passenger Record file structure of indexes and master records must be done concurrently with development of a similar structure for Seat Inventory Records. Whether it would be better for the same person or group to develop the Passenger Record subsystem first and then perform a similar function for Seat Inventory Records is a moot question. There is so much systems and programming work to be done that the activity must be overlapped if a reasonable schedule is to be followed.

Not only must the system be separated into logical subsystems by the technical planning staff to facilitate concurrent development; the entire managerial function of organizing, budgeting, staffing, and the like, is based on concurrency. And the schedule is the ultimate expression of this principle of concurrency.

There are limitations on concurrency, of course. To achieve a satisfactory installation, it is not enough merely to organize the work into several self-sufficient pieces at the outset and assign responsibility for each. This work is, after all, still closely interrelated and is being compartmentalized only in the interest of expediency in planning and programming. When the project moves into final system testing, one of the main preoccupations of the System Integration Team will be the recombining into *one* operational real-time system all the separate programs produced by groups and individuals working concurrently.

It is this interrelatedness that makes the establishment and control of a schedule so difficult. One unit of work, the writing of one program perhaps, that appears on the schedule as an assignment for an individual programmer, may depend for its satisfactory completion upon work being done not only by that programmer but by several of his colleagues as well. The system logic associated with indexing and filing an airline passenger's record is not just dependent upon the program that obtains the passenger's name from the agent via the terminal set; it is also dependent upon many other programs, which collect itinerary information, data about ticketing, telephone contacts, and other information. When this interdependence exists, the person preparing the initial schedule cannot establish a starting point for the passenger record indexing and filing program prior to the completion dates for the programs that collect the various data components of this record. And a delay in the specification of one of these predecessor programs delays the starting date of subsequent programs, even though all other programs scheduled concurrently with the one delayed are completed on schedule.

This interrelatedness applies equally to record specifications and to the work of groups as well as individuals, and has validity during all phases of system integration. System testing cannot be completed if the group responsible for producing the Control Program has fallen behind the group responsible for the Operational Programs.

What the schedule really implies, then, is a coordinated mixture of concurrent and sequential work to be done, with the degree of concurrency being established by a consideration of the resources available and the extent to which portions of the application can be attacked in parallel, that is, which are dependent upon the completion of one or more prior events and which are not.

It should be recognized that a delay in one portion of the system may have the effect of slowing down work in other portions on which it impinges. In many installations there is the classic example of the programmer whose job turns out to be seriously underestimated and who, after falling behind, begins to receive the solicitous attention of five or six levels of management, up to and including an executive vice-president, all of them aware that the project must remain pretty much on dead center until this luckless person solves his technical problems.

The idea of concurrency governs the work of the Controller and his technical planners in detailing the problems to be solved and developing the estimates and, with the participation of management, the schedules. Once system integration commences, the Controller should continually check for deviations from schedule in order to evaluate their impact on the overall mission of the System Integration Team. It is this continuing responsibility which underlies the need for a rapid, readily understandable, and accurate procedure for measuring, reporting, and evaluating progress. We shall look briefly at two such systems, the first a recent and relatively sophisticated approach to schedule control and the second involving more conventional techniques. The first approach merits mention because of its wide current interest and because of the need for caution in accepting it as a Controller's panacea. The second is presented to suggest a few items of information that should prove useful in measuring progress.

7.3 PROGRAM EVALUATION AND REVIEW TECHNIQUE

Because of the significance of concurrency in system engineering projects, in recent years great emphasis has been placed on improving techniques for schedule planning and control. Chief among the new approaches is the Program Evaluation and Review Technique (PERT) developed during 1958 at the Special Projects Office of the United States Navy and first applied to the development of the Polaris submarine. Today many variations of PERT are applied widely to both military and nonmilitary system projects. Many of the schemes now in use rely upon computer programs to perform the calculations and revisions required to set up and maintain PERT.[1]

An Explanation of PERT

In essence, PERT provides a method for diagramming a project by establishing a network which reflects all the concurrent developments to be accomplished by a project and which shows critical interrelationships. It is a pictorial representation of the events planned to take place in the project. *Events* are usually depicted by circles, which are connected by arrows representing the *activities* necessary to achieve the events. This network is the basic planning tool of the PERT approach. It identifies those check points which must be reached under the currently approved plan. If schedule target dates are utilized in planning the network, PERT becomes basically a reporting tool. If, on the other hand, planning the network is done without the constraint of target dates, PERT becomes both a scheduling and a reporting technique.

Figure 7.1 shows a simplified network of events and activities. The lines connecting each event show activities that must be performed before this event can take place. An activity line, therefore, links two successive events in a PERT network. An activity cannot be started until the event preceding it has taken place, and the event to which it leads cannot be considered completed until *all* activities leading to it have been completed.

In the preparing of a PERT network, estimates are generated for each activity based on estimated elapsed time for the performance of the activity, with some tacit assumptions about the resources available to accomplish each of the activities.

---

[1] IBM General Information Manual, *PERT . . . A Dynamic Project Planning and Control Method,* IBM Publication No. E 20-8067-1.

Usually, three time estimates—optimistic, most likely, and pessimistic—are obtained for each activity. The *critical path* in a PERT network, shown by the heavy black line in the figure, is the longest path through the network based on these estimates. When any event on the critical path falls behind schedule, it can be expected that the final event will also fall behind.

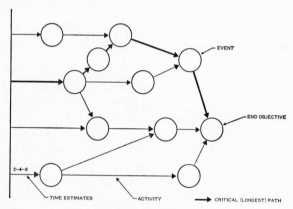

FIGURE 7.1. PERT NETWORK OF EVENTS
AND ACTIVITIES.

Once the project has been "PERTed," with the events laid out according to their interrelationships and the critical path established based on the estimated time required to complete each activity, the information on the diagram can be transcribed to punched cards as input to a PERT computer program. This program can do the following:

1) Provide listings by:
• Successor and predecessor event numbers
• Paths of criticality
• Latest allowable dates for activity completion

2) Cross-reference the network to calendar dates to indicate various completion deadlines and target dates.

3) Identify critical areas of *slack*, slack being the difference between the expected time and the latest allowable completion

time for each activity. (This is the length of time an event can be delayed without affecting the schedule. It indicates to the Controller those places where manpower and other resources can be diverted to a more critical portion of the project when necessary.)

4) Compute the effects of alternate courses of action.

With a PERT program available and with the inputs to the program being periodically revised to reflect actual performance against the schedule, a continuous stream of reports to aid in progress evaluation and schedule revision can be provided. Figure 7.2 shows a typical PERT system, with inputs in the form

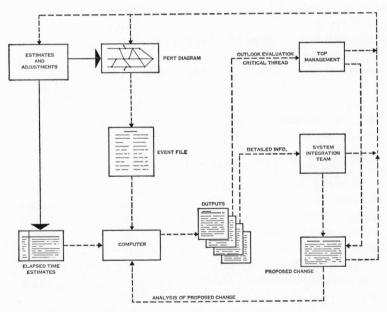

FIGURE 7.2.   PERT SYSTEM.

of an event listing and elapsed time estimates and with outputs in the form of reports for managerial and technical personnel.

What has just been outlined here in barest detail is sometimes called "PERT time." Other programs and procedures are available for developing networks showing different facets of a project's development. These include:

- Pert cost, in which the network is based on dollar estimates as well as time estimates
- PERT manpower, calling for estimates of man-weeks rather than calendar-weeks to complete

An extensive literature has grown up to describe the proliferating usages and methodology of PERT and PERT-like systems. Unfortunately, most of this literature is merely descriptive and assumes somewhat blandly that the adoption of PERT will be an unquestioned improvement over more conventional evaluation and control techniques. Although the literature abounds with suggestions about how to install and operate a PERT system, critical appraisals are somewhat lacking. There is reason to believe, however, that the efficaciousness of PERT can vary tremendously from one technological field to another. A technique that has had admitted success in missile technology will not necessarily be of comparable utility in the development of commercial data processing systems. What, then, are some of the pros and cons to be weighed before accepting PERT as a control mechanism?

Advantages of PERT in System Integration

Unquestionably, PERT has value in encouraging a methodical and thorough approach to planning, evaluating progress against plans, and revising plans when necessary. A great deal of information about alternatives and about the consequences of action and inaction is provided by the reports available as output from PERT programs. It is difficult for management to overlook a potentially troublesome situation when using PERT. And there is as well the benefit of *forcing* management to review its planning and scheduling on a regular basis rather than only when compelled to do so by the logic of events. Some of these advantages offered by the thoroughgoing and routinized nature of PERT are, admittedly, available in other procedures. Nevertheless, PERT has proved to be a powerful tool for planning and control in many situations.

One particularly adverse facet of scheduling a technical project that PERT can be of great benefit in eliminating is the tendency of many Controllers to revise only one portion of the schedule at a time, without careful analysis of the full effect of a change on other plans. When there is no network to show relationships and no critical path to be aware of, it may be easy enough to decide to delay the completion dates for twenty program specifications after a reappraisal of the difficulties in producing them, and yet inadvertently fail to delay the training program for ten new recruits who will, unless some action is taken, turn up as members of the System Integration Team, eagerly expecting to write programs based on the specifications that had been scheduled for completion coincident with their graduation from programming class. Similarly, the Controller might make an engineering decision to redesign the file control logic, yet neglect to delay by an equivalent amount of time the schedule for testing those programs which are dependent upon the availability of the file modules. It takes an exceptionally able Controller to be cognizant of these relationships and of the impact of delays and dislocations throughout the system, and to review his schedule and reallocate his resources accordingly.

Disadvantages of PERT

Discussions with the more ardent proponents of PERT cause one to wonder how large projects with very demanding schedules were carried out in the days before PERT was available. Yet the pyramids were constructed somehow and the Normandy invasion was successfully launched. The fact is that the manager of any large project has *always* had to be alert to the critical path leading to timely completion of the project. Fundamentally, PERT is little more than a new technique for organizing and presenting facts to management. There have been dazzling system engineering achievements long before the advent of PERT and there will doubtless be future system blunders abetted by PERT networks and diagrams. Given a choice between a mediocre Controller, armed with PERT charts and report forms, and an able Controller, who chooses more traditional methods of evaluation and control, it should be easy for most companies to select the right man.

Beyond the intrinsic merits and limitations of PERT lie more serious questions about its utility in software production. The early chapters of this book stressed certain points that should be recalled in evaluating the usefulness of PERT. There are, first of all, some fundamental differences between development of the equipment and the program subsystems that make preparation of the programs essentially the more intuitive and difficult task. The system Integration Team, with its Controller, is set up in recognition of the fact that computer programming, unlike computer engineering, cannot be classified as a science or even as a well-disciplined profession. What is good for hardware development (assuming of course that PERT is of value there) is not necessarily good for the programmers.

It has also been mentioned that a valuable result of preliminary technical planning is definition of the records and programs to be produced by the System Integration Team. The System Integration Team can be said to be proceeding from very general knowledge about software during the system design phase, into an intermediate state of knowledge at the time of technical planning, through a semifinal stage at specification writing time, and into final knowledge about what all the programmed system components will be at programming time (provided system test and conversion do not require extensive reprogramming).

But when is the PERT network most needed by the Controller? At the very start of system integration, that is, at the beginning of preliminary technical planning. But at this point, the only meaningful PERT network that can be drawn up is one showing only a handful of activities and events. And of course the Controller hardly needs a diagram and a set of reports to give him this information. What he really needs are all the details that only gradually become available as system integration progresses and the original half-dozen events develop into twenty records and 150 interrelated programs, each of which requires an investment of time and resources.

The danger of adopting PERT at the start of system integration is a temptation to generate detailed estimates to feed into the PERT process at the beginning, even though those generating the estimates have a confidence in them that is practically zero. This is akin to the difficulty already noted with simulation as a tool of system design. Both the PERT program and the simulator program *demand* information from the analyst on which they can operate; or, at least, they tempt the analyst to make estimates that he might not prudently make otherwise. Regrettably, answers thus obtained through the use of PERT during the initial stages of a project have a way of being retained in the consciousness of management even when, after successive revisions, the PERT diagram of a year later shows the project in an entirely different complexion and one in which the estimators have much more confidence. In such a case there is often the problem of persuading management to abandon its attachment to the original, less realistic schedule.

One final pitfall to be avoided is to "PERT" one part of the project but not another. If this piecemeal approach is taken, it should be understood by all concerned just what the limitations and ground rules are. PERT might, for example, be used very effectively by the plant producing the equipment to assure that the various hardware subsystems are being assembled according to schedule, but not used in scheduling the program subsystems because of the dearth of quantitative information to feed into the network. Good. So long as management does not adopt the view that programming can be expected to fill up the amount of time alloted by PERT for equipment development—no more, no less—and schedule target dates for the System Integration Team according to the plant production schedule.

7.4 ALTERNATIVE REPORTING SCHEMES

If it is decided not to proceed with PERT for purposes of measuring and evaluating progress, an alternative reporting and control system should be devised, one tailor-made to the project and well adapted to each phase of system integration. Assuming that the technical planning phase, which is inherently somewhat ill-defined, can be adequately supervised and controlled without a formal reporting structure, a reporting structure along the following lines could be applied to subsequent phases.

Specification Status Report

A report showing the status of each specification should be forthcoming on a regular basis from the organizational components responsible for specification preparation. This report should be prepared at least once and preferably twice a month. It not only serves as a means of measuring progress but provides as well an up-to-date summary of all record and program specifications currently known to be required. The pages of the specification status report will be rather barren initially, when few of the needed records and programs have yet been visualized—except for the major ones sketched out during preliminary technical planning. As work proceeds on known record specifications, the need for related record specifications and collateral program specifications is ascertained. The specification status report provides a vehicle for recognizing such newly identified pieces of work and inserting them in the schedule.

Often, in the initial specification status report, a large body of work is identified under a single program number and name such as the Sell Program. Later, this will be exploded into several programs, such as Sell Other Airline Space, Sell Large Party, Sell First Class, and Sell Jet, reflecting the detailed nature of the necessary programming. If an exceptionally good job of technical planning has been done, the target dates for all these pieces of the Sell Program will be comprehended by the one target date established initially for Sell as a general program. Usually, however, there will be many areas in which the true breakdown was not very accurately anticipated, where much more work is required on the subsidiary routines than was originally envisioned.

Once the format of the specification status report is decided upon, it should be set up in a manner that makes it easy to reproduce a fairly large number of copies. The report should be given wide distribution and not restricted to supervisory levels. Everyone who has some technical responsibility for specification development or programming should receive a copy. Because the specification status report contains an up-to-date listing of all specifications being written or planned, it offers a valuable means of disseminating technical information.

Some programs are common to more than one individual or group, no matter how the work is allocated. The terminal assembly area provides a good example of this, as does a routine for converting a calendar date received from a terminal into a day-of-the-year representation. Not all common records and routines can possibly be pinpointed in advance by the technical planning staff. The specification status report is, therefore, a good reference source for each System Integration Team member to consult when looking for records and programs that overlap or otherwise impinge on his own work. Perhaps follow-up with others will reveal a record or program on which two persons can collaborate, perhaps it will result in agreement to share a common routine to be specified by only one of the two, or perhaps it will identify clearly redundant effort and permit a more effective allocation of the work load. The specification status report thus serves as a communication as well as a control medium.

Each issue of the report offers an opportunity to focus the attention of the System Integration Team, and especially the supervisors, on the accomplishments and shortcomings of the preceding period. The Controller can extract maximum effectiveness from this report if he plans formal schedule review meetings with his supervisors, with the specification status report as the main agenda item. This can preferably be done before issuance of each report at a meeting in which each supervisor has an opportunity to comment on any change in status from the previous report. One result of regularly scheduled status report review meetings is a continued awareness of the importance of the schedule and an understanding that no slippage will go unnoticed or unaccounted for. The meetings also provide a good medium for information exchange between the Controller and his staff. Matters of technical coordination and identification of commonality and overlap can be brought out into the open. Questions of technical jurisdiction can, when they arise, be resolved by the Controller and reflected appropriately in the next report.

A typical specification status report might contain the following column headings. A complete picture of the status of a particular specification would constitute one line on the report form.

Program Number • The importance of developing a numbering scheme is discussed in Chapter 9 in connection with specification preparation. The number listed in this section of the report is the same one assigned to the specification. The numbering scheme should be devised in such a way that it continues to apply when one gross specification, or line on the status report, breaks out into several specifications.

Record or Program Name • A meaningful descriptor, which is also the title of the specification.

Latest Publication Date • Many specifications will be reissued fairly frequently during the specification phase. The issuing of an initial specification may be likened to the sending up of a trial balloon. The specification writer hopes that his colleagues working in related areas will see errors of omission and commission in his specification and call these to his attention. The latest publication date shown in the report for each specification should exhibit less and less change as the specification phase approaches its conclusion.

Assigned to • The member or members of the System Integration Team responsible for this specification.

Target Date • The scheduled completion date for this specification. *This date should not be changed* after it is first established, since, with each publication of the status report, it shows—when compared with the adjoining column—the variance between plans and actuality. This date can have a stimulating psychological effect on the specification writers, each of whom knows that his fellow workers are able to see how badly he is falling behind his original target. When one general specification breaks out into several subordinate ones, each of these should reflect the original target date.

Estimated Completion Date • This date may be expected to change as successive issues of the specification status report are compiled. When coupled with the corresponding target date, it gives an indication of how work is progressing. In dealing with completion dates, the question inevitably arises as to what is meant by "completion"—rough draft by the specification writer? reviewed and approved by those supervising the work? in typing? published? There may be substantial time differences between these stages of completion. No matter which is selected, the interpretation should be applied consistently by all responsible for compilation of the report.

Status • For each specification assigned but not yet published, some indication of current status should be forthcoming. Often a word or phrase can convey status. Better, an A-B-C-D code indicating quartile percent complete could be adopted. Without this, the Controller will not know that a completion date is going to be missed until he gets a copy of the report for the period covering the missed date. The status column should also provide the notation that a particular specification is "newly assigned" or "newly identified" with a particular issue of the report. The most satisfactory procedure here is probably to require an appropriate remark in the status column whenever there is *any* change in a particular line from the previous edition.

Programming Progress Report

Once a sufficient number of specifications have been written to allow programming to begin, the programming phase must be controlled by a reporting system that produces an acceptable measure of progress. Because more persons will be assigned during the programming phase, closer control is needed. Programming progress reports should be required of each group supervisor as often as once a week and certainly no less frequently than once every two weeks. If the program specifications are written in such a way that they provide estimates of the number of instructions each specification is expected to produce, this can become the basis for setting up the programming progress reporting system.

One real-time project established an arbitrary unit to be dealt with in reporting programming progress, rather than the actual lines of code produced. In this system, a "unit" was defined as one day's work and was derived by dividing the estimated number of instructions by 25, rounding up the result for safety and increasing by 2. The two extra units were added as the estimated amount of time that a newly assigned programmer would spend becoming familiar with the specifications pertaining to his program.[2]

As in the specification phase, the Controller should remain fully apprised of progress. A summary recap should be prepared for his scrutiny, containing a consolidation of all the programming progress reports to reflect the total number of units completed by all groups during the report period and to date.

One should expect to find in the programming progress report information such as the following:

Programmers Assigned • An identification, by name, of the programmer currently assigned to each program.

Programs Completed • A tabulation by program number and program name of all programs completed and the value of the units of such completed programs. The unit figures should be shown both for the original estimate as contained in the specification and for the actual units the program finally consisted of. This information about estimated and actual unit values of programs completed should be broken down into those completed during the current report period and those completed to date. In this way recent progress as well as cumulative progress can be evaluated. Some arbitrary definition of "complete" has to be made here just as in reporting on specification development. "Complete" could mean, for example,

---

[2] W. B. Elmore, Remarks at the IBM Systems Research Institute, August 1962.

tested by the programmer, approved by the group supervisor, fully documented, inserted on the master program tape. One such criterion must be selected and applied uniformly.

Programs in Process • This section should include the following kinds of information for each program not yet completed:

• Program number

• Date begun, with a clear distinction needed between the date "assigned" and the date on which work actually commenced

• Estimated units, from the specification

• Total units complete, as of last report

• Total units complete, as of this report

• Increment of units completed, since last report

System Testing Performance Report

In the same way that the programming envisioned by the specifications is translated into units of measure for reporting programming progress, it is desirable to establish some measurable unit to define and control system testing. One such measure is a complexity point scheme such as that described in Chapter 6, in which each programming "package" is given a complexity point value. This lends itself to a periodic system testing performance report showing the complexity point value of those program packages which have progressed through the various levels of system testing. For any level the report might indicate (1) the complexity point value of programs currently at this level, (2) how many points were scheduled to be at the level, and (3) the variance. As in the other reports, information should be shown both for the current report period and for year to date, that is, the cumulative complexity point value of all programs that have reached a given level of testing versus those scheduled to reach this level.

Under such a system, there will be an impressive sheaf of reports to examine during system testing, as there may be concurrent testing activity at most of the test levels established for progress reporting purposes.

7.5 PRESENTATIONS TO MANAGEMENT

Any reporting system, whether it relies upon PERT or upon more conventional approaches, contains much information that lends itself to reduction and graphical presentation for the benefit of management and others who may be interested in capsule or summary facts about system progress. Relationships between specifications and programs scheduled and those actually completed can be effectively presented in graphical form showing schedule dates on one axis and percent complete on the other. Figure 7.3 provides an example of this kind of rendering of data gleaned from the reporting system.

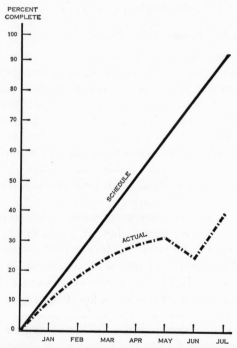

FIGURE 7.3. PROGRAMMING STATUS SUMMARY.

7.6 INDEPENDENT AUDITS OF PERFORMANCE

Let us suppose that, in implementing the decision to install a real-time system, management has assiduously followed every precept of system development which, based on a broad knowledge of its company, its customers, and its personnel, is believed necessary to assure success. A feasible system design has been developed and has not been overburdened by excessive demands from the operating departments. Management has selected a strong-willed and competent Controller and has given him ample support in planning, budgeting, and staffing. A realistic schedule has been set up and groups of reasonably well-qualified technicians have begun to address themselves to system integration. Biweekly specification status reports and weekly programming progress reports, supplemented by a truly formidable array of PERT listings, Gantt charts, and progress-versus-schedule curves are received from the System Integration Team. These indicate that the project is on schedule overall and, in several areas, is ahead of schedule.

Wonderful that everything is going so well—if true! But before relaxing, management should recall how much of the present and future well-being of the company is riding on the success of the system. Without doubt, the stake of the organization in the real-time system is immense. Conceding the technical competence of the System Integration Team, what will be the consequences of error, misjudgment, overoptimism? Are they sufficiently serious to prompt management to secure an objective outside appraisal of the performance of the System Integration Team, in somewhat the same fashion that a certified public accounting firm audits the company's own accounting department?

There have been data processing system fiascos in the past and there will surely be more as systems grow in complexity. It seems to be asking too much of the System Integration Team to demand that it be self-policing. A determination that a disk file subsystem is inadequate from both an access time and a reliability standpoint may be unwittingly concealed, even from the Controller, for an extended period. Those assigned to engineer this subsystem and produce a prototype may, until almost physically restrained, be convinced that their subsystem will ultimately work and that all it will take are a few revised loading calculations, a few changes in some of the circuit cards, a few more days, and—as the pressure mounts—a few more hours.

A similar situation may arise among the programmers. Possibly an elaborate and unworkable record organization plan has been built up by two programmers—one experienced and marginally competent, the other naive and opinionated. Their assigned area of record design is one that was underemphasized during technical planning—a blind spot of the kind that is bound to occur in system development. At any rate, the two have made a botch of it and, largely owing to a two-week absence of the Controller on a recruiting trip, the faulty record design creeps into the major structuring of the system, with the cursory approval of the Controller's deputy.

In all such situations, there is an understandable desire on the part of the technical people to be judged successful. No one likes to admit that his subsystem or program is a failure, even though in many projects the line between success and failure is only an ill-conceived schedule. In the theater there are commercial and artistic successes with no necessary coincidence between the two; in data processing there are systems that are truly miraculous in the ingenuity and creativity of system thought that goes into them. And yet they are failures, because somewhere in the system is a weak link that prevents implementation.

Since neither the engineering nor the programming personnel can be depended upon to rise consistently above their vested interests in evaluating their own segments of the project and since the Controller himself may not be immune from the virus of wishful thinking, management must protect itself by setting up a supplemental pipeline for the measurement of performance.

An outside consulting organization can fulfill this role if it is able to meet certain tests:

COMPETENCY • The consulting firm and its individual staff members should, by virtue of their experience and demonstrable ability, be able to follow a complex system integration effort without fear of being "snowed" about system features by members of the System Integration Team.

AVAILABILITY • The assignment of an outside consultant to audit a complex real-time system based on his presence at the account for only one or two days a month is totally unacceptable. No matter what the technical ability of the individual assigned, he simply cannot stay "on top" of a large system integration project by meager part-time participation. The consultant, for his part, should refuse to participate in a project in which he may be handicapped in his technical judgment. Management must pay the price in consulting fees to make the consultant's reports reliable and well informed.

Regardless of whether the auditing role is given to an outside consultant or to some highly placed staff group within the company, there is a compelling need for management to arm itself with independently derived facts about project status for comparison with reports emanating through channels from the System Integration Team.

Without an independent audit, management may continue to base major policy decisions on the scheduled availability of the real-time system. Only too late it may be discovered that there are technical flaws in the system that will cause costly delays and readjustments. Getting rid of the Controller *after* the facts are discovered can be very much like the process of dismissing a baseball manager—by then, it may be too late to correct the problem or improve the quality of the team.

7.7 SUMMARY

The basic objective of a reporting and measuring system is to identify potential troubles and delays as far in advance as possible so that alternative plans may be evaluated and corrective action initiated. PERT has performed this function for hardware development efforts but has yet to demonstrate the same effectiveness in the more subjective and nebulous working situation that characterizes real-time system integration. Alternatively, more conventional progress-reporting schemes may prove more suitable for system integration. With or without PERT there is no substitute for the good judgment of the Controller and for his ability to grasp the implications of what the progress-reporting system reveals. Without some well-defined reporting system for each phase, the Controller and his supervisors are powerless to direct the System Integration Team in the most effective fashion. When this is understood, it becomes a matter of personal proclivity, coupled with the nature of the real-time application, that governs the selection of a satisfactory method of controlling progress.

No matter what system for progress reporting is adopted, management should consider augmenting the information flowing upward from the System Integration Team with an independently derived appraisal of project status.

DEVELOPING STANDARDS | 8

8.1 THE WORLD OF STANDARDS

THERE ARE many kinds of standards applicable to system integration, either directly or indirectly. Certain of these are imposed by external forces and consequently are not controllable to any great extent. Others are generated by the System Integration Team itself and can therefore be cast in a manner most conducive to successful system integration. This chapter deals with those standards having a significant effect on system integration, regardless of whether they are established by the System Integration Team or applied from outside.

Before examining the standards that have the most immediacy for system integration, a perspective on standards in general should be established by noting the existence of the quasi-official organizations responsible for standards affecting automatic data processing. Computer standards bodies exist in many countries and usually contain representation from two main groups—professional societies and industrial organizations. In the United States, the American Standards Association, through its various committees and subcommittees, endeavors to develop standards that can be agreed upon within major industries and professional disciplines. In the field of data processing the American Standards Association has designated the Business Equipment Manufacturers Association (BEMA) to propose standards, and BEMA has in turn set up subcommittees to develop standards applicable to a wide range of equipment and programming matters. Some of these subcommittees are:

- Optical Character Recognition (X3.1)

- Coded Character Sets and Data Formats (X3.2)

- Data Transmission (X3.3)

- Common Procedure-Oriented Programming Languages (X3.4)

- Terminology and Glossary (X3.5)

- Problem Description and Analysis (X3.6)

- Magnetic Ink Character Recognition (X3.7) [1]

Certain of these subcommittees, such as X3.4 and X3.6, are primarily concerned with software standards, and others, such as X3.1 and X3.3, with equipment. It is, of course, manifestly impossible to establish equipment standards independent of programming or to promulgate programming standards without recognizing the potentialities and limitations of the equipment. Most of these committees, therefore, seek to obtain a wide base of representation in conducting their activities.

Below this broad level of standards development are other standards agreed upon by industry groups and associations having a common interest in more efficient utilization of computers for a particular purpose. There have been many impressive achievements in standardization at the user industry level, of which the following are illustrative.

Magnetic Ink Character Recognition

The American Banking Association has adopted a standard method for automatic sensing of characters placed along the lower part of checks. This system, initiated by the Bank of America and perfected at the Stanford Research Institute, provides a series of magnetically encoded numerals and special characters that are readable by both humans and machines. By 1958 the Bank of America, with the aid of character recognition and computing equipment produced by the General Electric Company, put Magnetic Ink Character Recognition (MICR)

---

[1] S. Gorn (Editor), "Structure of Standards-Processing Organizations in the Computer Area," Communications of the Association for Computing Machinery, vol. 6, June 1963, pp. 294-306.

into successful operation in the automatic performance of demand deposit accounting.

Machinable Airline Reservation Messages

Just as MICR provides a common language for standardizing banking operations, the Reservations Committee of the International Air Transport Association (IATA) has agreed upon a machinable message format for communicating reservation information among the passenger airlines that are its members. IATA had used standard interline teletype message formats for many years to facilitate communications among carriers, but, with the increasing usage of computers to perform reservation functions, it was discovered that messages which were perfectly understandable by humans were not sufficiently standardized for computer processing. In recognition of this shortcoming, a working group was established that produced an interline machinable message whose fixed format and identifying symbols are, like MICR, intelligible by both humans and data processing equipment.

Common Business Oriented Language

In the late 1950's the Department of Defense, a massive user of data processing equipment, became understandably concerned with improving the efficiency of programmers and sponsored a Conference on Data Systems Languages (CODASYL). This conference, the membership of which was drawn from data processing equipment manufacturers and user groups, produced the initial specifications for the Common Business Oriented Language (COBOL), which the equipment manufacturers adopted as a standard. The manufacturers, in conformance with this standard, now supply COBOL compiling programs, which operate on their various computers to transform into actual machine instructions the English-like sentences written by the COBOL programmer.

These are significant examples of the initiative taken by industry groups in recent years to provide needed standards for more effective utilization of data processing equipment.

8.2 SYSTEM STANDARDS

Any data processing system must be developed within an environment of national and industry standards which necessarily affect the definition of both the equipment and the program subsystems. In addition, more specific standards are needed to control a particular data processing project. These may be conveniently referred to as system standards. Certain of the system standards pertain to the overall operation of the system, others to the equipment and program subsystems in combination, others to the equipment alone, and still others to the programs by themselves.

Overall System Standards

Some of the overall system standards have already been discussed through reference to functional requirements. Fundamentally these application-oriented documents constitute a set of performance standards to be met by the system. A functional requirement may state that the typed response to a given terminal inquiry will be the phrase "OK" followed by the date in the form of day/month/year, with all this to be initiated within five seconds after the enter key is depressed by an operator. Such a functional requirement implicitly establishes several system standards, that is, equipment and program design objectives. A terminal device must have alphanumeric output ability to meet this standard, and the communication lines from the computer must be fast enough and the CPU and programs efficient enough to deliver a response to the terminal within the prescribed time.

Some data processing system contracts have written into them acceptance test procedures or other acceptance criteria to be met before final delivery of the system can be legally consummated. In effect, such acceptance tests are another form of system standard imposed upon the equipment manufacturer and the System Integration Team.

Equipment Standards

Many standards apply mainly to the equipment portion of the real-time data processing system. Some of these are established by the equipment manufacturer in consonance with his product test and quality control procedures for the equipment; others are developed by the using organization to assure that specially developed or modified equipment can do what is expected of it. Life testing of tape drives provides an example of an equipment standard set by the manufacturer. So does a production standard for CPU components to achieve a mean time to failure that will allow the computer to be marketed for the applications for which it was designed.

The prospective user may specify that reports produced by a high-speed printer achieve specified quality of legibility, containing no "ghosts" or "halos," or that the incidence of error on a communication line due to noise be held to some reasonably acceptable minimum. These equipment standards, once set by the user, must be applied by the manufacturer to the engineering and production of the hardware.

Programming Standards

The System Integration Team is concerned primarily with programming standards. Certainly, system standards and engineering standards are significant during system integration, but they usually impose prespecified and largely uncontrollable constraints on the System Integration Team. It was stated earlier that the Controller must sometimes demand changes in functional requirements in the interest of producing a balanced system or achieving significant economy in system development. Changes in pre-existing standards may also be necessary as a result of discoveries by the System Integration Team about the workability of such standards.

It is not conducive to timely system integration to search for ways to alter standards already in existence. The objective should be to undertake revision of standards only when the change is absolutely necessary or has a markedly beneficial effect. Except for changes instituted because the system would perform marginally without them or because there would be a substantial increase in performance or saving in developmental costs because of them, the System Integration Team should accept the system and equipment standards and concentrate on establishment of those standards which do not yet exist —the programming standards.

8.3 PROGRAMMING STANDARDS DEVELOPMENT

It would be impossible to install real-time systems without programming standards. If a Controller, through inexperience or ineptitude, should fail to set up a programming standards activity as a staff function, the standards would come into being anyway, created in an *ad hoc* manner by various programmers as the need arose. The difference between a System Integration Team with a well-planned standards function and one where this is lacking is akin to that between statutory national law and international law. Statutory law represents consciously established standards of conduct based on premeditated attention to the needs of the community; international law reflects only the comity of nations, those minimum standards necessary for the uneasy survival and perpetuation of the national "subsystems" that comprise the international system of nation states.

There are two basic principles underlying development of programming standards:

- Standards development is a continuing task.
- Standards must be developed phase-by-phase.

Some programming standards must be established at the inception of system integration. Others could not possibly be developed then, but instead must wait until more is known about the detailed problems facing the planning staff and the specification and programming groups. An example of the kind of standard needed at the beginning of system integration is the guide to preparing record and program specifications required to instruct and control the specification writers. Standards that must necessarily be developed on a more gradual standardize-as-you-go basis cover such matters as system testing procedures to obtain efficient utilization of the equipment. It would be desirable, of course, that the standards writer have sufficient foresight to anticipate all possible technical activities for which restrictions and guidelines are needed. But since this is manifestly impossible, the standards writer must occupy himself with first things first by establishing, as a minimum, the standards needed at the start of system integration. What normally occurs is that the "hard copy" representation of standards, as found in the Programming Standards Manual, evolves from a rather sparse collection of initial pages into a manual bulging with technical information about the conduct of the project, developed as the project itself develops.

Effective programming standards are not unplanned, that is, are not left to the whims of the various working groups for their establishment. Nor do they spring Venus-like from the brow of the technical planner. One individual should be assigned responsibility by the Controller for standards in order to provide:

1) A minimum initial set of standards to help the System Integration Team get started

2) A focal point for further standards development

Standards especially applicable to each phase of system integration are needed. Some of these, such as a write-up of the procedure for revising program specifications, apply primarily to the specification phase. Others, such as those establishing the number of test shots per program, are applicable only to system testing. The work-load curve for producing standards should show a high peak at the beginning, then a series of smaller peaks at the inception of each phase of system integration.

Even when there is a well-defined staff responsibility for programming standards, not all the labor involved in writing and issuing standards documents need necessarily be done by this staff member. The person responsible for standards may be merely a coordinating point, with much of the actual work on standards done by the personnel most familiar with the problem, under the guidance of the Standards Programmer.

At the opposite extreme from that in which the programming groups produce their own standards with staff guidance from the Standards Programmer is the situation in which a standards staff assumes some of the normal line functions of the operating groups. One real-time project, for example, established a System Evaluation and Control Group, which had the dual function of preliminary technical planning *and* standards development. Once the technical planning had been largely completed and the initial standards issued, the role of this group was transformed into one of (1) continuing to develop and maintain programming standards and (2) reviewing record and program specifications both for technical adequacy and for adherence to standards. This approach is interesting in that it consolidates the related functions of programming standards and technical planning. Although one can view these as organizationally separate, with the standards staff essentially responsible for form and the technical planning staff for substance, both are in a sense technical planning activities and can, therefore, be logically merged from an organizational standpoint.

Even where the Standards Programmer has no direct responsibility for technical planning or specification writing, copies of all technical planning documents and record and program specifications should be routed to him. It is through scrutiny of these documents that the need for additional standards can be pinpointed by an alert Standards Programmer. If it is noticed, for instance, that most draft file record specifications contain a field showing the date on which the record was created, then it may be worthwhile to insert this field in each file record and to standardize its location. The Standards Programmer, in reaching this conclusion, may be looking forward to a time when a file audit program has to be written to search through the file looking for "lost" records. The presence of a date field in a standard place in each record, irrespective of type of record, would be invaluable to such an audit program in finding past-date records that should be purged from the file.

8.4 STANDARDS PROGRAMMER

In large systems, there may be a standards group composed of working programmers with responsibility not only for writing material for the standards manual but for programming standard routines as well. Two types of programs could fall into this category:

1) Those common to the work of two or more programming groups

2) Those so frequently executed that they must be programmed in a highly efficient manner

An example of the first would be a routine for converting a date field received via a typewriter terminal into a number representing day of the year. This routine would be common to all record retrieval programs that use day of the year as an argument to obtain a file record, regardless of the different classes of records stored according to such a scheme.

An example of the second would be a program responsible for reading in from file and examining a terminal assembly area on receipt of an entry from a terminal. This is done to determine the validity of the entry, its source, and so on. Presumably it could be programmed as a separate routine for each entry, but if there were forty entry types in the system, there would then be forty separate TAA retrieval programs, varying tremendously in their relative efficiency. When a routine contributes heavily to the usage of file accesses, main memory cycles, or main memory storage or is subject to frequent revision, it is desirable to standardize the programming approach.

Active participation in programming by the standards group may occur at either the specification level or in the actual writing and testing of routines. At minimum, the standards group must remain cognizant of the development of specifications and the writing of programs in order to identify portions of the system for which standards are needed or for which standardized programs should be written. At maximum, the standards group would not only identify needs but would also specify and actually write the standard routines.

The responsibility for writing standard routines should be delineated by the Controller so that there is no misunderstanding on the part of the programmers. The Control Program, for instance, can be looked upon as a "standard" routine, yet few Controllers would consign it to the jurisdiction of the Standards Programmer, as it is a sufficiently sizable and complex program in its own right to warrant a separate programming group to concentrate on it single-mindedly. The same may be said of

Support Programs, such as those having to do with system test simulators and other program debugging aids. These programs are "standard" in that they are generally applicable to all Operational Programs, but their preparation is so formidable and costly a task that they should be assigned to a separate organizational component of the System Integration Team. Though the standards group may be geared to do programming, it should work only on selected system routines and should not do "bread-and-butter" programming. Its chief function is to serve as technical staff to the Controller in overseeing the work of the line programming groups and issuing standards to these line groups.

Depending upon how broadly its responsibilities are defined, the standards function might occupy several persons or, in a small project in which the scope is narrowly defined, it might involve only one programmer part time. The essential point is not so much *how* the standards function is set up but rather that it *be* set up. Assuming, and this should always be a valid assumption for a System Integration Team, that at least one person is assigned the title of Standards Programmer, what should his qualifications and duties be?

Qualifications of the Standards Programmer

Clearly he should be a senior staff member of the System Integration Team both in status and in experience. Probably he should report directly to the Controller. It is especially important that a well-qualified programmer be selected for this position if the Operational Programmers are mostly inexperienced trainees, chosen from within.

In addition to heavy recent programming experience on the computer selected for the real-time system, the Standards Programmer should possess several other technical and personal attributes:

- Experience on commercial data processing problems of considerable scope. Real-time systems experience is extremely desirable but hard to come by, and an otherwise well-qualified candidate should not be ruled out because he lacks such background.

- Exceptional ability to work with other programmers at all levels of proficiency.
- Experience in training or supervising junior programmers. Even though this may not be a direct responsibility in the position of Standards Programmer, the patience developed through such experience is desirable.
- Ability to describe narratively computer processes and programs. No matter how adept at personal relationships or how facile at programming, a person assigned to this job who cannot write English simply and precisely is doomed to failure.

Responsibilities of the Standards Programmer

The following general statements of responsibility are applicable to the Standards Programmer:

- Plan, develop, and maintain a Programming Standards Manual.
- Develop file conventions. This encompasses such matters as standardizing file record sizes for various programming purposes and setting up standard record labels, identifiers, and keys for all classes of records in the system.
- Develop standards for the preparation of record and program specifications.
- Maintain detailed familiarity with automatic programming languages such as COBOL in order to aid in evaluating the efficaciousness of various programming systems and languages.
- Prepare and follow up on standards for system documentation. This includes establishment of procedures for reproducing, distributing, revising, storing, controlling, and otherwise protecting all system documentation
- Evaluate the need for standard routines to be made available to the programming groups comprising the System Integration Team. With approval, undertake the programming of such routines.
- Establish standards and procedures for flow charting at

the system, the specification, and the individual program level.

- Establish a program numbering system to identify and control all programs through each phase of system integration, from technical planning through system testing. The numbering system should lend itself to automatic analysis of program status and the implications of program changes.

- Recommend to the Controller procedures for obtaining review and approval of specifications, programs, and test results.

8.5 STANDARDS MANUAL

One of the first concerns of the Standards Programmer should be the issuance of a Programming Standards Manual. In addition to deciding what the contents of this manual should be and what manual material is required immediately, the Standards Programmer must establish the mechanics for maintaining and distributing the manual.

Maintenance

It is prudent to obtain large-size (three-inch) ring binders to hold the standards material. The manual will have maximum visual appeal if an attractive cover is selected, individualized with the name or symbol of the system. Each page prepared for insertion in the manual should contain in a fixed format the number, title, issuance or revision date, and revision number of the standard. Manual pages are best prepared on a distinctive preprinted form that immediately identifies the page as containing standards manual material. It is also desirable to adopt some easily grasped method of identifying the changed portions of revised manual pages.

It must be understood by the members of the System Integration Team that the manual is under the jurisdiction of the Standards Programmer, who has responsibility for the editing and review of all material submitted for publication and for controlling the distribution of manuals and manual inserts. The Standards Programmer thus becomes the focal point for all questions having to do with the Programming Standards Manual.

In establishing the responsibility for standards, review and approval procedures for manual material should be spelled out, especially in a large organization. The Controller may, for example, wish to review personally all manual material, or material of a certain class, before it is issued. Alternatively, he may leave it to the discretion of the Standards Programmer whether he needs to pass judgment on manual material before issuance. In some situations, it may be found worthwhile to set up a Standards Committee, consisting of the Standards Programmer as chairman and the programming supervisors as members, to evaluate the need for, and to review, standards material.

Distribution

The Programming Standards Manual should be distributed widely, so that each member of the System Integration Team can have his own copy. Interested organizations not directly a part of the System Integration Team, such as those engaged in equipment engineering and manufacturing, contract programming, and consulting, should also receive copies, as there will doubtless be standards directly affecting their activities. If it is impossible to give each individual his own copy, then each first-line organizational component of the System Integration Team should have a copy for the common use of persons in that group.

Distribution of certain sections of the manual may be selective, on a "need-to-know" basis. For example, only persons at the level of group supervisor and higher might be on the distribution list for standards material having to do with premium pay, office hours, and expense allowances.

Chapter Headings for the Standards Manual

The following are representative section headings behind which information pertaining to standards might be filed. Naturally, there will be as many variations in this outline as there are system projects. The essential objective is to set up a well-organized repository for information to be conveyed to the System Integration Team in the form of technical "do's" and "dont's."

RECORD AND PROGRAM SPECIFICATION GUIDES • The record and program specification section contains detailed guides to the uniform preparation of record and program specifications. The guides themselves should be supplemented by samples showing record formats and programs that have been specified in accordance with them. In addition to these instructions and supporting samples, this section includes directions for the following:

- Specification numbering
- Review and approval of specifications
- Reproduction and distribution of specifications
- Revision of specifications

STANDARD FORMS • In the standard forms section are found samples of record layout forms and other forms specifically tailored to this system. Typically, there are special forms pertaining to both specifications and programs. This section also includes specimens of standard forms supplied by the equipment manufacturer for use in programming and program documentation. All these samples should be accompanied by instructions about when and how each form will be used, if these are not self-evident or are not indicated on the form itself.

FLOW CHARTING • Flow charts are necessary at the technical planning, specification, and programming phases, with the degree of detail increasing as the descent is made to the next lower level of documentation. Because of the special character of real-time planning and programming, flow charting standards promulgated by professional associations or equipment manufacturers usually have to be adapted for real-time use. For this reason, standards for flow charting merit a separate section in the Programming Standards Manual. Figure 8.1 shows a very simple standard adhered to by one real-time project in preparing flow charts to accompany program specifications. This relatively simple standard was found to be considerably more effective than an exhaustively detailed one previously used on the same project.

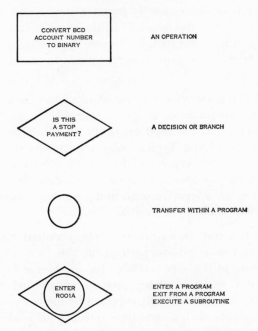

FIGURE 8.1.   GENERAL LOGIC DIAGRAM
SYMBOLS.

FIELD DEFINITIONS • The section on field definition is applicable only to those projects which undertake to control, at a level below that of record specification numbering, the contents of system records, as was done in the SAGE Systems Communications Pool (COMPOOL). If major components of records, and items and fields within those components, are named symbolically and if the symbols are intended to have common usage, then this section contains the current listing and description of such common fields. In large systems the procedure for controlling programmers' references to fields and records has been automated, as in the SAGE system. This is, however, a complex and costly undertaking and the same results may be achieved in smaller systems through manual control under the supervision of the Standards Programmer. Regardless of how automatic, if an attempt is made to identify commonly used and referenced data this section of the manual can serve as the clearing house of field definitions that have been made, to be consulted by any specification writer or programmer engaged in record definition or modification.

STANDARD CONVENTIONS • The standard conventions section is a repository for issuances, normally prepared by the Standards Programmer when the need arises, to establish common programming procedures. Typical subject matter covered includes tape labeling, establishment of file record identifiers, standard error-checking procedures, location of standard fields (such as date) within all system records, and common procedures for logging system statistics in records.

STANDARD ROUTINE DESCRIPTIONS • The standard routine section contains descriptions, perhaps in the form of program specifications, of routines available for use by the Operational Programmers. Some of these, such as generalized sorts and utility programs, are normally supplied by the equipment manufacturer; others, such as real-time routines for reading in the terminal assembly area, must be produced within the System Integration Team.

CONTROL PROGRAM DESCRIPTION • Often the Control Program description is distributed in its own special manual. This is particularly true when the Control Program to be used is a generalized one, already written by the equipment manufacturer. But even when such documentation is already on hand, this section of the Programming Standards Manual should be reserved to describe modifications or extensions of the Control Program. If, for example, certain macro instructions are written to supplement those provided by the Control Program, they should be fully described here.

SYSTEM TESTING • Standards governing all aspects of system testing are provided in this section, which includes detailed requirements for initially testing individual programs as well as later testing, up to and including the requirements for insertion of program changes into an operational system.

Final Documentation • Collected in the final documentation section are standards each programmer must fulfill before the documentation of his work can be considered complete and his program accepted as a permanent addition to the system. Enough unfortunate occurrences in commercial sytsems have resulted from failure to document programs to make the need for this section of the manual self-evident.

Bibliography of Reference Material • The System Integration Team assigned to a project of fairly long duration should begin to build up a technical library for the benefit of its members. This might include texts on programming and system engineering, technical periodicals, and manuals supplied by equipment manufacturers. The Programming Standards Manual should contain a bibliography of such material.

Glossary • Because of the special aspects of real-time systems and the inexperience of many of the technical staff with such systems, a specialized glossary may prove very useful if the time can be found to prepare one. A glossary is especially worthwhile if there are engineers engaged in designing new equipment with the aid of the System Integration Team, or if there are newcomers either to programming or to the application itself. Under these conditions the glossary should include engineering and equipment terminology, real-time programming terminology, and application terminology.

System Control • Basic technical information about the overall system is contained in the system control section. Decisions, particularly those made during technical planning, fixing the location and methods of accessing major classes of records, should be spelled out. High-usage reference tables, constants, and programs that must be kept in main memory at all times should be listed and described. Since the individual specifications for each record and program are usually too voluminous to be kept in the Programming Standards Manual itself, this chapter should provide a convenient general picture of the technical outlines of the system. A logic level system flow chart might appropriately be placed in this section, if its length and format make it suitable for inclusion.

STATUS REPORTS • The status reports section provides a place for current copies of specification, programming, and system testing status reports. Some Controllers may wish each staff member having a standards manual to receive such reports; others may wish them to go only to supervision, in which case this can be a limited section distributed and maintained only for certain copies of the manual.

In addition to these sections, an up-to-date table of contents and an index should be included.

A good Programming Standards Manual requires considerable planning and effort, not only to set up initially but also to maintain as a current system control tool. But the effort pays off handsomely—in enhanced effectiveness of the technical personnel once system development ground rules have been codified for their benefit.

8.6 SUMMARY

There are numerous standards on many different levels that affect the System Integration Team. Although overall system standards and equipment standards have a direct impact, the System Integration Team is most immediately concerned with programming standards. These must be developed to set forth technical guidelines and constraints for each phase of system integration. A Standards Programmer is required for this purpose and his activities may extend to the programming of standard routines as well as preparation of standards. The Standards Programmer is also reponsible for preparation and maintenance of a Programming Standards Manual as the repository for the technical information needed to control system integration.

IV

DIRECTING
  THE SYSTEM
INTEGRATION
  EFFORT

RECORD AND PROGRAM
SPECIFICATIONS | 9

9.1 SYSTEM DOCUMENTATION

IN TERMS OF a chronological view of system integration, Chapters 4 through 8 have constituted a sizable digression from the main sequential path. This was necessary to identify the administrative and technical problems associated with establishing the System Integration Team. We shall now return to consideration of another of the phases of system integration—that of preparing a set of documents in detail that describe the system records and programs. These documents, designated here as record and program specifications, are based on the work already accomplished during preliminary technical planning. And in turn, the work of the specification writers provides the basis for the preparation of programs during the programming phase of system integration.

Given an initial software subsystem design as the product of technical planning, how does the System Integration Team go about specifying, in programmable terms, what remains to be accomplished? It has already been noted (in Chapter 3) that several kinds of documentation will typically be required in real-time system integration. Let us now place record and program specifications in their proper perspective by describing the nature and purpose of various system documents that have an immediate effect on programming.

Functional Requirements

Functional requirements produced by the company that is to use the system (which, it will be recalled, is not necessarily responsible for system integration) describe the data process-

211

ing job to be done and set forth the performance requirements to be met by the system. They are not programming oriented and may in fact be completely machine independent. Frequently they are a reflection of the inputs and outputs required of the system. In an airline reservation system, there might be a functional requirement establishing what actions must result when the Sell button on the agent's terminal is depressed. The document would describe the action to be taken by the system in the event space was or was not available, the action required in case of agent error, the format of the response, and the allowable time limit for giving the response. Often, functional requirements take the form of an acceptance test.

In many instances the functional requirements may not have been set forth in sufficient detail to guide the programmers in a useful way. This complicates matters for the System Integration Team, which must then guess at the system requirements or find out about them somewhat haphazardly.

Record and Program Specifications

Record and program specifications define the system in programmable terms. They transform the functional requirements into a technical description that controls the programming phase. It is these specifications, covering both the records needed by the system as well as the required programs, which are the keystone of real-time system integration. They represent a level of specification not usually found outside real-time systems. The main purpose of this chapter is to suggest general guidelines for producing such specifications.

System Flow Chart

An overall system description or schematic is a virtual necessity in real-time programming and usually requires a great deal of ingenuity to produce. The system flow chart should ideally be available at the *beginning* of the specification phase but frequently is not. It may well be a general rule that a system flow chart which is *meaningful to the programming staff* cannot be produced until after considerable effort has been invested in specifications. The system flow chart may be in conventional

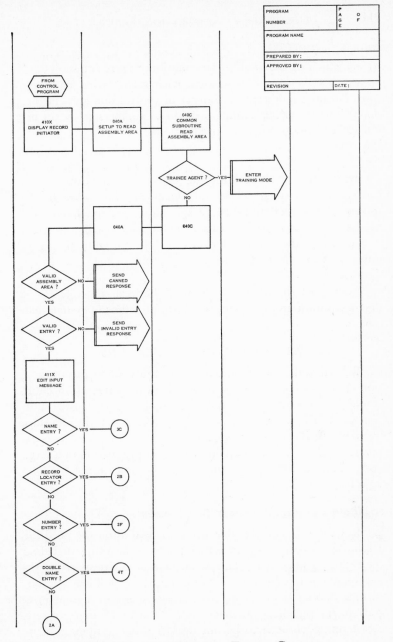

FIGURE 9.1. SYSTEM FLOW CHART.

213

form, as was the case of the SABRE system, or it may be tabular, as was much of the SAGE documentation. Figure 9.1 shows one approach to system flow charting. Each vertical line across the page indicates a descent or transfer of control one level farther down into the programming structure. Numbers in boxes are cross references to Program Specifications.

Other Documentation

Below the level of both the program specifications and the system flow chart exists the documentation normally required of any well-managed programming group. There will be detailed flow charts produced in conformity with the specifications, and there will, of course, be the program listing itself—the ultimate document in this entire scheme of things.

Figure 9.2 shows the relationship between these levels of documentation and indicates the downward flow of system definition.

9.2 PURPOSE OF SPECIFICATIONS

Record and program specifications are vital to the integration of a real-time system. Without them the integration effort would be very difficult, if not impossible, to standardize and control. Perhaps the most compelling reason for the development of specifications has to do with the principle of *concurrency*, which, it will be recalled, states that production of a large body of system description and documentation cannot be done serially.

Facilitate Concurrent System Development

In Chapter 3 considerable stress was placed on the need for a relatively small group of senior planners, working to define the technical bounds of the system. One objective of establishing this small initial group is to minimize the problems of concurrent development during subsequent stages of system integration. In fact, the basic *raison d'être* of a preliminary technical planning phase is to permit heavier reliance upon concurrent development during the specification phase, after the technical planning staff has made the basic system decisions that cannot be relegated to a larger and necessarily less well coordinated effort.

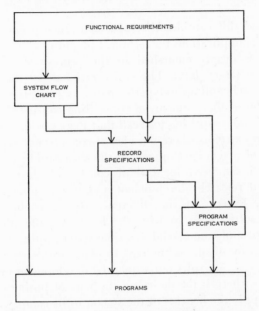

FIGURE 9.2. LEVELS AND SOURCES OF SYSTEM DEFINITION.

How many people should be involved in preliminary technical planning? in specification writing? in programming? Ideally, there should be one person only in each phase, and this should be the same person from one phase to another. This has been possible now and then in the past on some systems, particularly on some scientific problems, but it is usually out of the question on today's file-oriented real-time systems.

Generally, the more people assigned during each phase, the more concurrency in system development and the greater the danger of misunderstandings and inefficiencies. The System Integration Team normally expands from a few staff members during technical planning to a larger but still relatively small group at specification writing time to a sizable task force at programming and system test time. If a workmanlike job of specification is done during the earlier phases, the project can best permit concurrency when it is most needed—during the final phases.

Beyond this consideration of concurrency from the standpoint of its implications for technical planning, the idea of concurrency is deeply enmeshed in the process of establishing completion target dates. The entire rationale of the PERT approach to scheduling and performance appraisal is based on recognition of the problems of controlling concurrent development. It is not surprising to recall that PERT was first developed for military systems where the idea of concurrency, with its implication of system development at the most rapid pace possible, underlined the need for careful control of the progress of overlapped research, development and production of military hardware. Except for the differences brought about by the need for software to go with the hardware, the concurrency characteristic of commercial real-time system integration is not unlike that of missile technology. In place of the overwhelming national need that rules out sequential development of military subsystems, there is the desire on the part of business management to apply the benefits of the system to its company's operations just as soon as possible.

It is hard to visualize a Controller who would be able to abandon the principle of concurrency entirely. Even if the installation target date so permitted, computer technology is changing with such rapidity that any system developed one subsystem at a time would be obsolete before it was installed, because of changes not only in the equipment but also in the operational environment. It must be concluded then that concurrency in the development of software subsystems is not only necessary but desirable. Control must, however, be asserted to assure that independently fabricated software subsystems will be compatible and will, when put together, interact to produce an efficient total system. It is a primary purpose of record and program specifications to provide this assurance by describing objectively the details of each record and program in the system for the guidance of the programmers.

In addition to facilitating concurrent development of programs, specifications provide other benefits for the System Integration Team. Even where there is relatively little emphasis on concurrency, these other advantages will result from a well-defined program specification phase.

Aid in System Design

As the specification phase begins, few concrete details are known about record content or program logic. Writing and issuance of specifications enables each specification writer to dovetail his own specifications into those already issued and to suggest changes and modifications to others' work based on what he has been doing. In this way important program and record relationships are worked out before any program steps are actually coded.

Break the Problem down into Programmable Pieces

Entirely apart from concurrency, a group of programmers cannot simply be thrown a job estimated to require some 50,-000 to 150,000 machine instructions and told to start programming. Specifications are required to compartmentalize this task into easily manageable units of work.

Provide an Organized Means of Programmer-to-Programmer Communication

While informal communication among programmers on technical problems is inevitable and, within reasonable limits, desirable, it can also seriously impair productivity. One purpose of specifications is to formalize such communication by concentrating much of it in a phase precedent to the actual programming.

Permit Effective Use of Inexperienced Personnel

The real-time system, as has been noted earlier, is almost certain to involve the recruitment of inexperienced personnel for training and assignment as programmers. Specifications serve to prevent these novices from making momentous system decisions. Record layout, file organization, optimum file accessing schemes—all these are worked out in advance by the specification writers, who should, of course, themselves be experienced programmers. In effect, the specification writers serve as a buffer beween the system configuration and the programmers.

9.3 DEVELOPMENT OF SPECIFICATIONS

Based on an initial system design, including the specifications for the equipment and for the Control Program (which may for purposes of this discussion be viewed as an extension of the equipment), what must be done to produce a set of record and program specifications? First of all, guides for specification writing should be prepared. Section 9.5 presents two such guides in generalized form. Each real-time project should develop its own guides, tailor-made to recognize such variables as type of equipment, application, Control Program logic, and the technical proficiency of the programming staff. These guides will aid in standardization of written specifications and will, if carefully prepared, establish the level of the specifications. It should, for example, be determined and built into the program specification guide whether the specifications are to be *programming* or *coding* specifications; that is, should they contain detailed flow charts or should this be made the responsibility of the individual programmer? In addition to the guides for specification writing, other aids to specification development include a set of functional requirements and a system flow chart, if available. With these documents at hand, work may commence on record and program specifications.

At the risk of stating the obvious, a word of caution is in order here. Specifications should be maintained in some easily updated looseleaf manual form. They should *never* be issued in bound volumes. A procedure for easy revision and reissuance, preferably by page, should be devised, as the specifications may be expected to change throughout the life of the system.

This tendency toward obsolescence is especially pronounced during the specification-writing phase itself, since one purpose of issuing specifications is to inform the other specification writers how a particular record is being laid out or how the logic of a particular program is being planned within a certain processing area. The specification writer thus *expects* changes as the result of suggestions from others. A second reason for change involves modifications to record specifications when the programs that must operate on these records come to be specified. Third, the nature of the application may change during the period of specification production, causing a change in the functional requirements, which, in turn, triggers a change in the specifications. Finally, change in specifications may be expected during the programming phase as the programmers, in seeking to translate the specifications into code, discover inconsistencies and inefficiencies in the specifications. The continuing need to update specifications should be anticipated by the system planners. Figure 9.3 illustrates various patterns of change in system definition that may occur in a real-time system.

9.4 CONTROL OF SPECIFICATION DEVELOPMENT

In a system like SABRE, which required more than 500 specifications (not including revisions) of the type outlined in this chapter, some manageable method of identifying and controlling the specifications has to be devised to assign work and to measure the progress of those assigned to produce specifications. It is necessary, therefore, during the initial planning of the real-time system, to establish procedures for review and approval of specifications and to design a specification numbering procedure.

Review and Approval of Specifications

An effective review and approval procedure for specifications should serve a twofold purpose:

1) Determine functional adequacy. Does this specification satisfactorily accomplish the processing demanded by the appropriate functional requirements? Does it contain any features that distort or undermine the *intent* of any functional require-

ment? An edit program which is specified with the limitation that an entry will always be in a fixed format is making some rather far-reaching assumptions about the manner in which a terminal operator enters data into the system. The ability to backspace or to space the carriage a variable distance for format purposes may be precluded by such a narrowly specified program.

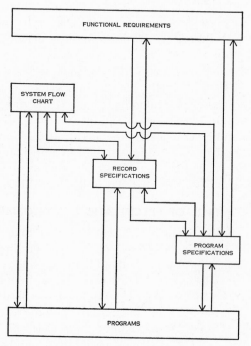

FIGURE 9.3.   SOURCES OF CHANGE IN
SYSTEM DEFINITION.

2) Determine technical adequacy. Does this specification conform to the standards set up to govern Operational Programs? Does it violate Control Program restrictions? Is it markedly inefficient in its usage of main memory or file storage? Such questions of a technical nature must be answered for each

specification entirely apart from questions about its adherence to functional requirements.

Lest these comments give too negative a connotation to the review process, it should be mentioned that there are also positive benefits to be obtained from review of specifications by technical management. As the result of review, System Integration Team management can remain continuously aware of the problems being encountered as specifications are produced. This technical cognizance can be maintained on an informal basis during technical planning, when few persons are involved and when the technical problems are mostly of the "big picture" variety. When the specification phase commences, there must be a more routinized way for technical management to remain "wired in" on progress and problems. Specifications provide an ideal vehicle for this when they are submitted for review.

In setting up the review procedure, emphasis can be placed either on extensive review before issuance or on revision of documents following publication. If there is only limited review before initial issuance of a specification, the chances of later extensive modification are great. If, on the other hand, there is considerable scrutiny of the specification in draft form before its first publication, some revision can still be anticipated but should be minor compared to the changes that might have occurred if the specification had not been carefully examined before issuance.

No matter what the procedure, *some* review of specification must be made before their initial issuance, to exert at least minimal quality control over the specification. Among those who might be expected to have review and approval responsibility are:

- The supervisor of the group in which the specification was prepared
- The application analyst cognizant over the functional requirements touched upon by the specification
- The Standards Programmer.

If the System Integration Team is composed of personnel from different companies, the review procedure may have to be set up along organizational lines, so that a representative of each company "signs off" on the specification. The guide for specification preparation should give consideration to the number of people who must review specifications and to their needs and backgrounds, as specifications can be written, "formatted," and reproduced in a manner that either facilitates or impedes review, depending upon how much thought has been devoted to the purposes and mechanics of review.

If, for example, more than one or two persons have pre-publication review responsibility, it may be prudent to produce multiple copies of drafts for review so that the time consumed in review can be overlapped. Such drafts might carry a suspense date, by which the specification will be issued *unless* an objection is raised by any of those with review responsibility. Even when the review procedure is intended to take a specification up through the managerial hierarchy, there is no need to send it up one level, then back for revision; up another level, then back two for revision; up one level more, then back three for revision, and so on. To avoid bottlenecks and delays, it is necessary either to limit the extent of review or to apply the concurrency principle to review.

It is also worthwhile to distinguish *type* of specification in setting up the review path. Some "internal" specifications have no need of functional review, as their impact upon the external world of terminal operators is nil. Certain record specifications, such as those for indexes, are more basic than others and should be reviewed more closely.

It is difficult to suggest general rules for intelligent review steps. Perhaps the best that can be done is to caution that cumbersome or "knit picking" review mechanics have a demoralizing effect on those preparing the specifications. And, of course, whatever procedure is adopted, it should be one that can be readily changed after more experience has been gained in trying to implement it.

Specification Numbering

A specification numbering system should provide some readily grasped means for identification by humans, as well as encoded information useful in machine analysis of specification status. In illustration consider the following hypothetical record specification number for an index record called "Index to Inventory Status."

$$I225XD$$

- "I" indicates the functional grouping to which this record belongs. Work on records may be divided among several groups, only one of which specializes in inventory functions.

- "225" is a number uniquely identifying this record within the inventory functional area.

- "X" indicates that this record serves as an index to other records, namely those containing inventory status.

- "D" identifies the location of the index as being on disk.

Thus, a capsule profile of the Index to Inventory Status Record may be obtained merely by examining the specification number.

If such a descriptive numbering system can be set up and if certain additional information contained in the specifications can be encoded, a powerful analytical tool becomes available at the cost of a few passes on EAM equipment or a relatively simple computer program. Two illustrations suggest some of the possibilities:

1) Simulation shows that System A is in potentially serious trouble during peak hours because of heavy references to disk storage. A record description file containing information about the location and size of each record in the system (obtained from the Record Environment section of the specifications) is run against data on disk file throughput figures for each transaction type and the most frequently referenced disk records identified. Some or all of these records are now candidates for promotion to faster access storage.

2) A change in a field in one set of records in System B has been proposed. Since this field, like all fields in the system, has its own

unique symbol, a pass of a symbol reference file is used to extract the numbers of all record specifications that utilize this field. A second pass, this time on the record description file, produces a list of all programs that refer to each record containing the affected field. Thus, the impact of the proposed change can be rapidly and thoroughly considered in advance.

This type of automatic control over specifications can be as straightforward or as elaborate as the size and complexity of the system demand. The value of such a disciplined approach to system analysis and maintenance has already been demonstrated in the Communications Pool (COMPOOL) utilized by the SAGE system.

9.5 GUIDES FOR PREPARING SPECIFICATIONS

The material outlined in the following guides is presented to provide suggestions that may aid in specification of real-time records and Operational Programs. It is based on an equipment configuration including alphanumeric terminals and drum, disk and tape storage, in addition to fixed word length, binary core storage. It also assumes the existence of a Control Program that provides the environment within which the other programs operate.

In examining these guides, it should be kept in mind that they are designed to instruct an imaginary technical staff member in the art of specification writing. Consequently, their style is imperative. The guides require that all section and subsection headings be included in each specification with the comment "not applicable" where necessary.

File Record Specification Guide

As mentioned in Chapter 3, records may be classified into certain arbitrarily defined categories, such as file, index, output, and linkage.

File records are the basic records in the system, enabling it to fulfill its functions. It is this type of record that the File Record Specification guide refers to.

Index records are records used to obtain other records, primarily file records.

Input records are records describing inputs received from the external world, such as messages or inquiries. A special input record specification guide, while not described here, will very probably have to be issued as a standard.

Output records are records describing outputs generated by the system, such as responses to inquiries. A separate output record specification guide will probably also be required.

Linkage records are, essentially, housekeeping records used to transmit intermediate data and results from one program to another.

The file record specification guide described here may be found suitable for specifying index and linkage records; if it is not, additional guides will have to be promulgated.

I. SUMMARY

The summary section of the specification should contain a brief statement, in nontechnical language, of the purpose and contents of the record. It is intended to facilitate review and approval by application analysts who may not be familiar with programming. Great care should be exercised in its wording.

A. PURPOSE

Normally one sentence should suffice.

B. CONTENT

A terse paragraph or two should be sufficient.

II. ASSUMPTIONS

A complete statement should be provided of any assumptions underlying development of this record specification. Such assumptions may be either functional or technical and are collected in this section of the specification so that their implications will not be overlooked during review. An example of a functional assumption would be that a dispatcher will desire to interrogate one portion of a file very frequently and the remainder infrequently. Such an assumption might dictate the splitting of a file between drum and disk storage with major throughput and file maintenance consequences. An example of a technical assumption would be that a thousand contiguous words of drum memory will be available in which to store an index.

III. RECORD ENVIRONMENT

The Record Environment section of the specification will contain many mandatory subsections intended to define the role of a particular class of record and its impact on the overall system. The section is designed in such a way that its contents lend themselves to tabulation by means of either punched cards or an off-line computer program. In this way, much valuable information for analysis and control of the programming system can be obtained.

A. FUNCTION

Indicate the kind of record being specified, together with any explanatory comment that may be appropriate.

B. LOCATION

Specify the normal record location. Where the location is unknown or variable, an explanation should be provided. An example of a record whose location is variable would be one of a file comprised of individual records, some of which are stored on drum and others on disk.

C. CYCLING

Provide an explanation of the life cycle of the record, with specific comment as to the logic of its creation and removal. For example, a daily Seat Inventory Record might be created on receipt of the first customer demand for a flight and removed the day after scheduled completion of the flight. Note here all daily or other periodic actions affecting the record, such as the turning on of a bit indicator in a record at 2:00 A.M. local time each day. Note also the method of creation and removal of a record, if known, such as read-in from cards, write-out to tape.

D. ADDRESSING

Describe in detail how the record may be obtained: through computation, through an index, through chaining. Whenever possible, specify the exact method, such as "computation of a fixed disk address using the last four digits of social security number."

E. SIZE

1. *BASIC SIZE* • Indicate whether the record is of fixed or variable length. If fixed, mention the exact size of the record. If variable, indicate maximum, minimum, and normal size, with the basis for determining size. Since certain systems organize all data into fixed-size record blocks some recognition of the differences between "physical" and "logical" records should be made. Following are two such considerations:

• As a rule, a logical record starts at the beginning of a physical record. If it does not, define its exact location.

• If a physical record contains more than one logical record, detail the number and size of each logical record.

2. *EXPANSION* • Indicate any provision for expansion and the basis for such provision.

F. STORAGE REQUIRED

For drum, disk, and tape records, state exactly the number of physical records required for this class of logical record. Describe the basis for determining the number required and define whether this number is actual or estimated. Indicate any provision for expansion and the basis for planning expansion requirements.

G. CORE LOCATIONS REQUIRED

If any words of core storage are pre-empted in connection with the addressing or cycling of this record, such locations should be named symbolically and described. Usage of such core locations should be approved in advance of issuance of the specification.

H. SEQUENCE

If this specification governs a sequenced file, table, or index, state the sequence.

I. INFORMATION REPRESENTATION

Indicate whether the record contents are binary, binary coded decimal (BCD), or mixed.

J. RECORD RESTRICTIONS

Note any restrictions on usage of this record. For example, "This record may be modified only by an entry from a terminal used by a supervisor." Or "This record cannot be removed from disk to tape until Program R323X has been executed."

IV. DATA DESCRIPTION

The Data Description section is the most important part of a record specification in that it describes and locates every field of data within the record. The overall organization of this section will vary depending upon the record being described. If the record has major sections such as Header, Body, and Trailer, these should be the subsection headings in the Data Description section.

When a record is made up of more than one section, each section should be defined as to size and general content. If any section is variable, the formula used to locate the first, last, or intermediate parts of the section should be defined. Each separate field in a record should be individually and precisely identified and described according to the outline below. A field is defined as the smallest significant piece of information contained in a record. A date change indicator (one bit) would be a field, as would an airport code (three characters).

A. DATA SYMBOL

Up to six alphanumeric characters. The Standards Programmer will maintain and periodically issue a list of data symbols. It will be each specification writer's responsibility to review this list to see if a standard symbol already exists for the field he is describing. Any revision to a data symbol must be furnished to the Standards Programmer, who is charged with responsibility for maintaining this list.

B. STARTING BIT POSITION

Word and bit within the word where this field commences.

C. ENDING BIT POSITION

Word and bit within the word where this field ends.

D. SIZE

Expressed as a bit or bits, characters, or words. If the field occupies part of one word or more than one word, this size should be the total bits, characters, or words, whichever is most feasible to use to describe the complete field.

E. INFORMATION REPRESENTATION

Binary, BCD, or mixed.

F. MAXIMUM VALUE

If this field has a numeric value that would limit the information stored, then the maximum value should be stated.

G. NAME OF FIELD

A descriptive name assigned by the specification writer.

H. DESCRIPTION

A brief statement that fully defines the purpose and usage of the field.

I. FIELD RESTRICTIONS

Absolute or conditional prohibitions covering display or modification of this field. This normally identifies the class of terminal operator who may have access to this field for either display or modification. A data description item should be provided for blank fields in a record. This will consist of symbol name ("Blank"), starting bit position, ending bit position, and size.

Example of a Data Description section:

A. *Header*

Six words, starts at word zero and ends at word 5. Contents: General Schedule information.

1. Word Zero

a) *Blank*	*0-11*	*12 bits*	
b) *ITSAV*	*12-19*	*8 bits*	*binary*

Seats Available for Sale.
This field reflects the actual number of seats for sale. Its ini-

tial value is obtained from Field ICAPAC of the General Schedule at the time the record is set up. Field includes sign. Minus condition indicates overbooking.

Restrictions: When this field is zero or minus, bookings will be accepted only from a terminal manned by a supervisory reservations agent.

V. CROSS REFERENCES

This section will provide a current listing by program number and name of:

A. *Programs That Use This Record*
B. *Programs That Modify This Record*

VI. LAYOUT

A record layout, prepared by the specification writer on a master layout form, should accompany each specification. Depending upon space available in the layout, each field should contain the following information in descending order of importance:

- Field name

- Data symbol

- Number of bits in field

For clarity, certain specifications may also include a simple chart to reflect the overall file layout for one or more classes of records.

Program Specification Guide

For purposes of specification writing, each Operational Program should be classified. Programs could, for instance, be designated from a priority standpoint as real time, deferred, off-line.

REAL TIME • High priority programs that must be initiated without delay on receipt of an entry or other occurrence that triggers their activation. Such programs are typically those which must provide a response to a terminal before further entries can be accepted from this terminal.

DEFERRED • Programs whose initiation may be deferred until a specified time or until adequate time is available. Usually such programs involve batch processing, which may be done when convenient, or the processing of entries for which an immediate response is not critical.

OFF-LINE • Programs not intended to run on the real-time processor and which are not, therefore, programmed within the real-time Control Program environment.

The following program specification guide applies primarily to real-time programs.

I. SUMMARY

The Summary section of the specification should contain a brief statement of the purpose and scope of the program in nontechnical language. It is intended to facilitate functional review and approval, and great care should be exercised in its wording.

A. PURPOSE

Normally one sentence should suffice.

B. SCOPE

A terse paragraph or two should be provided outlining the functions to be performed by the program and the general method employed to accomplish these functions. This is basically a plain-English capsule version of the Logic Description section of the specification.

II. ASSUMPTIONS

A complete statement should be provided of any assumptions underlying development of this specification. Such assumptions may be either functional or technical. An example of a functional assumption would be that a program will remove certain file records not less than twenty-four hours after scheduled completion of a flight. An example of a technical assumption would be that there will be a standard routine for determining the validity of flight origination and termination points.

III. PROGRAM ENVIRONMENT

The Program Environment section will contain many mandatory subsections intended to define the role of a particular program and its impact on the overall system.

A. KIND OF PROGRAM

Designate the kind of program. When a program, such as a standard routine used by many other programs, may fall into more than one category, it should be designated according to its highest priority.

B. ESTIMATED NUMBER OF INSTRUCTIONS

Provide a realistic estimate of the number of instruction and constant words required for this program. This should represent the specification writer's best judgment based on his close knowledge of the program logic.

C. RECORD ACCESSES

Estimate the number of physical record accesses required to process a single action through this program. Where the number of accesses varies depending upon branching within the program, the minimum, maximum, and average number of accesses should be estimated. Accesses should be tabulated as follows:

1. Drum
   * Read

   * Write

2. Disk
   * Read

   * Write

3. Tape
   * Read

   * Write

D. DRUM, DISK, AND TAPE STORAGE REQUIRED

1. *TEMPORARY* • Estimate the number of physical drum, disk, or tape records required in the course of *one* execution of this program. Where use of such temporary storage varies depending upon branching within the program, the minimum, maximum, and average number of records should be estimated. (The requirement for this kind of temporary storage will be exceptional, as most programs utilize main memory storage

for this purpose. Programs that add items to a temporary file or queue will be the main users of temporary file storage. For example, a program to check airline ticket time limits might examine all Passenger Records for a given date and store those records containing expired time limits in a temporary file to await cancellation action by an agent.)

2. *PERMANENT* • Specify the number of drum or disk physical records permanently associated with this program. Such a record might be required to hold cumulative statistics concerning the frequency of usage of this program or for storage of infrequently used variables (such as a beginning file address) that are not regarded as important enough to be held permanently in main memory. When the need for such permanent storage is determined, its format should be described in a record specification.

E. MAIN MEMORY STORAGE REQUIRED

1. *TEMPORARY* • Provide an estimate of the amount of main memory storage required in the course of one execution of this program. Where the use of such temporary storage varies depending upon branching within the program, the minimum, maximum, and average amount of storage used should be estimated.

2. *PERMANENT* • Determine the amount of main memory storage permanently pre-empted by this program. Such storage might be required for control words, statistical tallies, and frequently used tables. Since main memory is the most expensive storage medium, an effort should be made to store permanently needed information on drum or disk unless this is prohibitive in terms of access time. When a main memory word or series of words must be used, their usage should be approved in advance and a symbolic name assigned. The Standards Programmer will maintain and periodically issue a list of such permanently assigned memory main locations.

F. PROGRAM MODIFICATION

Where small tables or sets of parameters are to be carried within the program as constants, include a statement in the Program Modification section to identify such data so that the program can be modified when this information changes. An example of such program constant information would be a brief list of types of aircraft, one word per each type, which would have to be modified each time a new type of aircraft is added to the system.

G. ENTRY CONDITIONS

Indicate how the program is entered, the circumstances or processing sequences under which it is entered, and any other information which, in addition to the input formats and locations, should be known before transfer to this program can be made.

H. EXIT CONDITIONS

Indicate the method of exit (return to using program, exit to Control Program, transfer to next program in a series) and provide any special details on each normal and error exit possible for this program.

I. ERROR AND EXCEPTION DETECTION

Individually summarize all tests to be made on the validity of input and file data and specify action to be taken by the program when errors are encountered. (This subsection is concerned primarily with showing Operational Program action on receipt of incorrect input, rather than action resulting from equipment malfunction. It is intended to assist in the development of standard error detection and correction routines and procedures.)

J. RESTRICTIONS AND SPECIAL REQUIREMENTS

Note any internal or external restrictions on usage of this program not described in the previous subsections. For example, "This program may not be activated more than once every 24 hours" or "This program should not be activated before 2:00 A.M. daily because of the large numbers of accesses involved."

IV. INPUT

Input should be described under two subsections as follows.

A. INITIAL

Data available upon initial entry to the program for the purpose of processing a new action. Such input may be contained in a register or in main memory. Drum, disk, or tape records are not regarded as initial input unless they happen to be in main memory at the time the program is activated. Initial input should be broken down and described as linkage or record.

1. *LINKAGE* • Data provided in one or more registers. This type of input usually consists of parameters or indicators for which a record specification may not exist. For each such input a complete description at the bit level should be provided, as well as information about its location (accumulator, index register, and so on).

2. *RECORD* • Data existing in main memory. This type of input is ordinarily a file record read in by some predecessor program or an input received from a terminal. For each input, the record specification number and name should be listed.

B. INTERMEDIATE

Data obtained for itself by *this* program during the course of an execution. This intermediate or "internal" input consists normally of one or more records described in a record specification. The number and name of each such specification should be listed.

V. OUTPUT

Output should be described under two subsections as follows.

A. FINAL

Data produced by the program on completion of processing. As in the case of initial input, final output may be located in a register or in main memory storage. Final output should be broken down and described as linkage or main memory.

1. *LINKAGE* • Data produced in one or more registers. This type of output usually consists of parameters or indicators for which a record specification does not exist. For each such output a complete description at the bit level should be provided, along with information about its location.

2. *MAIN MEMORY* • Data existing in main memory storage. This type of output is ordinarily a file record previously read or generated in main memory. For each such output, the record specification number and name should be listed.

No records that have been disposed of by filing before exit should be included under final output. It is possible for a program which, let us say, updates and files certain records and then exits to the Control Program without generating a response to a terminal to have no final output.

B. INTERMEDIATE

Data filed by this program prior to completion of its processing. The number and name of any record that has been so disposed of should be listed.

VI. LOGIC DESCRIPTION

The Logic Description section is the most important part of a program specification in that it describes in considerable detail the processing steps to be accomplished by the program. The objective of this section is threefold:

• To provide a reasonably thoroughgoing narrative outline of the basic program logic.

• To specify particular techniques or requirements where, in the interest of efficiency, the programmer should be required to attack the problem in a certain way. For example, in processing a Sell action, it might be specified that the terminal identifier be checked for legitimacy before seeking the Seat Inventory Record, thus saving an access in the case of erroneous identification.

• To prohibit the use of techniques or methods deemed undesirable or inefficient by the specification writer. For example, the programmer might be told *not* to check date for validity, as this is already being done by some predecessor program.

VII. CROSS REFERENCES

The Cross References section provides a current listing, by record or program number and name, of the following:

A. RECORD REFERENCES

1. Records used (but not modified)
2. Records modified
3. Records created

B. PROGRAM REFERENCES

1. Programs that may transfer control to this program
2. Programs to which this program may transfer control

VIII. GENERAL LOGIC DIAGRAM

A general logic diagram, prepared by the specification writer, should accompany each specification to supplement the Logic Description section. This diagram, or gross flow chart, should not contain excessive detail, as it will be supplemented later by a detailed flow chart prepared by the programmer. *The general logic diagram for each program should normally not exceed one page.* Figure 8.1 shows a set of symbols that could be used in standardizing the preparation of such a diagram.

9.6 SUMMARY

Traditional approaches to data and program description are not adequate for development of real-time programs. Real-time systems demand levels of description and quantities of detail within these levels beyond what has normally sufficed for other systems.

Preparation of record and program specifications makes several contributions to real-time system integration:

- Facilitates concurrent system development.
- Aids in system design.
- Helps to break the problem down.
- Provides a means of communication.
- Permits use of inexperienced personnel.

Many procedures and controls underlie the successful completion of the specification phase. Requirements for review and approval of specifications must, for example, be established and a specification numbering scheme set up. Most important of all, guides must be prepared to instruct those assigned to this phase in the art of specification writing.

PROGRAMMING | 10

10.1 MULTIPROGRAMMING

OF ALL THE technical decisions to be made during system integration, by far the most portentous one has to do with whether the system will be multiprogrammed. This dictates the basic structure of the Control Program (or indeed whether a Control Program is needed at all), how the Operational Programs must be specified and coded, the allocation of main memory, and the methodology of system testing. For some applications there may be no choice available between multiprogramming and sequential handling of inputs, as the response requirements or file reference volumes may be so demanding as to dictate a multiprogrammed approach.

What is multiprogramming and why does it have such a far-reaching effect on the real-time system? Like so many other terms in current usage among computer specialists, it has taken on a variety of shades of meaning. In this discussion a multiprogrammed system is defined as one in which several actions may be in process at the same time inside the central processing unit. This is in contrast to a sequentially programmed system which disposes of actions one by one, not permitting a new action to enter the processing cycle until the current one has been completely processed.

Figure 10.1 illustrates how a multiprogrammed system operates on inputs received from several outlying terminals. An entry is received from Terminal 1 and is immediately subjected to analysis by the Control Program to determine the type of action required. This processing is interrupted by receipt of an entry from Terminal 2. After the same preliminary action

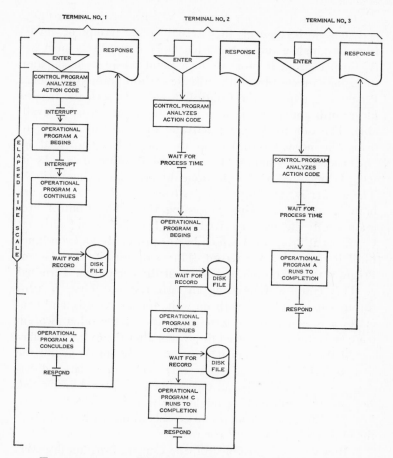

FIGURE 10.1. MULTIPROGRAMMED OPERATION.

code analysis of this second entry, the Control Program completes its scrutiny of the first entry and activates Operational Program A. Operational Program A is interrupted by receipt of an entry from Terminal 3, which must be given the same preliminary action code analysis as were the two preceding entries. On completion of this analysis, the Control Program again reactivates the program that has been interrupted, namely Operational Program A.

Operational Program A has by now been twice interrupted —each time because of an external event: receipt of entries from terminals 2 and 3. Now that Operational Program A has regained control, it proceeds to a point where it must pause to request a record from the disk file. At this point Operational Program A requests the Control Program to seek the needed file record, and relinquishes control until the record is available. The Control Program activates the access mechanism to bring the needed record from the file address provided by Operational Program A. The Control Program then asks itself, "Is any other work to be done during this waiting period?" The answer is "Yes," since entries from Terminals 2 and 3 are both in queues awaiting processing time. The Control Program selects the entry received from Terminal 2 and activates Operational Program B, which begins processing and continues until it requires a file record. This wait permits the Control Program to initiate the processing of the entry from Terminal 3. This entry is interesting in two respects. First, it runs through to completion with no waits for file records, and generates a response to the terminal ahead of the other two entries, even though it entered the system after them. It also makes use of the same program (Operational Program A) as did the first entry, but because of a difference in the input data a different processing path through Operational Program A is selected. Both entry 1 and entry 3 might, for example, be Sell entries, but 3 might perhaps contain an erroneous date, which obviates the need to consult any file records.

After entry 3 is disposed of, the Control Program discovers that the file record requested by Program B is now ready, and so control returns to this program, which almost immediately relinquishes control with a request for a second file record. This is a rather typical occurrence, in which the first record requested might be an index containing the file address of the second, or master, record. At any rate, during this second wait, Operational Program A can be reactivated, as the file record requested by it some time ago is now ready. The availability of this record permits Operational Program A to process entry 1 through to completion.

All that now remains is to dispose of entry 2. This can be done as soon as the second record requested by Operational Program B is available. Note, however, that there is a transfer of control from Operational Program B to Operational Program C, which contains the logic for operating on the newly obtained record and for preparing the response to Terminal 2.

Several revealing inferences can be drawn from this example:

1) The usage of relatively slow disk storage with the resultant waits for records to be fetched into main memory constitutes one of the principal reasons for multiprogramming. Essentially, the idea is to let some other program make use of the central processing unit while the access mechanism is seeking file records.

2) There are two sources of interruption of an Operational Program—receipt of input from the outside world and receipt of input from the file on completion of a seek by the access mechanism.

3) The processing sequence and the time required to process a given input are dependent upon what other inputs also happen to be undergoing processing. If, in the example, entry 3 had *not* come into the system, entries 1 and 2 would not have been interrupted as frequently. And if the entries from the three terminals had been received in a slightly different sequence, say 2-3-1, we would have to redraw the schematic entirely to gain a picture of the processing operations. This processing variability has some disconcerting implications for system testing.

4) A Control Program is essential to determine what must be done next by the system.

The schematic is, of course, greatly simplified. There may be tens or hundreds of terminals associated with a system, each capable of generating any one of two or three dozen different kinds of entries. And the reference files in the system may be on several modules of disk storage, on drums or tapes, or on all these in combination. Multiprogramming can make a file-oriented system efficient but at the same time dangerously complex in its operation. And the planning, programming, and system testing required to produce this efficient but complex operating system are technically formidable and costly.

Must the system planner make a clear-cut choice between multiprogramming of the type just described and processing in a serial one-by-one fashion? Not necessarily. For many systems, there is a middle way, which reduces somewhat the complexity of multiprogramming while retaining much of its overlapped efficiency. In a file-oriented system the chief advantage of multiprogramming is the overlapping of central processor time with file seek time, a buffering advantage forfeited by sequential processing. It might, however, be possible to overlap file references while processing only a limited number of entries at a time. By allowing only n entries (where n is some number greater than one) into the system at once, file overlap can be obtained in processing this batch of entries, but such parameters as storage devoted to entries, file records requested by entries, and waiting lists of various programs in process have known limits and are therefore somewhat simpler to analyze and control. In a system possessing an input/output multiplexor, it should be possible to accumulate a batch of entries, then send these to the central processing unit to undergo processing. Depending upon the type of input and file data being dealt with, it might be possible to relieve the multiprogramming burden of the central processor even further by organizing the batches of entries into groups containing similar action codes or into file number or priority sequence. Regardless of the equipment involved or the application, attention should be concentrated on ways to eliminate or at least to simplify the difficulties associated with multiprogramming.

10.2 CONTROL PROGRAM FUNCTIONS

As was mentioned in the discussion of multiprogramming, a real-time system need not necessarily have a Control Program, if a way can be found to avoid the problems of processing several entries simultaneously. Systems have been put into operation for such applications as airline reservations and savings bank accounting that are not multiprogrammed. In one airline reservation system, inventory information is stored on magnetic drums of sufficient speed that the lack of overlapped processing and access time can be tolerated for the transaction rate experienced. Often in savings bank accounting the inquiry rate from the terminals is sufficiently light when balanced against computer and file access time that there is no need to venture into the treacherous waters of multiprogramming.

Even in these systems, however, a Control Program may come into existence as a work scheduler and interrupt processor. This is especially true of systems with low inquiry rates, which are designed to do non-real-time processing when there is no real-time inquiry work to be performed. In such instances a vestigial Control Program is set up to obtain control from the non-real-time program, see to it that an inquiry is processed, and then return control to the interrupted non-real-time program.

Recognizing that the performance requirements of many real-time systems are sufficiently lenient to need only a very primitive Control Program, let us examine the functions that would be lodged in a Control Program of some complexity. The most elaborate of Control Programs will encompass all the following functions; the least elaborate perhaps ony one or two.

Control of Input from Terminals

This portion of the Control Program regulates the receipt and assembly of entries from the remote terminals. It might include:

- Code-to-code conversion
- Long entry assembly
- Action code analysis
- Preliminary editing
- Polling of terminals, that is, signaling of terminals to transmit their entries.

It there is an input/output multiplexor, these input control functions would be performed by it; otherwise, they must be handled by the central processing unit.

Control of Output to Terminals

Transmission of responses and other outputs from the central processor to the terminals is included here. This may extend to:

- Code-to-code conversion
- Assembly of outgoing long messages
- Transmission of unsolicited output
- Attachment of routing characters to outputs
- Network awareness, that is, maintaining a checklist of those locations presently in communication with the computer

Control of File Input/Output

All requests for file records made by Operational Programs are serviced by this portion of the Control Program. This may include file address conversion from symbolic to absolute, redirecting of file accesses in a system having duplicated records when the primary copy is unavailable, removal of file modules from the system on either a planned or an unplanned basis, and restoration of file modules to the system. If there is a file multiplexor in the system, such as that described in Chapter 2, most of these input/output functions would be performed there.

Operational Program Read-In

Besides controlling the input and output of data contained in the system files, the Control Program is responsible for reading from file the programs needed to process particular entries received from the terminals. This is essential in those systems which cannot contain in main memory all the Operational Programs needed to process each possible entry. Basically the Control Program is responsible for bringing together in main memory an entry and the program or programs needed to process that entry.

Waiting List Control

In a multiprogrammed file-oriented system, several queues of items awaiting processing action must be maintained. The following are representative:

- New entries awaiting assignment to an Operational Program for processing
- File record requests not yet accomplished
- Records read in and now awaiting further processing
- Programs awaiting read-in from the file to process particular entries
- Programs read in from file and now available for processing
- Responses awaiting transmission to the terminals

Various Control Program techniques have been developed to manage these lists, most of them closely dependent upon the logic of particular pieces of hardware.

Administration of Processing Priorities

In some systems, administration of processing priorities turns out to be an extremely complicated function. Every Control Program must contend with priority problems, if only to the extent of deciding whether to give precedence to a newly received entry or to one already partially processed, when both are competing for available processing time. Besides this kind of priority, externally established priorities may have to be adhered to—one action code over another, one terminal ahead of another, and real-time work ahead of non-real-time, for example.

Storage Allocation

This involves control of available main memory as well as file storage. In addition to the lists of programs and data awaiting processing, there are lists of available storage to be maintained by the Control Program.

Error Checking

The Control Program must have the ability to identify and report, and possibly diagnose and compensate for, recurrent and transient equipment malfunctions—whether in the computer, the multiplexors, the files, the communication lines, or the remote equipment.

Operator Communication

Since a file-oriented real-time system is not closed loop, a comprehensive method of communication with the central computer operator is needed. Many systems use a terminal as the communication medium in place of the standard computer console. Handling of error conditions, switchover in a duplex system, fallback to a diminished equipment configuration, initiation or termination of real-time processing all call for Control Program/operator communication.

Switchover

In a duplex system, the Control Program must be capable of shifting operations from the on-line to the standby computer in an orderly manner and in one most protective of work in progress in both computers. In the case of emergency switchover, it is not always possible to preserve the integrity of all data, but in many instances of scheduled switchover this can and should be done.

Fallback and Recovery

The responsibility for removing a terminal or an entire communication line from service comes under the category of fallback and recovery, as does removal of a drum or disk module from service and its subsequent restoration. Like switchover, fallback may be on a planned or an emergency basis, with Control Program action differing substantially depending upon the case it is dealing with.

Intercomputer Communication

Where there are multiple computers in the real-time system, such as a central processing unit and an input/output multiplexor, special routines are needed to control the interaction of these computers. An exchange of control information must be made, for example, between the host computer and its input/ output multiplexor following a change in terminal status. If a terminal is taken out of service by the multiplexor, the host computer should be apprised so that it will not generate unsolicited outputs for this terminal. Communication between computers is also necessary to control fallback, restart, and switchover in a duplex system.

There are many variations in the kinds of Control Programs possible and in the relationship between Control and Operational Programs. The development of Control Programs is a new and burgeoning art and it is possible here to suggest only a few of the characteristics that might be encountered in a present-day real-time Control Program. It is reasonable to expect that a new generation of equipment, engineered from the ground up for real-time processing, will in the foreseeable future have many of these Control Program features already built into the hardware.[1]

10.3 CONTROL-OPERATIONAL PROGRAM RELATIONSHIPS

The Control Program exists to service the Operational Program and to simplify the job of the Operational Programmer by freeing him from concern over complex real-time housekeeping routines. In return for this assistance, the Operational Programmer gives up much of his freedom to deal directly with the hardware, as he would do in a conventional system.

The facilities offered by the Control Program and the constraints it exercises are often embodied in a special set of macro instructions to be used by the Operational Programmers. These differ from macros as the term is commonly understood by system programmers in that they do *not* result in the insertion, as part of the code of the Operational Program, of instructions to carry out the macro functions; instead they result in a transfer of control from the Operational Program to a group of instructions that exist as part of the Control Program. This distinc-

---

[1] Since this was written, announcement of the IBM 360 series and the GE 600 series confirms this prognosis.

tion becomes important when it is borne in mind that in a multi-programmed system, the coding for a macro exists in one place only—the Control Program—rather than in each individual Operational Program that may encounter the need to execute this macro. The macro thus contains coding common to all programs but which does not exist in any of them; rather it exists in the Control Program itself.

Control Program Macro Instructions

To indicate how Control-Operational Program communication by means of macro instructions works, a few typical macros are defined below:

READ FILE RECORD • Obtain from file storage the record whose address is provided by the Operational Program.

READ FILE RECORD AND WAIT • Obtain the designated record from file storage but do not return to the Operational Program until the record has been read into main memory.

WRITE FILE RECORD AND BLAST • Write to the file a record now in main memory and blast (release) the main memory write-out area on completion of the write.

GET FILE ADDRESS • Provide the Operational Program with the address of an available record slot in file storage. The Operational Program in this case probably wishes to set up some temporary or permanent record in file.

RELEASE FILE RECORD • Return the file record at the address indicated to the pool of available file storage records. The Operational Program has decided that certain information is no longer needed in the system. Perhaps this is a record that contained information about a depositor whose account has been closed out.

SEND MESSAGE • Transmit a message from the main memory location designated to the terminal specified. This may be a response generated by an Operational Program or it may be an unsolicited output.

START ANOTHER OPERATIONAL PROGRAM • The Operational Program currently in control can no longer process this entry, and control must be transferred to another program to continue processing.

SET UP FOR TIME INITIATION • Activate the designated Operational Program at the time specified. The program currently in control has decided that further processing must take place *h* hours from now and is requesting the Control Program to set up the mechanism for activating an Operational Program at that time, perhaps for the purpose of doing low-priority batch processing.

RETURN • The program executing this macro is really like an open subroutine. Some other program executed a Start macro to get this program activated, and now this program has decided that control must be returned to the predecessor program.

EXIT • All processing associated with a particular entry has been completed, and the final Operational Program in a series is now terminating. All main memory assigned to this entry for program and data storage should therefore be blasted.

These are representative of the macro instructions used in a real-time system to knit the Control and Operational Programs together into a cohesive and well-articulated running system. Each macro performs a preplanned housekeeping function, designed by the authors of the Control Program in a manner that permits the Operational Programmers to concentrate their energies on solving the problems of the application rather than those of the equipment.

Constraints Imposed on Operational Programs

In exchange for the services available through the Control Program, the Operational Programmers are required to live within certain programming restrictions necessary to the successful functioning of the Control Program. Some of these are imposed in order to centralize and standardize key functions, such an input/output control. Others have to do with multiprogramming, which places restrictions on usage of storage areas to permit them to be shared by several programs. Among the constraints likely to be encountered in a multiprogrammed real-time system are the following:

1) Input/output commands may not be executed by Operational Programs. This applies to commands pertaining to terminals and other remote devices, as well as to tape and random access subsystems. Input/output facility is achieved by an Operational Program through insertion of Control Program macros into the Operational Program.

2) Only certain areas of main memory may be referenced by an Operational Program. Because several programs, with their associated data, may be located in various portions of main memory at any instant in time, no one program can refer to locations beyond the predefined boundaries of the area assigned to it by the Control Program. In some systems the equipment is designed to provide an error interrupt, which returns control to the Control Program if an Operational Program ventures outside the bounds of its assigned area in main memory.

3) If there are multiple index registers, certain of these may be reserved for the exclusive use of the Control Program.

4) The Operational Program may be required to save information contained in the accumulators or index registers when control is temporarily relinquished to the Control Program, as in the case of a request for a file reference. This is because some other Operational Program may be activated before control is returned, and this second program will no doubt be making use of the same registers.

5) Operational Programs may be terminated arbitrarily in some systems if their running time exceeds some predefined period. This is more common in scientific than in commercial systems, as programs in the latter can usually be depended upon to make a file reference fairly soon after their activation and consequently will not pre-empt an undue amount of processing time at the expense of other users of the system. In scientific systems, where the emphasis is on computation, there may be provision for an interrupt after a given period, say 500 milliseconds, which causes control to revert to the Control Program, which may then activate some other Operational Program. Scheduling algorithms in such systems take into account the running time of Operational Programs, the amount of time they have already used up,

the amount of storage they take up in main memory, and kindred factors.[2]

6) Programs may be forbidden from modifying their own instructions, a technique used for decision branching in non-real-time programming. This prohibition is essential in systems employing program relocation, in which a given program segment or group of instructions may be read into different areas of main memory by the Control Program, depending upon what area happens to be available at the time execution of a particular Operational Program is demanded. This procedure makes it impermissible for an Operational Programmer to let his program loop back on itself or perform other gyrations through modification of instructions. This restriction is doubly important in those systems in which an Operational Program is liable to be "erased" when a wait for a file record is encountered. This might happen during the period of the wait if some higher priority program demanded processing time and was brought into the main memory area held by the original program. Later, when the original program is read back into main memory from file (along with the record it requested in the first place), it will resume life as a "fresh" copy and any instruction modification that took place during its earlier existence in main memory is, of course, lost.

7) There may be limits on the total amount of main or auxiliary memory that any given program can tie up for data storage. Without such a limitation, the system might become "locked up" by a program that greedily obtains memory storage until the available supply is exhausted.

8) In addition to being restricted as to the amount of computer time that they may pre-empt, Operational Programs may be restricted as to their length; that is, they may have to be split up into segments of uniform size. Point 7 has to do with the total main memory space taken up at execution time by a given Operational Program for *data*. This restriction is aimed

---

2 F. J. Corbato, M. Merwin-Daggett, and R. C. Daley, "An Experimental Time-Sharing System," *Proceedings of the Spring Joint Computer Conference,* San Francisco, May 1962.

at the length of the *program* itself. To facilitate program relocation and read-in of programs from auxiliary storage, many systems divide their Operational Programs up into standard blocks or segments of arbitrary length, such as 256 instructions in the SABRE system. The programmer is then required to make certain that each such program segment is self-sufficient. For instance, he would have to ascertain that his program did not involve a loop which extends across segment boundaries, as he has no assurance that more than one of his segments will be permitted in main memory at any one time in the course of a particular processing cycle.

9) In those systems capable of generating outputs of uncontrollable length, the Operational Programs may be required to chop the outgoing data into portions, to conform to the error levels of the communication lines, physical limitations of the transmitting equipment, or logical limitations of the Control Program. In effect the Operational Program must break these outputs up into individually transmittable pieces and feed them, one by one, to the Control Program for transmission. This procedure can become quite involved, as some of the data to be transmitted may be in main memory, and the rest in file storage, at the time transmission is initiated. Supervision must be exercised to assure that the output portions are transmitted in the correct sequence. Further, some ability has to be built into the Operational Programs to repeat a long output, either from the very beginning or from the start of the current portion. This requires that portions be saved somewhere— probably in auxiliary storage—subject to retrieval and retransmission in the proper sequence.

10) An analogous situation exists on receipt of an incoming long entry from a terminal, when the equipment—for buffering or other purposes—may arbitrarily divide a long entry into portions of perhaps fifty or one hundred characters. Each portion received must be preserved and tested to see whether it is the first, the last, or an intermediate portion. If it is any portion other than the first, a mechanism must be provided to associate it with the previous portions, usually through consultation of the terminal assembly area. This is an

acute problem in systems in which data may be coming in simultaneously from several terminals, with the possibility that each portion of a long entry may be separated by totally unrelated entries arriving from other terminals.

In some systems, supervision of the transmission and receipt of unusually long entries is handled by the Control Program. In others, however, the Control Program's role is interpreted more narrowly as extending only to getting data into and out of the system according to the hardware definition of message length (arbitrarily fixed) rather than the application definition (variable or uncontrollable length).

Control-Operational Program Interface

A logical separation between the Control Program and the Operational Programs in a real-time system is far from self-evident. There is usually a sizable "no man's land" between the two. This was alluded to in Chapter 2 in the discussion of software/software tradeoffs. The proper determination of which software functions are to be allocated to the Control Program and which to the Operational Programs becomes especially important in those situations in which the organizational responsibility for program specification and programming is to be split according to this determination. When the equipment manufacturer is committed to provide the Control Program, and the purchaser of the system the Operational Programs, decisions about where functions will be performed take on a dollar-and-cents connotation for both parties. This situation is unfortunate from a technical standpoint, as it encourages the making of system decisions based on the amount of economic and psychological leverage that various individuals and companies are able to exert on each other rather than on an objective analysis of where system functions should be placed to enhance the efficiency of the system or ease the total programming work load.

In some systems, particularly of the smaller nonmultiprogrammed variety such as those for savings banks, the Control Program is little more than an interrupt processing routine, concerned only with satisfying the conditions that permit data to be received by the computor and relinquishing control to the Operational Programs for the other scheduling and data processing functions. At the opposite end of this extreme are Control Programs performing all the functions listed in Section 10.2, plus a variety of others such as "look ahead" to determine in advance which Operational Programs will be needed and in what sequence, then reading these in to process a particular entry. The objective of the technical planner is to posit a Control Program somewhere between the extremes, on the one hand, of doing very little to help the Operational Programs perform their application-oriented processing and, on the other, of venturing too far in providing processing features that are highly application dependent and, for that reason, more logically in the province of operational programming.

In some systems the equipment selected contributes substantially to a definition of the responsibilities of Control and Operational Programs. If there is an input/output multiplexor like that shown in Figure 2.2, it may be easy to establish that, by definition, all processing performed by this multiplexor is the responsibility of the Control Program development group. This has the effect of restricting the gray area to the central processing unit. It should be remembered, however, that what seems to be a clear-cut separation of functions at the conceptual or planning phase is not always so easily achievable during the specification and programming phases.

Ideally, the separation between Control and Operational Programs should be such that only the Control Program would have to be modified as a result of a change in the system equipment and only the Operational Programs would have to be modified as a result of a change in the application. This is, of course, an ideal never realized. One must, therefore, consider those aspects of a real-time system which are frequently difficult to classify as either Control or Operational.

LONG-MESSAGE PROCESSING • The problem of long-message processing has already been mentioned in the discussion of Control Program restrictions. The controlling of incoming and outgoing messages might be performed by either the Control

Program or the Operational Programs. In systems containing an input/output multiplexor, an arbitrary decision may be made that those long-message processing routines assigned to the multiplexor are part of the Control Program and those assigned to the central processing unit are part of the Operational Programs. In other systems this line of demarcation is not so clear, and it may be specified that the Control Program is responsible for the accumulation and transmission of long messages up to a certain number of portions, beyond which it is an Operational Program responsibility to keep track of multiples of this agreed-upon number of portions.

There are enough possibilities, as the inputs and outputs begin to be defined for each system, to prevent generalization about possible divisions of labor between Control and Operational Programs with respect to long messages.

MESSAGE ROUTING • Not every system has long messages to process, particularly if the system does not have alphanumeric input/output capability at the terminals, as is the case with many savings bank systems. There is, as a consequence, great variability in the approach to message routing. The more primitive systems, which process only one action at a time and generate no unsolicited output, do not find message routing a great problem. A more complex system, which must generate unsolicited messages and transmit them to many points, requires a sizable program to look up and assign to each output the appropriate routing characters.

The supplying of these routing characters when they are not, as in the conversational code, obtainable from the message-origin section of the entry, cannot be handled exclusively either by the Control Program or by an Operational Program, though the bulk of the job may fit more logically into one than into another. The presence of a multiplexor affects this software/software tradeoff, with all message routing functions performed by the multiplexor likely to be considered a Control Program responsibility.

Another split might be to have the Operational Programs route at the symbolic or application level and the Control Program route at the absolute or machine level. An Operational Program might determine, for instance, that an unsolicited message is to be sent to Mr. Jones in San Francisco and convert this into a standard symbolic routing code for this individual and this city—perhaps JSFO—which it would turn over to the Control Program along with the message itself. The Control Program, by consulting its communication tables, would select the routing characters to which the communications equipment and terminals would respond in order to reach Jones's terminal in San Francisco. Routing characters at this machine level might be 1*324, in which "1" represents the communication trunk line from the processing center to San Francisco, "*3" designates terminal buffering gear in the San Francisco branch office, and "24" designates Jones's terminal.

According to such an arrangement, the Operational Program is responsible for the routing processes most closely akin to the application: (1) that a message should go to Jones, (2) that Jones is in San Francisco, and (3) that his code is JSFO; whereas the Control Program is responsible for actually getting the message to its destination, conceivably varying the routing path, depending upon which pieces of communication and terminal gear are up and which are out of service at the time the routing request is received from the Operational Program.

INCOMING ENTRY ANALYSIS • In a system designed to process more than one type of entry, a decision must be made at the very beginning of the processing cycle for each entry as to which Operational Program or series of Operational Programs is required to process this particular entry. The program making this decision may be complex or simple, depending upon whether it must pre-establish the entire processing sequence that will ensue, or whether it is concerned merely with activating the very first program in a chain, with this first program then being responsible for deciding which program will be its successor in the sequence of getting an entry through the system. Regardless of its degree of complexity, the program that makes the initial determination after locating and analyzing the action code in the incoming entry may be classified either as the last of the Control Program routines having to do with incoming entries or the first of the Operational Programs.

PROGRAM-TO-PROGRAM TRANSFERS • Where Operational Programs have been segmented to facilitate main memory allocation, there is the problem of determining what the next segment in the chain should be, and of establishing the mechanics for passing a partially completed inquiry (with related file data) along from one program segment in the chain to another. Some systems—particularly where branching decision points are not encountered very often—rely upon the Control Program to establish the processing sequence in advance and send the entry confidently on its way. But in systems where processing is based on a large number of decision path possibilities, it is more efficacious to determine the processing chain as the programs are executed, that is, to "improvise" what will be done next to this entry. When this is the approach, it is an open question whether the decision making about which program will be activated next should be done by the Control Program or by the Operational Program which discovers what additional processing is needed. Either approach is feasible. One represents tight centralized determination of the processing sequence with control reverting to the Control Program whenever a processing impasse is reached. The other represents more diffusion in decision making about the conduct of the processing of each entry, as any one of several Operational Programs may be eligible to make branching decisions. (We are not discussing here the question of whether there should be Control Program macros such as Start, Return, and Exit, which are mandatory in a multiprogrammed system. We are merely considering what the *meaning* of these macros should be to an Operational Programmer.)

Conceptually it might seem more desirable to centralize this kind of supervision in the Control Program, but this has the disadvantage of making the Control Program quite application oriented, in that it must take cognizance of all the processing paths available for any action type entering the system. On the other hand, if program activation decisions are buried in

each affected Operational Program, the planning of system testing and the evaluation of the impact of system changes on the
processing sequence become extremely difficult.

CONTROL OF FILE INPUT/OUTPUT • Just as there is latitude in
the distribution of those control functions which place the system in communication with its external environment, there are
similar choices to be made about the extent to which Operational Programs become involved in obtaining data from the
files. It may be quite feasible in many systems to remove the Operational Programs from any close knowledge about what is
happening in the file subsystem, particularly if the system has a
file multiplexor (Figure 2.3). With such a configuration, a request for a file record might be communicated symbolically to
the Control Program in the multiplexor, using the file name
rather than its true physical address. The Control Program
would then do the necessary conversion plus the seeking and
reading of the record. In other systems, the Operational Programs might be required to furnish to the Control Program the
physical record address, as obtained through computation,
table lookup, or consultation of an index, with the Control Program's rule thus more narrowly demarcated.

In systems employing a duplicated record approach to improve reliability, it is desirable to relieve the Operational Programs of concern when one of the two copies is unavailable or
cannot be read. The Control Program could, as a service to
the Operational Programs, automatically seek the duplicate if
it cannot obtain the original. Similarly on execution of the
Write File Record macro, the Control Program could take over
the task of writing both the original and the duplicate to their
appropriate physical locations in file storage. (This implies
that the entire record organization plan in a system employing
duplicated records should be such that the address of one copy
is mathematically derivable from that of the other. This places
a considerable restriction on the technical planner, especially
when he attempts to develop fallback schemes to cover the loss
of storage modules.)

These illustrations indicate the types of trade-offs that must be evaluated in determining the interface between the Control Program and the Operational Programs it services. Decisions about where a processing chore can best be performed are necessary at almost any point at which the two program subsystems interact. In essence, the set of Control Program macros, precisely defined, provides a description of the interface between Control and Operational Programs, once all decisions about performance of data processing functions have been made.

There have been instances in which, for expediency or because of lack of understanding of Control-Operational Program relationships, a decision about which program would perform some major function is deferred. This may be the result of a situation in which the technical planners working on the Control Program and those working on the Operational Program both ignore a problem on the assumption that it is not within their respective provinces. Eventually when a decision *has* to be made, usually the subsystem to which the responsibility is assigned may—because of absence of adequate preliminary planning—have great difficulty in absorbing it into the other routines already specified and perhaps programmed. The result is either a patched-up version of the subsystem or time consuming respecifying and reprogramming.

10.4 OPERATIONAL PROGRAMS

Operational Programs are here defined as all those which must function within the data processing environment provided by the Control Program. As was mentioned in Chapter 3, this encompasses not only the real-time response programs developed to process entries from terminals and reply with an appropriate response; it also includes lower priority programs, such as those for administrative message switching or other processing not carried on in the conversational mode. It may even comprehend batch processing on a time-available basis. This background processing is planned for many systems in which on-line entry processing is only a minor part of the work load, with the bulk of the system's attention focused on conventional batch processing. In such instances the Control Program functions like a monitor or work scheduler much of the time and concentrates on getting the batch processing jobs on and off the computer expeditiously, but interrupting them whenever a real-time entry occurs. Thus, the term "Operational Program" covers a wide gamut of routines operating according to different time constraints and on different volumes of data. Their common characteristic is their subordination to a Control Program.

In contrast to the Control Program, the Operational Programs are application oriented. This characteristic has some interesting implications for system integration. First of all, it is likely that the company acquiring the system will, in the absence of special agreements, have to write these programs. In this sense they are like the application programs that, in most non-real-time systems, the customer has to specify and write (though often with substantial assistance from the equipment supplier).

Second, these Operational Programs are the routines most prone to modification as the functional requirements of the system change. In fact, if the Control Program as well as the Operational Programs must be modified whenever there is change in the application, this is a sign of a poorly designed and unmodular system.

A third characteristic of Operational Programs is that numerically they are more important than the Control Program. When measured according to number of instructions written, Operational Programs tend to outnumber the Control Program by at least ten to one, depending of course upon the way in which the two types of programs are defined.

On the basis of developmental complexity, however, it seems that, instruction for instruction, the Control Program is about twice as difficult to produce; that is, it requires about twice as many man-years to specify, program, and test as does an Operational Program of equal length. One reason for this difference is that each routine of the Control Program, sometimes each instruction in a routine, must be scrutinized carefully to assure its efficient usage of both main memory space occupied and memory cycles required during each execution. This care is necessitated by the relative frequency with which most parts of the

Control Program are called upon during processing, in contrast to the usage of each routine and instruction in the more specialized Operational Programs.

Having thus demarcated the role of the Operational Programs, let us examine a typical specimen of such a program as illustrated by Figure 10.2. This is a somewhat simplified representation of the processing path taken by a Sell entry in an airline reservation system. It assumes the existence of a Control Program and the execution of a Control Program macro whenever required to obtain programs or records from file storage. The method of processing shown would occur whether the system were multiprogrammed or not, the main difference being that in a multiprogrammed system operations would not follow each other immediately in time. In a multiprogrammed system each file access would doubtless signal the interruption of this Sell Program in order to execute instructions belonging to some other Operational Program engaged in processing an entry from another terminal.

On receipt of the Sell entry, the first processing occurrence after the data collection is a test on action code. (This is in the trade-off area discussed previously, with the test being performed under the aegis of either the Control Program or an Operational Program, depending upon the particular application and the proclivities of the technical planning staff.) The Sell path resulting from the action code test represents but one of several paths possible in an airline reservation system, some others being List, Cancel, Enter Name, Enter Phone Number, Provide Ticket Information, and a variety of more obscure but necessary exception-type entries.

To commence the Sell processing, the first segment of the Sell Program must be read in from drum storage by the Control Program if it is not already in memory as the result of some previous Sell action. Once it has been fetched in, it is given control of the processing. A test is made by the Sell Program to determine whether the entry is for a flight thirty days or more into the future. This is necessary because the record organization has been set up to provide faster access to the more frequent action paths—that is, requests for space within the

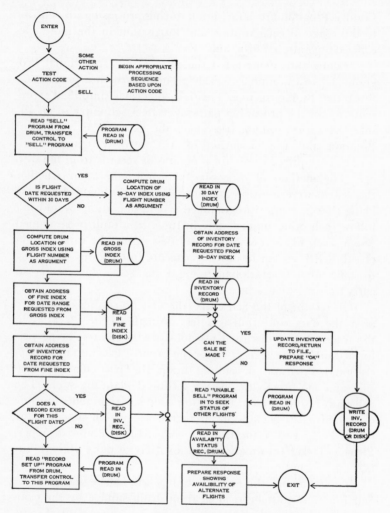

FIGURE 10.2.   PROCESSING OF AN AIRLINE
SYSTEM "SELL" ENTRY

next month—and the processing logic within the Sell Program
varies accordingly.

If the requested flight is within thirty days, a Thirty-Day Index Record must be read into main memory from drum storage by the Control Program. To accomplish this, the address of the index is computed by the Sell Program, using the current date as a base date and modifying the record address according to the number of days from the current date that the request indicates. The Control Program reads in this index and, when it has been read in, reactivates the Sell Program. The Sell Program consults the index and obtains from it the address of the appropriate Inventory Record for the flight number and the date requested. At this point the processing becomes common again with that for a request for thirty days and beyond.

This exceptional path of thirty days and beyond, shown running down the lower left-hand portion of Figure 10.2, involves more file accesses than does the within-thirty-days path. The address of a Gross (preliminary) Index is first computed by the Sell Program, then read into memory by execution of the Read File Record macro. The only purpose of the Gross Index, organized according to flight number, is to provide the address of a more detailed Fine Index containing an item for each future date for the flight number demanded by this inquiry. The Fine Index, in turn, provides the address of the Inventory Record having the information for the flight number and date contained in the entry. Both the Fine Index and the Inventory Record in this thirty-day-and-beyond case are in disk rather than drum storage because of the small proportion of times that the Sell Program will follow this processing path.

In seeking records well into the future, an Inventory Record may not yet exist for the flight/date requested. The request may, for example, represent the first booking for this particular flight/date. In this circumstance an Inventory Record has to be created in real time before processing can continue. We show, therefore, in the lower left-hand corner of the figure an additional program read in to main memory from drum in order to activate the specialized Record Setup Program needed to create a new Inventory Record.

The two processing paths then converge again and a query is made whether enough seats are available to consummate the sale. If sufficient seats are available, the Inventory Record is updated by reducing the Number of Seats Available Field and is returned, via the Control Program, to file. Otherwise, if the answer is "unable," an additional program segment and an additional record must be read in from drum storage to ascertain the availability of other flights for the same date that might be of interest to the passenger. Finally, in either the "OK" or the "unable" case, a response is prepared to be sent back to the agent, and the Sell Program makes its final exit. This has the effect of blasting all main memory storage containing the index and other records no longer needed now that processing is completed.

Although this example is couched in airline parlance, it typifies the variations in processing paths that an entry can evoke. The number of program segments needed differs as the result of testing at various junctures within the Sell Program, as does the number of file records referenced. The same would be true, though it is not shown by the figure, of the amount of computation time used. As has been stressed before, the technical planning staff must optimize the main path through the system for the sake of balance and efficiency. The most efficient Control Program possible cannot help very much if the more frequently used Operational Programs are specified or coded in a manner wasteful of main memory space, processing time, or record referencing time. This is true of both multiprogrammed and sequential processing systems. In fact, it is most important where multiprogramming is not employed and file seek time cannot be overlapped with processing time.

10.5 SUPPORT PROGRAMS

In addition to the real-time programs—Control and Operational Programs of various kinds—another set of programs is necessary to an operating system but executed off-line either when the central processing unit is not connected to the terminals or in the standby processor of a duplex system. Support Programs are needed before, during, and after conversion.

We have noted that Operational Programs loom considerably greater than the Control Program on any scale of system development cost based on total number of instructions required, even though, instruction for instruction, the Control Program is more difficult to produce. Support Programs would fit into this scheme of things either on a par with the Operational Programs or perhaps outranking them when measured by number of instructions required. Because Support Programs are a nonhomogeneous lot, it is somewhat dangerous to generalize. Some, like the schedule change programs in an airline system or the interest calculation routines in a savings bank system, are highly application oriented; others, like the test simulators used in the early stages of system testing, are quite equipment oriented. Some support programs, such as test edit programs, are logically straightforward and relatively easy to produce; others, such as disk file audit programs, may rival the Control Program in complexity.

Besides this wide variety, Support Programs have another characteristic that is equally alarming: they tend to be downgraded, if not entirely overlooked, by the system designers and by the System Integration Team because of their preoccupation with the Control and Operational Programs. There are understandable reasons for this. Since the need for Operational Programs and for the Control Program is fairly obvious, these tend to receive the lion's share of personnel commitments and technical attention. If the System Integration Team personnel are inexperienced, or have only non-real-time experience, they may not realize that the difficulty of system testing and conversion is much greater in a real-time system than in other systems of comparable size and, as a consequence, requires extra programming support.

It is a false economy to assign Support Programs a back seat in allocating programming resources because these Support Programs seem somewhat intrinsically less important than the real-time routines. More damage is probably done to real-time project schedules because of delays in Support Program development than for any other reason.

Unless a genuine effort is made to speed the development of Support Programs in parallel with the real-time programs, they may be incomplete at the times when they are needed. The Controller should assure at the beginning that attention is devoted to identifying all Support Programs that conceivably may be needed. Some of these requirements are sufficiently obscure that they will not come to light unless there is a constant probing coupled with an awareness that many classes of programs besides the glamorous real-time subsystems are required.

System Development Programs

In Chapter 3 a classification of Support Programs was made according to whether they were needed to make the system operational or to keep the system running once it becomes operational. We shall now expand somewhat on this classification, dealing first with the system development programs.

SYSTEM DESIGN AIDS • General- or special-purpose simulators are useful if not essential during the design stage to help develop the basic system configuration. A general-purpose simulator program may have to be modified to suit the needs of the particular system being studied, or, if this proves impossible, a specially tailored simulator program will have to be written.

In Chapter 9 the desirability of automating the contents of certain parts of the record and program specifications was suggested in the interest of configuration control. Like the periodic rerunning of a simulation program as system design parameters become more solid, the ability to perform automatic analysis and reanalysis of records and programs is a valuable means of evaluating the impact of proposed changes on the system not only during system integration but also after the system is converted.

It would, in fact, prove beneficial on large projects to invest sufficient support programming effort to link together the system simulation and the specification analysis programs, since much of the information in the specifications regarding number of instructions, number of file events, and related information, is precisely the same data needed to perform accurate system simulations.

ASSEMBLERS AND COMPILERS • There are some profound technical difficulties in this area, so far as real-time systems are concerned.[3] Most of these have to do with the fact that the programming requirements of real-time systems are still so new that a torrent of programming aids similar to those available for non-real-time systems has not yet been loosened by the equipment suppliers. Often the Controller is confronted with the following alternatives in trying to select the "language" in which the System Integration Team will program.

1) He can use an obsolete but machine-oriented assembler or compiler. Real-time programs must be quite economical of both memory storage and instruction execution time. This efficiency is not yet attainable in the requisite degree through use of the more "sophisticated" procedure-oriented COBOL-ALGOL type compiler in which an English or algebraic statement is transformed into a collection of machine instructions. These instructions are efficient enough for many non-real-time purposes but not for real-time usage. Even when a relatively primitive assembler or compiler is chosen, it may have to be modified extensively. Presently existing compilers, whether they be the COBOL variety or of the more mundane symbolic type, have the common characteristic of having been conceived originally for magnetic tape-oriented rather than random access file-oriented systems. Where such compilers have been extended to work with disk file systems, their entire logical structure continues to be based on the concept of sequential magnetic tape batch processing in contrast to the specialized record ordering and addressing schemes that characterize random access file-oriented systems. The record indexing and retrieval schemes of real-time systems, the Control Program macro structure, and the dynamic memory allocation procedures are all alien to the concepts underlying development and usage of present-day compilers.

2) He can write a compiler suitable to the real-time system's needs. A generously financed System Integration Team may, after considering the limitations of what is available, decide to undertake the writing of a brand-new compiler well

---

[3] Robert V. Head, "New Challenge for Programming Systems," *Datamation*, February 1963, pp. 39-41.

suited to their own system. The only word of advice that can be offered here is "caution." There is likely to be a net loss of system integration energy by adopting such a course. It may be aesthetically less satisfying to the programmers to revert to a relatively humble assembler language such as Basic Autocoder, which provides only one instruction per symbolic statement, than to program in a special language well adapted to their real-time programming needs. Here the Controller must make and enforce the most practicable decision from the *system* viewpoint. He simply may not be able to dissipate scarce human resources in the writing of compilers, even though the dollars are forthcoming. Further, the availability of financial support may not overcome the unavailability of schedule time to produce a brand-new compiler, particularly if some of the other Support Programs have to be neglected because of a diversion of qualified people.

Fortunately, this question of "going it alone" arises only on a few projects, with most Controllers limited to choosing the best compiling tools available and making do with these. In a few years compilers designed to satisfy real-time needs will no doubt begin to emerge, thus alleviating today's problem.

TEST SUPPORT PROGRAMS • Test support programs will be discussed in Chapter 11.

CONVERSION PROGRAMS • Conversion programs will be discussed in Chapter 12.

System Maintenance Programs

System maintenance programs are needed to keep the system in operation once it has been tested and converted. Some are application dependent; others are equipment dependent; still others represent a mixture of the two, as illustrated by a diagnostic program designed to detect communication line errors. Such errors are a reflection of the reliability of the communication and modulation equipment, but they are also a function of the length of the messages being transmitted, which in turn are a result of the functional requirements.

FILE MAINTENANCE PROGRAMS • File maintenance programs are designed to keep the file subsystem in current and usable condition. These programs vary all the way from the extremely application oriented to those suitable for any real-time system with random access storage.

In savings bank systems a routine for periodic posting of interest to depositor records is a good example of a file maintenance program that is application dependent. Among airline reservation systems the classic example is provided by the programs written to introduce schedule changes into the file records. At least twice each year, during the changeover from standard to daylight saving time in the spring and back again in the fall, the airlines undergo a major schedule change. This involves much more than just an hour's change in departure times. Basic patterns of aircraft routing and crew assignment and scheduling are also subject to change. Airlines with a north/ south pattern of service—such as New York to Miami—increase the frequency of their service during the winter; and airlines with an east/west pattern augment their service during the summer.

What does such adjustment mean in an automatic reservation system? It means that special-purpose file maintenance programs must be written:

- to revise the contents of those Seat Inventory Records already set up beyond the selling date of the new schedule. This is necessary to reflect changes in the departure and arrival time fields contained in these records.
- to purge from the files the Inventory and Passenger Records for all flights to be discontinued.
- to set up new records for flights that will begin to operate for the first time.
- to identify those passengers who previously booked space but who are now canceled owing to the schedule change.
- to identify those passengers who still hold space but who, because of the differences in departure and arrival times resulting from the schedule change, will no longer be able to make their connections.

These are the most rudimentary aspects of schedule change processing, but they do indicate the scope of file maintenance programs having nothing to do with day-to-day real-time processing but vital to the continued successful operation of the system. In any application exhibiting a similar file-oriented nature, an equivalent of the "schedule change problem" is almost certain to present itself.

As stated previously, the Control Program usually has responsibility for controlling the status of file storage and assigning available physical records to an Operational Program for purposes of temporary or permanent data storage. To illustrate another kind of file maintenance program, let us suppose that a Control Program maintains "directories" of two kinds of available disk file storage, records containing thirty-two words of storage (single records) and records containing sixty-four words (double records). This contributes to system flexibility and helps optimize usage of file storage by giving each Operational Program a choice of the size of record it may request for a given processing purpose. An airline passenger with a short round-trip itinerary might have his data stored in a single record, whereas one booking four or five flights might have to go into a double record. There must be, under such circumstances, provision in the Control Program to replenish its supply of available single records, should it become exhausted, by "splitting" double records apart by removing the address of a record from the double-record directory and inserting this address *and* this address plus 32 in the single-record directory. (When we say that the Control Program "gives" a single or double record to an Operational Program, we really mean that it provides the file *address* of such a record to the Operational Program.)

Eventually, under this procedure, the necessity arises of replenishing the inventory of available double records by sorting and recombining the single records that have been relinquished by the Operational Programs over some processing period. The programs needed to do this recombining are representative of file maintenance programs.

There is also in most systems the practical problem of "dirty" files, that is, the possibility of available file records being lost or allocated to contradictory users as a consequence of equipment malfunction or program errors. What is needed as a remedy here is a Support Program of the file maintenance type that periodically scans through the file looking for records that should have been returned to the Control Program's directories of available records but which for some reason have not been. Like most Support Programs, the need for this one should be anticipated during technical planning, so that standards for establishing record identifiers and other format aids to detection of lost or misplaced records can be developed. The technical planning staff should be sufficiently aware of such file maintenance requirements to establish, for example, that each record will have an identifier in a standard location within the record. This generic information may have to be supplemented by other standard fields in a fixed location, such as date of record creation or date of record obsolesence, to permit a file audit program to operate effectively. Unless it can be confidently assumed, and it almost never can be, that the file subsystem is completely adaptive and self-correcting, a file audit program has to be written to compensate for errors affecting the operation of the system files.

FALLBACK AND RECOVERY PROGRAMS • Fallback and recovery programs will be discussed in Chapter 12.

DIAGNOSTIC PROGRAMS • The advent of real-time systems has provoked a controversy among diagnostic programming specialists similar to that which preoccupies the apostles of various programming languages. In this case the question is: what is the efficaciousness of previously useful diagnostic programs when they are extended into the realm of real-time systems? All suppliers today offer, as an aid to the technicians who maintain the equipment, programs falling into the general category of diagnostics. The following programs are included in this category:

1) Programs designed to make main memory and other hardware components fail. For a given equipment complement, memory "pounders" and other programmed exercisers are avail-

able to assure the maintenance technician that, once the diagnostics have been run successfully, the equipment is ready to begin processing live data. The purpose of these programs is to prevent system malfunction by advance detection of marginal components.

2) Programs designed to locate a malfunction once it occurs in an operational system. Diagnostic programs are needed not only for preventive purposes but also to pinpoint trouble *after* it occurs in any of the equipment subsystems.

What seems needed in real-time systems is yet a third type of diagnostic to supplement the other two. This would provide a means of *correcting* or bypassing an error condition in the system in order to keep the system in operation. In a sense this should not properly be called a diagnostic routine but rather a curative or restorative program. In fact, the real-time correction of errors caused by either the equipment or the programs need not be performed by a program at all. At least some of it could be done equally well by equipment or by a combination of programs and equipment. The venerable UNIVAC I computer, with its duplicated arithmetic and logical circuitry, is an early example of a machine possessing hardware features engineered to compensate for equipment malfunctions. Today, self-correcting input/output devices are available in which dropped bits or changed bits are detected upon read-in, with the reading mechanism capable of regenerating missing bits based on the pattern exhibited by those known to be correct.

Most real-time systems have the programmed ability to take any terminal out of the polling sequence by testing the error-free quality of the characters being received from that terminal (that is, of course, if some sort of self-checking is built into the characters or messages being transmitted). If too many messages have to be repeated or if all messages are garbled, the program will correct this situation by refusing to poll the offending terminal until maintenance is performed on it. Such a system may be described as adaptive, adjusting itself to terminal equipment malfunctions.

At present, real-time system adaptability is generally limited to terminals and peripheral storage, with little ability to correct or bypass arithmetic and other errors in the central processing unit. These malfunctions usually force the system down, even though they may later turn out to be trivial and isolatable. Presumably, the development of real-time diagnostic programs will, in the future, concentrate on adapting the system to these CPU malfunctions in such a way that maximum system availability is achieved. To accomplish this the equipment design engineers must become more fully impressed with the objective of having the system, by programmed means or otherwise, not only analyze what has gone wrong with itself but immediately "patch" its way around the trouble.

These three types of diagnostic programming are closely analogous to medical science's endeavors at prevention, diagnosis, and cure to keep the organism—in this case the real-time system—in robust health or, failing that, at least in some state of working order. Today's computer diagnostic routines are mostly in the nature of autopsies, being performed after processing has been terminated, either on a preplanned or an emergency basis.

To the extent that standard diagnostic programs available to the user of a real-time system do not fully exercise the system, the System Integration Team will have to write its own diagnostics. Some of these will be special real-time programs and will look very much like Operational Programs or parts of the Control Program; others, particularly the preventive exercisers, will be more off-line in nature and more accurately fit within the category of Support Programs.

Apart from the question of extending the breadth and depth of diagnostic programs to make them more suitable for real-time processing, the System Integration Team may have to rewrite the conventional diagnostic programs because they do not fully cover the equipment configuration being installed. There is usually an ample supply of diagnostics for standard equipment configurations, but where this equipment has been modified for real-time purposes, the diagnostics, too, must be modified to perform their functions effectively. If the equipment manufacturer is unwilling or unable (perhaps because the equipment of more than one manufacturer is interconnected) to supply the required special diagnostics, they will have to be programmed by the System Integration Team.

10.6 MAIN MEMORY ALLOCATION

Comments made earlier in this chapter about the relationship between Control and Operational Programs and about the processing responsibilities of each may be made more clear by examining the usage to which main memory, a storage medium common to both kinds of programs, is devoted in a real-time system.

It is a real-time axiom that the Control Program is master of all main memory storage and that it is impossible for an Operational Program to get such memory for any purpose—to store an input message, to contain a file record, indeed even to contain itself—save by requesting it from the Control Program. Once the Control Program has made available a block of main memory to the Operational Program, however, the use of this area is entirely according to the way in which the Operational Program is specified. The Operational Program thus controls its currently assigned main memory blocks in the same sense that it controls the computer circuitry during its processing, once it has been permitted by the Control Program to initiate processing.

Main memory of the central processing unit in a real-time system is frequently divided into several major areas that reflect the various purposes to which it can be devoted.

Control Program

In the Control Program area are stored the routines of the Control Program itself, including the coding for the macro instructions executed by the Operational Programs.

Permanent Operational Programs

On the basis of manual or machine analysis of execution frequency, storage may be provided for Operational Programs whose usage is so heavy that they are permitted to remain in main memory at all times. Some of these will be "gray area" programs such as long-message assemblers, others will be commonly used subroutines.

Some real-time systems are self-adjusting in that a program can be promoted into the "permanent" category on the basis of the current frequency of demand for its execution. Then, should there be a change in the "mix" of entries, the programs most often requested would be most readily available.

Because of the need for flexibility in deciding which programs inhabit the permanent area, whether this be done automatically or by external decision, all Operational Programs which are candidates for this area should be written in such a way that they can be relocatable if they should lose their special status entitling them to a permanent place in main memory.

Relocatable Operational Programs

Most of the Operational Programs compete for the relocatable portion of main memory, an area not large enough to contain all of them at once. Two main approaches to relocating programs are currently favored. In the simpler of the two, each program is reassembled several times, say a half dozen, with the instructions of each version specified to begin in a different memory location. These several copies of the program are stored in auxiliary memory and, when the program is required, the Control Program makes a decision about what (if any) copy may be read in, depending upon which portions of main memory allocated for this purpose are available. This rather cumbersome method is wasteful of auxiliary storage space and is inconvenient to maintain.

Alternatively, all programs may be assembled relative to zero, that is, the first location in main memory, and then modified by special hardware or by the Control Program to fit into *any* portion of main memory that happens to be available for program storage when a program is required. This approach, while more flexible, makes more demands on the real-time capability of the system to perform the housekeeping associated with real-time relocation.

In either case, there is frequently an underlying requirement that a program be defined as some arbitrarily long segment of coding, such as 64 or 256 instructions. The programmer, or the compiler if it has such capability, is required to compartmentalize what appears to be a logical program (an interrelated, cohesive, and pretty much self-sufficient grouping of instructions) into fixed lengths to adhere to the restrictions of the relocation scheme. A program specification, representing a logical breakdown of work as conceived by the specification writer, might call for anywhere from 100 to 1000 instructions to get a particular entry processed. This means that some specifications may require only half a segment, others several such relocatable segments.

These comments about the unsatisfactory nature of relocatable programs apply primarily to the larger multiprogrammed systems calling for perhaps a dozen or more programs to coexist in main memory at any one instant. Restrictions on the length of the segment and other restrictions pertaining to its relocatability, such as not being able to use an instruction as a constant, can be minimized or eliminated in smaller systems that need to contain but one or two Operational Programs in memory at the same time. Such processing is serial or semiserial, and program execution can be delayed sufficiently long to free all or most of the Operational Program area of main memory for use by a single program.

Developmental problems associated with planning relocation procedures can often be eliminated by the purchase of sufficient main memory to accommodate *all* instructions. When there are 15,000 words of main memory for Operational Program storage and only 18,000 words of Operational Program instructions, the trade-off of simplified program development, as well as a more efficient running system versus the cost of the extra memory, can probably be justified. But in a SABRE-like system in which the application requires some 100,000 instructions, it will no doubt make sense economically to suffer the tribulations of program read-in rather than make an enormous investment in main memory storage.

Any System Integration Team that solves the program relocation problem by taking advantage of low-inquiry volume to avoid multiprogramming or by adding main memory must remember that the application may change sufficiently to force another solution on the system at some time in the future. Today's serial processing may be tomorrow's multiprogramming and today's 20,000-instruction application may be tomorrow's 35,000 instructions. Because of this, it may be preferable to swallow the program relocation pill at the beginning, since to do so after conversion can produce a disruptive change in programming philosophy.

Regardless of the simplicity or complexity of the program read-in plan, the Control Program is responsible for determining the status of the read-in area and controlling its contents. This includes the reading in and overlaying or erasing of programs, usually at the behest of the Operational Programs themselves.

System Status Information

A small but vital part of main memory, the area of system status information contains various indicators that define the current operating status of the system. Here one might find the current polling list, with a bypass indicator for Indianapolis (for example) if this office happens for some reason to be presently disconnected from the system; disk file module status indicators showing which modules are up and which are down; the system calendar, showing time of day, day of week, calendar date, and day of year; preliminary index locators, showing which section of a file index should be consulted to process an account number falling in a particular range.

Most of the information in this area is of sufficient importance that it should be copied out onto auxiliary storage whenever it is changed. By so doing, restart and switchover are facilitated.

Entry Blocks

In a system in which entries can be received from several communication sources simultaneously, each entry must be placed in a storage area to await further processing. These entries are queued for subsequent processing by the Control Program, which inserts the address of the main memory block assigned to the newly arrived entry into a list containing the addresses of previously received entries, or which, alternatively, attaches the storage main memory block assigned to the newly received entry onto a "chain" of previously received entries. This chaining is accomplished by inserting the address of the current entry block into a field set aside for this purpose in the block holding the entry received just before the current one. In either case, a first-in first-out collection of entries is maintained, scattered throughout the entry storage area without the burden of shifting the entry data itself around inside memory. When the program needed to process an entry is read in, the Control Program gives it the address in the entry storage area of the entry to be processed.

The SABRE Control Program design makes the entry block the focal point for controlling the entire processing sequence and storage assignment for each entry. The entry block might contain not only the inquiry or message as received (including action code and message origin) but also the main memory addresses of all Operational Programs read in or requested and the main memory addresses of all file records needed to process the entry. The entry block may also be the repository for intermediate results carried forward from one Operational Program to another and may serve as the area in which the response to an entry is built up and from which it is transmitted.

File Record Blocks

Like the entry storage area, the main memory area allocated for file records contains a number of blocks, each destined to be the repository for a record read from file during the course of processing an entry.

Some interesting questions are involved in the planning of this area. First, there must be compatability between the physical size of a record on file to be read in and the record block in main memory designated to hold it. This often leads to specifying standard-sized file records (called "physical" records to distinguish them from the less easily controllable application information they contain, called "logical" records) and standard-sized main memory blocks into which they will fit. Thus, all disk file records in a system might be specified at 150 characters, and all main memory record blocks at 200 characters. In this way, it is assured in advance that any file record will fit into any available main memory block devoted to this purpose with fifty characters left over for controls and working storage.

A price is extracted for such a solution, of course. One hundred fifty characters might be chosen as an optimum-sized file record for an application, but with the qualification that chaining in file will be employed if a logical record exceeds this physical length, as it might, let us say, for any depositor who had more than three stop payments against his account. When such a case is encountered, the initial record in file may contain a flag indicating that the remainder of the logical record for this depositor is located in a second 150-character physical record block elsewhere in file storage. The Operational Program in this instance has to initiate a second seek and read, and the Control Program has to set aside a second record block in main memory and chain it to the first. When the second record is available from file, the Operational Program has the job, probably accomplished through use of index registers, of working on a logical record sitting in two nonadjacent portions of main memory.

It may be questioned why the Control Program cannot allocate two contiguous blocks of main memory to these two physical records, which contain the one logical record, and in some systems this can conveniently be done. But such allocation, in effect, necessitates a buildup of two standard-sized blocks into one larger size in main memory in real time. Perhaps this procedure could be followed for a single requesting Operational Program, but if several programs made a similar request about the same time there would be a queueing problem. There might also be a problem if an Operational Program requested not two, but three, four, or five contiguous blocks of main memory to process an abnormally lengthy logical record. In certain circumstances an Operational Program or Programs might, through their excessive demands for contiguous blocks, lock the system up and prevent it from performing further processing.

Another question that must be resolved in planning file-oriented systems is whether it is more economical for the Control Program to associate a main memory block with a file record at the time the seek is begun than it is at the time the read is given. If the main memory block is committed to a particular file request at the time the record search is initiated, then this main memory block essentially lies around unused during the relatively lengthy period it takes the random access mechanism to find the needed file record. Meanwhile, perhaps some other use could be made of the main memory space. If on the other hand, it is decided not to commit a main memory block for the needed file record until the seek is completed and the read-in of the record begun, then the Control Program must have some assurance that a main memory block will in fact be available in which to deposit the file record when it is ready to be read in, as all blocks may at that instant be associated with other jobs existing inside the computer.

Often the main memory sections devoted to entries and file records can be combined into one area if their block sizes are reasonably compatible. This contributes greatly to system flexibility, for, instead of two or more pools of main memory storage for specialized purposes, there is only one. Any main memory block in this larger area may be assigned to *either* an entry *or* a file record. It may be possible to go even further and combine the program read-in area with the entry/file record pool if a size common to all three types of storage can be worked out. This is potentially a powerful solution, as there can then be almost any distribution of main memory blocks among programs, entries, and file records, depending on the nature of the processing jobs currently occupying the system. Moreover, the housekeeping burden of maintaining control over available main memory blocks is relieved considerably. The Control Program would need to maintain only one list rather than three lists of available main memory blocks. The Control Program would, of course, still have to maintain cognizance over which entries require processing, which programs are to be or have been read in, and which file records are, or are needed, in main memory.

10.7 SUMMARY

The single most important decision to be made during system integration is whether the system will be multiprogrammed. Sometimes the requirements of the application are so demanding that a multiprogramming approach must be taken.

Several basic functions are usually found in a Control Program, although such programs vary markedly in their scope and complexity even among multiprogrammed systems. The points of interface between the Control Program and the Operational Programs are found in a series of macro instructions made available to the Operational Programmer.

The Control Program may be said to be equipment oriented and the Operational Programs application oriented. There are, however, many "gray areas," such as long-message handling, that could be made part of either the Control Program or the Operational Programs.

In addition to the Control Program and the Operational Programs, there are Support Programs, which are essential to development and maintenance of the real-time system.

An understanding of the way in which main memory is allocated in a real-time system and the methods employed to control utilization of main memory helps to clarify Control-Operational Program relationships.

SYSTEM TESTING 11

11.1 SPECIAL CHARACTER OF REAL-TIME TESTING

CHAPTER 1 presented some reasons why real-time systems, at the present stage of their development, differ substantially from other systems and as a consequence present significant new problems in system integration. Some of the factors that contribute to system complexity in a real-time environment were mentioned in Chapter 2 as items to be considered during system design. All these previously discussed aspects of real-time systems heighten the difficulties of system testing, a phase of system integration that is the least amenable to control, even in the non-real-time world.

"System testing" here means whatever work must be performed by the System Integration Team from the completion of programming until the system achieves operational status. This is not limited to checkout of the various real-time programs; it extends also to the necessary checkout of the equipment subsystems and to the integrated testing of combinations of equipment and programs. Final system testing and the subsequent period of system operation require a thoroughly checked out and reliable combination of equipment and programs.

It may be suggested with validity that the programming portions of a data processing system present a greater testing challenge than do the equipment portions, this contention resting on the familiar ground that programming is more art than science and that, furthermore, the equipment is subject to manufacturing quality control procedures which are easier to define and enforce than are equivalent standards for software development. And since it is the programs that bear the brunt of transforming the application as described in the functional requirements into a system-in-being, they constitute our main preoccupation here, recognizing that in an operational sense programs cannot be divorced from equipment and that in a developmental sense the System Integration Team is frequently responsible for the complete testing of both equipment and programs.

Because the real-time system tends to be applied to the more vital facets of an organization's operation and because, as a consequence, any malfunction of the system causing it to become totally or partially unavailable has an immediate and potentially disastrous effect, there must be more painstaking testing than has sufficed in the past.

Many non-real-time systems can be converted even when there is abundant evidence that the programs still harbor a large number of errors. Conversion under such conditions may be decidedly ill considered because of the amount of rerun time consumed when bugs are encountered, but the risk of damage to the customer's operation is usually not extremely high. Moreover, it has been demonstrated in non-real-time systems work that not all bugs can or need be found even during a protracted system test. To become completely error free, programs must be subjected to "live" operations and to all the permutations in data and operating conditions that occur over a fairly long period of productive system operation.

Although it is doubtful that any real-time System Integration Team will ever be able to warrant a system as error free, it will have to go far beyond satisfying the testing standards that sufficed for prior systems in order to permit the real-time system to go into operation with a high degree of confidence in its workability. There will be the same "moment of truth" in real-time system development as in conventional systems, when the Controller declares the test phase ended. But in real-time systems, this declaration must be based on much more solid evidence of error-free programs than in the past.

Chapter 1 cautioned that management must be prepared to face disruptions during conversion and the early stages of operation until both the equipment and the programs achieve the requisite level of reliability. At the same time the System Integration Team, through its approach to testing, must try to prove that a pessimistic attitude on the part of management is unwarranted. The System Integration Team can best do this by going to virtually any reasonable length to purge the programs of errors.

One of the most pitiable collusions imaginable in real-time system development is that between top management and the Controller in agreeing to go ahead with cutover prematurely simply because the schedule calls for it or because "we planned it that way." If this attitude prevails, a great deal of time is bound to be lost through confusion and frustration caused by trying to make a system work when it is just not yet ready to work.

The real-time system presents the System Integration Team with a twofold testing problem: (1) more intensive testing is mandatory to achieve reliable operational status and (2) it is more difficult to satisfy this heightened testing standard. Let us now look further into this dilemma to identify those attributes of a real-time system which, on the one hand, fortify the need for preconversion testing and, on the other, make such testing harder to carry out.

Magnitude of Programming Effort

Many real-time systems are of such size that there are dozens and even hundreds of programs to be tested and fitted together. One large file-oriented system contained, in addition to its Control Program and Support Programs, over 100,000 real-time Operational Program instructions. These were divided into some 800 programs, which were produced in accordance with the contents of 400 program specifications. These 800 programs were brought together in varying combinations to form some eighty input-oriented "packages" of related programs needed to process various entries. The personnel who worked on this system were organized into four basic groups, each doing a portion of the job divided along the following functional lines, with many programs being common to more than one group:

- High-speed (high-priority) input processing
- Low-speed (low-priority) input processing
- File-oriented processing: type A file records
- File-oriented processing: type B file records

Misinterpreted Specifications

It is during system testing that the specification and programming work performed by each individual and group must be gradually tied together into a unified operational skein. Considering the Operational Programs alone and ignoring Control and Support Programs, there are numerous interfaces to be tested at both the specification and the programming levels. Even assuming (and this is extremely unlikely) that all specifications are consistent among themselves—that is, that incongruities in specifications impinging on each other have been discovered and corrected prior to the start of testing—it is necessary to assure that each programmer involved:

- understands the specifications
- understands the *interpretation* placed on the specifications by his fellow programmers
- reflects both these understandings in his program

When one recognizes the shortcomings in the methodology of preparing specifications and the ambiguities inherent in both narrative descriptions and flow charts, he can anticipate that misunderstandings, great and small, will be built into the Operational Programs. System testing must eliminate these misunderstandings.

As was noted in Chapter 5, the System Integration Team will have to utilize many inexperienced programmers. This situation is sometimes cited as the reason for the increased difficulty of testing a large software subsystem. There is ground for disputing this argument, however. True, the neophyte may write a less *efficient* program from an operational standpoint and indeed may engender more clerical errors, which must be uncovered during the early stages of testing. But beyond this the novice is actually no worse off than his more experienced colleague, in that both will be hampered by the same misunderstandings that prevent separately fabricated programs from fitting together properly at system testing time.

It is a combination of the imperfection of written specifications and the fallibility of those who program from them that results in the cutting and fitting required to achieve a workable system.

Inability to Repeat Errors

On detection of a program error in a conventional system, as typified by a magnetic tape batch processing application, the usual procedure is to locate the error (with the aid of instruction traces, printouts, memory dumps, for example), attempt to correct it, and then rerun with the same inputs as before to see whether the correction "took." This general procedure is followed not only during system testing but also beyond, when bugs are encountered in production runs.

Unfortunately such a relatively straightforward debugging method is not feasible for real-time systems. Entries generated at remote terminals in random and asynchronous fashion often cannot be repeated in exactly the same sequence needed to make an error condition repeat. Although the difficulties resulting from this limitation on repeatability are not insurmountable, they are formidable. They necessitate employment of terminal simulator programs during the early stages of system testing in order to exercise the programs independent of this uncontrollable terminal input. Later, when testing has progressed to the point where terminals are placed on-line for more realistic tests, data logging programs and procedures must be devised to capture the input in its original form and sequence. Even then, in a multiprogrammed system, it may be impossible to make all errors repeat, because of variations in allocation of main memory, lengths of main memory queues, and varying status of relocatable programs.

These complexities make real-time programmers yearn for the days when input tapes could be remounted and a repeat run initiated under constant conditions following insertion of a program "patch."

Equipment Interaction: Multiprocessing

In a real-time system there may be several equipment sub-systems, each with stored program capability, as illustrated by Figures 2.2 through 2.7, which depict systems having stored program multiplexors or similar ability to perform processing simultaneously in more than one computer. This multiprocessing potential imposes extra demands during system testing because of the necessity of real-time communication among processors. This may include the communication of data, as in the case of entries originating at terminals and passing first into an input/output multiplexor and thence to the central processing unit. Or it may involve communication of control data, as in the switchover procedures for a duplex system. In any case the sub-systems must exchange information at least occasionally and, in many systems, frequently. This means that all interfaces must be tested not just from a hardware standpoint but to make certain that all specifications and assumptions about the format and condition of data have been correctly understood by the programmers working on either side of the hardware interface in developing their respective software subsystems.

Not surprisingly, there is a tendency in multiprocessing systems to organize the programming along machine lines. The presence of a stored program multiplexor, for example, offers a convenient way to begin making a division of programming labor. Once established, machine-oriented groups work more or less in isolation to produce their programs. Eventually there must be testing of all these subsystems operating in conjunction with each other. It is here, when pieces are put together to form the overall processing system, that the consequences of a multiprocessing approach begin to make themselves felt in the form of program errors and inconsistencies.

This tendency toward work-load assignment along machine lines may be heightened by the geographic or organizational separateness of the programming groups. The equipment manufacturer might, for example, undertake to program the input/output multiplexor, leaving the task of programming the central processing unit a customer responsibility. In this event one programming group might be based at the manufacturing plant and the other at the eventual computer site. In such a situation it is frequently the line of least resistance for people to fail to communicate during the specification and programming phases. At system testing time the consequences of this lack of communication come to the surface.

Program Interaction: Multiprogramming

Where several programs share the same computer at the same time, each engaged in processing a different transaction, the possibilities of error due to unplanned and illegal program interaction are enormous. System testing must channel this interaction into the patterns demanded by the Control Program, the Operational Program specifications, and the programming standards. Conditions whereby one program operates on the data of another are suggestive of the kinds of errors that occur. Many of these would immediately put the system out of operation if they were to arise during productive processing.

Some equipment protection may be available to safeguard the system against the depredations of a real-time program gone amuck. A memory-protection feature can be obtained to guard certain areas of main memory by causing an interrupt and reversion of control to the Control Program if an illegal reference is made by an Operational Program beyond a permissible range of main memory locations. An interval timer can aid in endless loop detection by causing an automatic interrupt and transfer to the Control Program if any one Operational Program usurps the computer by failing to execute one of the Control Program macro instructions periodically.

The nature of a multiprogrammed system also complicates the problem of repeatability. At a given instant when the system "hangs up" in some Operational Program, it may be impossible, without special debugging aids, to determine what processing preceded the activation of this particular program and whether the predecessor processing was logical or illogical. Often one may attempt to reintroduce the same entry conditions without success because the exact string of program segments executed the second time differs from the original string, perhaps only because the variation of a few milliseconds in file access time due to a different positioning of the disk access arms causes one Operational Program rather than another to be activated and its file request fulfilled sooner than before.

Inherent Logical Complexity

Commercial data processing systems, whether real time or not, are sometimes regarded a trifle superciliously by those engaged in scientific computation. The feeling seems to be that, while there are challenging aspects to commercial system analysis, the programming of such a system is trivial when compared to the difficulty of programming a large scientific problem. Comparison invariably reveals that the arithmetic steps in an accounting application are pitifully simple when contrasted with those in a typical scientific problem. Yet despite this, the coding in a commercial system may be more difficult to test than that in the scientific program.

Behind this seeming paradox is an interesting characteristic of commercial systems: There are usually many *more decision points* in an accounting application than in a scientific computation problem of equivalent length. No one has yet done a comparative study of this phenomenon, but scrutiny of even the simplified example shown in Figure 10.2 reveals several major decision points in processing a real-time action. At a more detailed level, the number of decisions and branches becomes truly impressive. Thus, while arithmetically primitive, the logic and decision-making potential of commercial programs may be very complex. And where such logic dictates a branch to a new program that must be read into main memory and linked to the one already there, the error possibilities begin to abound.

Random Access Storage Limitations

One feature of non-real-time systems that permits them to go into operation after only minimum testing is the relative invulnerability of magnetic tape files to program-produced errors. In testing and initial conversion of a batch processing system, it is often the practice to keep "grandfather" copies of mas ter files as well as the corresponding activity tapes. Then if an error is discovered, a rerun can be made to produce a revised current master file free of error. This protection of data through tape retention is certainly not foolproof, as a posting error may not be discovered until so many cycles have been gone through that the regeneration process cannot be repeated. (Perhaps the "great-grandfather" tape has been "scratched," perhaps the rerun time would be prohibitive, perhaps statements containing the erroneous data have already been issued and must be corrected by reversal procedures rather than rerun.) Nevertheless, rerun to correct erroneous master file records is feasible more often than not in tape systems.

By contrast, it is impossible to do this in a real-time system employing random access storage. Here there is no periodic updating of a master file by running batched and sequenced transactions against it, but rather an unpredictable consultation of master file records caused by entries randomly generated at terminals and requiring immediate processing. A real-time program error affecting master records may be difficult to discern in the normal course of processing and may fail to leave a trail showing which records have been updated in error. Consider, for example, an exception path in the airline system Sell Program. Suppose that whenever the "seats available" field in an Inventory Record shows just four seats remaining, the number of seats requested by the current entry is erroneously and arbitrarily decreased by one seat before the Inventory Record is updated and the response sent back to the terminal. The result of this error will be a nagging and persistent overbooking condition that may hamper the system for weeks before detection. And once this type of error is discovered, one cannot revise the erroneous Inventory Records by rerun. For it cannot be determined which of the many flight/date Inventory Records maintained by the system have experienced the erroneous updating and which have not.

Another example could be found in a program that in error returns an unneeded disk file record to the Control Program's list of available storage *twice* instead of once. The Control Program, assuming that nothing is amiss, places the address of this record in its list of records available for reuse twice and eventually gives the same address to *two* completely unrelated Operational Programs which, one after the other, have requested an empty file record. Hence, we might, in a banking system, have the balances of Jones and of Smith scrambled into a single record. If this occurred, the condition would be detected fairly quickly but not before other duplicate record assignments had been made by the Control Program, perhaps to some more obscure Operational Program than the Balance Posting Program. Often the only cure for the consequences of such an error is to reinitialize the files completely, a process that can be more readily undertaken during testing than after conversion.

11.2 LEVELS OF REAL-TIME TESTING

The System Integration Team has planning responsibility for the identification and definition of the levels of testing to which the real-time system must be subjected before it can be stated with confidence that an acceptable standard of error-free performance is attained. The structuring of the system testing will, of course, vary from one system to another, depending upon such factors as size of the programming effort, number of equipment subsystems to be interconnected, and degree of reliability expected from the operational system. It may be useful, however, to describe generally the testing that a real-time system might go through, with emphasis on the Operational Programs. The emphasis is placed here because these programs constitute the major portions of the system that must be subjected to testing. Figure 11.1 illustrates levels of Operational Program testing as well as the testing required for the other programs needed to activate a duplex system with input/output multiplexors.

Simulated Environment

At the beginning of testing, it is neither necessary nor desirable to undertake Operational Program debugging with the real-time equipment or even with its software extension, the Control Program. And often, as a practical matter, the equipment has not been manufactured, let alone delivered, and the

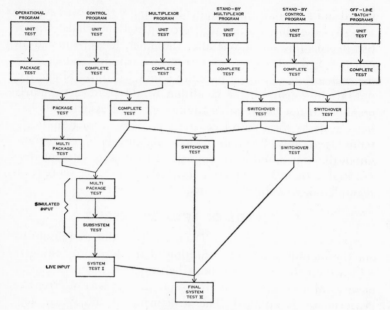

FIGURE 11.1. DUPLEX SYSTEM TESTING
SCHEMATIC.

Control Program has not yet been tested at the time the first
Operational Programs become available for testing.

During this initial stage, input to the programs in the form
of inquiries is simulated, that is, obtained from punched cards
or magnetic tape rather than from the remote terminals. Similarly, requests for file records may be simulated by pulling data
in from tape instead of random access storage.

Often then, initial testing is performed with the use of a
special test simulator program that duplicates, more or less, the
functions of both the hardware and the Control Program. In
this testing mode, which is usually run on some non-real-time
computer of the same family as the one to be installed, the execution of a Control Program macro instruction by the Operational Program causes the Control Program simulator to produce almost the same result as would the Control Program and
to return control to the Operational Program just as though

the system were functioning under real-time conditions. A Read File Record macro, for instance, might result in the needed data being read in from tape rather than from a disk file by the Control Program simulator in such a manner that it looks as if the data actually came in from a certain location on the disk file.

In addition to serving as a substitute for the Control Program and the real-time hardware before these are available, the test simulator program provides special debugging facility not found in the Control Program. For example a macro trace feature could, on completion of an Operational Program test shot, produce a record of all the Control Program macro instructions executed by the Operational Program in the course of the test. Many useful debugging features can be built into the Control Program simulator, since there is no urgent necessity for completing the execution of an Operational Program with the same rapidity with which it must be executed in a true real-time environment. In order to provide extensive debugging facility, the simulator may not return control to an Operational Program for several seconds after execution of a macro, whereas the Control Program must in an operating environment return control within milliseconds. The extra time may be used by the simulator for tracing, dumping registers and memory locations, and so forth.

Testing in this simulated environment usually divides itself into at least two distinguishable levels, through which each program must pass. One ground rule in establishing these and other testing levels is that *if an Operational Program chronically fails at a given level, it should be "demoted" to the previous level for additional testing.*

SIMULATED UNIT TESTING • In simulated unit testing, each individual program or program segment is tested as an individual entity. Frequently unit testing is considered part of the programming phase, with the person who wrote the program responsible for its unit testing through use of the Control Program simulator.

SIMULATED PACKAGE TESTING • Whenever a sufficient number of related programs or program segments have successfully undergone unit testing, they may be combined into a logically related entity of larger size, sometimes called a package. In order to display an airline passenger's record, a dozen or more programs or program segments may be needed to process the various types of inquiries, some of these representing exception paths in the Display Record Program (such as "No Match on Name"), others representing the main line ("Edit Record for Display"). All these program segments, having been found to work satisfactorily as individual units, must be tested to assure that they work correctly together. Data must be passed across segment boundaries, and segments must call and transfer control to each other. Normally all the program segments needed for a package are not written by the same programmer and as a consequence suffer from misunderstandings, overlooked relationships, and other logical and clerical inconsistencies. Also, it may be that not all the program segments needed to form a package are covered by one program specification, in which case misunderstandings are to be expected at both the specification and the program levels.

Packages are usually defined in terms of the inputs and outputs of the system, and in this respect represent a reversion to the method of system description employed in the functional requirements but abandoned during the technical planning, specification writing, and programming phases of system integration. Now, with these phases completed, the System Integration Team once again begins to view the system as the designers did initially: according to what information must be put into it and what obtained from it.

Testing with the Control Program

Those program packages which successfully pass the first level of testing—in which not only communication with the external world is simulated but communication with the file subsystem and with the Control Program as well—are ready to be tested in conjunction with the Control Program. Testing at this level is distinguished by the addition of the Control Program to the test environment. This can satisfy the dual purpose of debugging both the Operational Programs and the Control Program if the latter is not a pretested, proven piece of coding. At this level, the Operational Programs take a long step closer to final operating reality by being exercised with the Control Program and with the central processing unit.

Testing here exemplifies another important axiom of real-time testing: *Take only one major new step at a time, holding all other environmental factors constant.* Thus, the testing does not yet include "live" input generated at the terminals. This comes later, after the initial tie-in with the Control Program has been successfully accomplished. For the moment, it is sufficient to go from the Control Program simulator to the Control Program itself while continuing to use simulated input of the same type used at the previous level. Indeed it may be the very same input as was used previously.

PACKAGE RETESTING • Every package that survived testing with the Control Program simulator must be subjected to another test to detect errors in the packages not discovered by the simulator. The complexity and the duration of this package retesting using the Control Program depend upon the degree of sophistication built into the Control Program simulator, that is, the extent to which it truly reflects the logic and restrictions of the Control Program and the real-time equipment.

MULTIPLE PACKAGE TESTING • In multiple package testing in a multiprogrammed system, *groups* of packages that have negotiated package testing and retesting are run concurrently for the first time in a multiprogrammed manner. Even though the input source continues to be simulated, the entries are now fed into the system not one at a time, as was appropriate to the testing of a single package at a time, but in groups representing a heterogeneous mixture of input types. Whereas before, when testing a package like the airline system Sell, a variety of Sell actions with different flight numbers and dates, differing numbers in party, and other information, might have been fed in to be run against the Sell package of programs, now not only Sell actions, but Wait List, Cancel, Display Passenger Record, and many more can be admitted as their corresponding processing packages are added to the system.

Subsystem Testing

As soon as multiple package testing reaches the point where all packages have been proved to work within a multiprogrammed environment, the Operational Programs are ready for a full-fledged subsystem test. Depending upon the equipment configuration, this level may also consist of sublevels.

MULTIPLE PACKAGE TESTING WITH MULTIPLEXOR INPUT • If an input/output multiplexor is part of the system equipment, this would be the time at which such a device and its stored program might be integrated into the testing. Heretofore, the simulated input for test purposes might have been fed directly into the central processing unit from one or more tape drives. This was done in order to isolate program errors as belonging to either the central processing unit's packages under test or to the Control Program, without introducing the more complex possibilities of the error being lodged in the program of some other computer, namely the multiplexor. The time must come, however, when the system testers, satisfied with the performance of the Control and Operational Programs of the central processing unit, start to admit data generated by the input/output multiplexor, accepting the possibility of this device as a source of error. This broadening of the equipment base for further testing still does not mean that live input need be admitted to the system. It simply means that the input/output multiplexor becomes the source of input, which could be generated by a special program in the multiplexor or pulled in from tape units attached to the multiplexor.

In systems employing a file multiplexor (Figure 2.3), an analogous phasing-in of this multiplexor must also take place at an appropriate juncture in the system testing, perhaps even before the phasing-in of the input/output multiplexor, depending upon the necessity of making use of the system files rather than simulating the presence of file data. At the time of subsystem testing, if not before, use should be made of the random access files associated with the system in place of simulated file records drawn from magnetic tape. This is not to say that the random access storage subsystem must contain actual operational system records, such as might be obtained by conversion. The records stored on file should, however, resemble as closely as possible live system records.

HIGH-VOLUME TESTING • In high-volume testing, the external input, though still not live, is admitted under considerably less control than before. In earlier testing, incoming entries, while mixed to contain a variety of action code types, were received in a predetermined and known sequence. This was done for two reasons: (1) not all packages were available, some not yet having graduated to the subsystem testing level; (2) it was desirable for purposes of analyzing test results to know exactly the kinds and sequences of actions being processed by the available packages. Now these barriers can be lowered by removal of some of the limitations on the input volume and mix. The multiplexor and central processing unit programs are inundated with inputs having these characteristics:

- Any package may be called, as all are assumed to be checked out and all possible inputs can be processed.
- The mix and sequence of inputs are unknown, just as in productive operation.
- The volume of input is not controlled, and so the programs have to compensate for overload conditions.

Another tenet of system testing is that the entire test phase is characterized not only by levels in which more programs and equipment components are admitted gradually into the test, but at the same time *the volume of test entries and test file records should gradually expand*. At the conclusion of subsystem testing, the equipment and programs should be able to deal with the kind of volume that must be processed during maximum operating peaks projected over the life of the system. One of the biggest testing problems of the System Integration Team lies in generating or otherwise obtaining test data in sufficient quantities to satisfy this requirement.

System Testing

Subsystem testing as just described concerns primarily testing of Control and Operational Programs as major subsystems. Testing of all the other subsystems should take place concurrently to speed the day when all pieces are put together for the grand climax—a final, integrated test of the entire system. At this level, two separate steps may be taken, the first involving data generated at the terminals and the second a fully integrated final test.

TESTING WITH TERMINAL INPUT • The Operational Programs, having reached the final system testing stage, are now required to cope with input generated at the terminals, which have presumably been linked to the central processing site and debugged from an equipment standpoint before this time. In actuality, the lines of demarcation we have been drawing here between the various testing levels and sublevels are not always so clear cut. One level will normally blend into another in such a way that testing of at least two kinds goes on simultaneously. The processing of terminal-originated actions may, therefore, in some systems begin quite early in the testing cycle. However, one fact that differentiates the earlier from the later stages of system testing is that live terminal input is *not necessary* to perform initial testing and may, if introduced in large quantity and for purposes other than experimentation, even be detrimental. During the final testing stages, however, the transition from artificial to live test data must be made in order to flush out error cases not detected by using simulated input. Thus, while terminals may be used as test data sources almost from the beginning, they *must* be used and used very heavily during the final stages in order to provide entries in a mix, a sequence, and a format and content that closely resemble operating conditions.

FINAL SYSTEM TESTING • In the more complex systems, such as those of the duplex variety, the real-time portion of the system has to be tied into the off-line portion to assure that the two interact correctly at all points of conjunction. Switchover programs must be fully tested at this time and assurance gained about the proper functioning of the off-line Control Program and batch processing programs when they are subjected to interruption by the real-time system. What should emerge at the conclusion of this final system testing is a system capable of operating in a sufficiently reliable manner to permit conversion and productive operation.

11.3 ORGANIZATION AND STANDARDS FOR TESTING

Attention during the entire system integration effort to the way in which testing is to be organized and conducted will produce dividends when the testing phase itself is reached. From the start of preliminary technical planning, the responsibility for system testing should be placed with a designated individual or group within the System Integration Team. Initially, this may be a staff assignment having to do with preparatory planning for the testing phase and gradually expanding into a line activity as the testing is begun. Some of the aspects of system testing that should receive early recognition to assure an efficient testing phase are the following.

Test Data Requirements

Determinations must be made regarding the kinds and amounts of test data, both terminal input and file, that must be available for each level of testing. Once these requirements are known, a decision can be made about the most economical and rapid methods of obtaining the test data.

Testing Standards

A decision is also required as to the point at which testing ceases to be the individual programmer's responsibility and comes under the formal jurisdiction of the test group. In some projects, the person who writes the program is accountable for unit testing, on completion of which his program is made part of the Operational Program system tape. After that, the system test group assumes responsibility and the individual programmer is no longer held responsible for devising test data or conducting tests but is responsible only for repairing his program when errors are discovered by the test group. The prime reason for taking the program away from its author and turning it over to the test group is to gain objectivity in testing. It constitutes the imposition of a form of quality control over the products of the various programmers.

To the extent that the programmers do participate directly in testing either at or beyond the unit test level, standards must be imposed to obtain a uniform degree of testing accomplishment. Without the promulgation of standards covering not only *what* must be tested (test data requirements) but also the methodology of testing and the documentation of test results, the early levels of testing that involve the programmers' individual efforts will not furnish the needed foundation for more intensive later testing.

TEST SHOT PROCEDURES • Programs should be expected to pass beyond the unit test level after n shots on the computer, where n is some pragmatically determined standard based on the complexity of the program segments and the good judgment of the system test specialists. Then, if an individual programmer consistently requires twenty test shots per program segment debugged when the standard is five, corrective action can be taken.

All the preparation requirements for performing testing, such as format of correction cards, procedures for logging computer time used, and control of test tapes, must of course be clearly outlined for the guidance of the programmers.

DOCUMENTATION OF RESULTS • Where the initial testing is not the direct responsibility of the test group, as will likely be the case during unit and possibly package testing, the programmers performing the tests must be given well-defined standards for uniform documentation of test results. Tangible evidence is necessary to assure (1) that the minimum required tests have been made, (2) that exceptions have not been ignored, and (3) that in the event of future trouble certain error sources can, after review of the documentation, be ruled out as already tested.

Planning and Scheduling of Test Support Programs

Test data generators and test simulators have already been mentioned as among the programs needed to support system testing. In many real-time systems, a sizable collection of programs has to be written for the sole purpose of aiding the System Integration Team in testing. Careful planning is mandatory to make certain that these programs are available when they are needed. Otherwise the System Integration Team may find itself in the somewhat frustrating position of having arrived at a given level of system testing, only to discover that the tools needed to go on the next level are not available.

Exception Test Planning

Often the System Integration Team, in planning for testing, tends to concentrate on real-time Control and Operational Program testing, ignoring or slighting similar planning for lower priority real-time programs and off-line programs. This planning bias can be disastrous, for the real-time system, when put into operation, will be only as strong as its least-tested program. A duplex system which operates very satisfactorily until there is occasion to switch over and which then flounders because not all the switchover programs have been thoroughly tested defeats the whole purpose of adopting the duplex configuration in the first place. Similarly, a system in which the fallback and recovery programs have not been adequately tested will work well enough without them until the first system-down situation is encountered (probably on the first day of productive running after cutover).

The operational programmers cannot be relied upon to identify these exception programs and schedule them for testing so that all needed portions of the system are ready at the proper time. This is a responsibility of the Controller, who may, of course, delegate it to the system test group. This group must certainly be mindful of the necessity of testing not just the main line routines but every exception routine as well.

11.4 TEST SUPPORT PROGRAMS

Special programs are needed to accomplish real-time testing, some designed to operate in the real-time environment along with the regular real-time programs, and others intended to operate in an off-line mode. The extent of this special software varies considerably from system to system, tending to increase substantially in those which are multiprogrammed. Frequently there are trade-off opportunities between programmed approaches to system testing and manual "brute force" methods. Test cases in the form of inputs and file records can, for example, be generated by programs specially written for this purpose, or they can be hand-prepared by the programmers or by clerical personnel from the affected operating departments. However, even in a small real-time system that is not multiprogrammed, at least some investment in support programming has to be made. To indicate the possible scope of such programming, let us briefly describe some representative programs required to support system testing.

Control Program Simulator

The Control Program simulator is the routine mentioned earlier that supplants both the Control Program and the real-time equipment in the early stages of testing. Basically, each Control Program macro instruction executed by an Operational Program when working with this simulator results in a transfer of control to the simulator rather than to the Control Program. Usually in making use of the simulator, the programmer supplies not only his program to be tested but also his own test data, which can be made known to the simulator by means of special set-up cards or instructions. Sometimes these test cases are held in main memory by the simulator rather than in their normal auxiliary storage locations. One area in main memory may be set aside for "terminal entries" that have been preloaded along with the Operational Program; another area may be set aside for file records to be consulted by the Operational Programs in the course of processing an entry. Data will then be picked up from main memory by the simulator as required, obviating the need for true terminal input or auxiliary storage.

The Control Program simulator can afford to be more wasteful of main memory space and computer time than can the Control Program itself. It can be more wasteful of main memory because the testing of program segments and packages is, at the stage when the simulator is employed, single- rather than multipackage. It can be more wasteful of computer time because it is under no obligation to respond to the terminals within a specified interval, as would the Control Program in an operating environment.

Besides taking the place of the Control Program and the equipment at a time when they may not be available and besides establishing more controlled and limited conditions for testing than would otherwise be possible, the Control Program simulator provides (or should provide) special debugging features to aid the programmers in testing. A partial or selective macro trace should be built into the simulator, preserving the contents of registers and the status of other storage areas each time the Operational Program executes one of the Control Program macro instructions. The simulator may, further, detect illegal procedures being followed by an Operational Program, such as failing to store registers, modifying instuctions across a wait, making illogical file record requests, or incorrectly transferring control to another program.

Control Program Exerciser

If the System Integration Team has to write its own Control Program, a special simulator may also have to be written to aid in checking out the Control Program. This simulator does for the Control Program what the Control Program simulator does for Operational Programs. It serves as a substitute for the demands that the Operational Programs will make on the Control Program. In this way Operational Program requests for main memory and file storage, for record reads and writes, for input message editing, and for output message transmission can be fed into the Control Program without resorting to usage of the Operational Programs themselves, which at this level of

Control Program testing are probably not even written, let alone tested and available to help debug the Control Program.

Test Data Generators

No one has yet devised a formula for predicting the number of errors that may creep into a system in the form of program bugs. In a large commercial system containing many decision paths and a variety of inputs and file records, the potential sources of error are numbered in the billions. Although no amount of testing can ferret out *all* the bugs, the vitality of real-time systems places on the System Integration Team a special burden to try, during testing, to detect and correct as many errors as possible, thereby gaining maximum assurance that the system will be capable of sustained operation after cutover.

Because of the necessity of conducting as exhaustive a series of tests as possible, it is usually not feasible to depend exclusively upon manually prepared test data. Instead, the System Integration Team must write special programs to generate such data. Program-generated test data offers two powerful advantages over manually prepared data.

1) Generator programs can be used to flood the system with massive amounts of test data. If, for example, 10,000 deposit transactions for varying amounts and for a range of account numbers are automatically produced and stored on magnetic tape by a generator program, then many more errors —particularly on the very unusual exception paths—will be detected than would be if an analyst had spent a great deal of time manually devising perhaps 500 test cases that he felt were both typical and atypical.

2) Computer-generated test data are free of human bias. Suppose that, in an airline system, the Sell Program contains an error evidenced only when conditions are such that space is requested on the last day of February of an even-numbered non-leap year and when the Inventory Record involved is for a flight making three stops with a date change occurring between stops one and two; suppose, further, that the error manifests itself only if the request is for three seats to form the re-

turn portion of a reservation. This is but one of the myriad error possibilities in an airline system. Many are not logically predictable by the operators of the system or by the programmers. The more data that can be generated and pumped into the system during testing, the more of these obscure errors will be detected and corrected. Otherwise, an error like that mentioned will probably manifest itself, to the consternation of everyone, one day along about the fourth year of system operation.

Not only input but file records as well may be produced by specially written generator programs. The latter may be more difficult to generate, especially if there are multiple levels of file record indexing or other complexities in getting at the file records. Nevertheless, an investment of System Integration Team effort in writing file generator programs as well as input data generators can help to insure future bug-free operation.

Input/Output and File Simulators

Even when the Control Program has been linked with the Operational Programs for more advanced system testing and when the use of a simulator to take the place of the Control Program has been discontinued, there will need to be simulation of some parts of the equipment. The Control Program may, for example, call upon magnetic tape rather than disk storage to obtain records requested by the Operational Programs and may, therefore, be tied into a simulator that reads the required records from tape. Similarly, it is not until the final stages of testing that the remote terminals need be depended upon to provide substantial volumes of input for testing purposes. In the meantime these inquiries are fed into the Control Program by terminal simulator programs designed for such purposes.

These special-purpose simulators could be connected to, or could even be a part of, the data generators mentioned previously. Then when it is time, let us say, for another input to enter the system as though from a terminal, the terminal simulator program could activate the generator, which would produce an entry of the kind desired. This entry would be transformed by the simulator into the exact format it would exhibit if it had originated at a terminal.

Data Logging Programs

Because of the problem of repeatability of errors, particularly when testing has progressed beyond the use of simulated input and terminals are permitted access to the system, there must be a program to log the entries as received by either the input/output multiplexor or the CPU if there is no multiplexor. In this way it may be possible, when the system has been halted because of error, to repeat the conditions that caused the system to go down by reading in from the logging tape (or disk) the group of entries most recently received. In its simplest form such logging may consist merely of preserving the exact format of all entries from the terminals in the sequence in which they are received.

There are, of course, circumstances—particularly in a multiprogrammed system—where even with such data logging an error cannot be forced to repeat. This is because the error may have modified the files or because the Operational Program that produced the error, being relocatable, may end up in a different section of main memory when the retry is attempted. Or the length of queues maintained by the Control Program may vary during the retry. Data logging cannot, in short, be depended upon to recreate *all* the conditions present when the error first occurred in the multiprogrammed system. But with such logging, the offending input message is at least still present for a retry or several retries in an attempt to duplicate the error conditions. Even with data logging, the problem of repeatability is still severe; without it, the problem is virtually insoluble.

Data logging programs and procedures should not be abandoned once system testing is over, but should be continued at least into the initial period of conversion when confidence in the system performance may not be high. They can then be used to help find errors resulting from input of productive work into the system.

Data Reduction Programs

If generators are employed to produce massive amounts of test data, the results of testing may be so voluminous as to defy analysis by those assigned to evaluate test results. Accordingly, programs have to be written that take the output results of large-volume system testing and reduce them to a size and format meaningful to the test analyst. Essentially, a test data reduction program operates on an exception basis, digesting the contents of magnetic tapes, one of which might be the data logging tape containing a copy of each entry or simulated input message, and another an output tape giving results of the processing in the form of response messages and updated file records corresponding to each entry. From these, the data reduction program might select only those inputs which caused an "abort" in an Operational Program so that no output was produced, or which resulted in the production of abnormal output according to some prespecified definition. The data reduction program would then edit this information and prepare an edited tape for the printing of items deemed worthy of human scrutiny.

A data reduction program is primarily an off-line program that transforms the nondiscernible results of system testing into a form suitable for human analysis. At its most primitive, it may be a simple edit program. In more complex form, it may be a highly sophisticated information-retrieval program.

Control Program Modifications

Many of the debugging aids built into the Control Program simulator should also be made part of the Control Program itself, preferably in "pluggable" form so that they can later be removed during peak-volume operation when instruction execution time comes at more of a premium. Macro-tracing ability is a necessity during early usage of the Control Program, as is the ability to take a "snapshot" of all or part of main memory to facilitate rerun. The debugging features required in the Control Program are so similar to those built into the Control Program simulator that these two programs should desirably be written by the same group. If the two differ, either in their debugging ability or, more significantly, in their interpretation of the meaning of the macro instructions, Operational Programs that successfully meet the testing standards at the level of the Control Program simulator may fail when first put together with the Control Program.

11.5 ACCEPTANCE TESTS

Heretofore, we have been speaking about the imposition of quality control over error detection and correction to make certain that the product of the System Integration Team is a good one and that the system will not be hampered by bugs which continually force it into a condition of marginal performance. There is another aspect of system quality control, however. This has to do with evaluating not *whether* the system is capable of performing productively but, assuming that it is more or less bug-free, how *well* it is performing when measured against the functional requirements. Sometimes an acceptance test is contractually required to provide the user with assurance on this vital question.

The occurrence of program errors may cause the system to fail an acceptance test. But the absence of these errors constitutes no guarantee that acceptance test criteria concerning response time and system availability will be met. Even where a formal acceptance test is not provided for in the contract, there is invariably a tacit condition of acceptance: to be acceptable a system must be able to accomplish the productive work of the application in a manner resembling that originally intended by the system designers.

The point to be made here is that there is a considerable difference between system testing as discussed in this chapter and acceptance testing. The successful system test provides an error-free system as the basis for further acceptance criteria to be applied either before or after conversion.

11.6 SUMMARY

The testing requirements for real-time systems are unusually demanding, because the system must not be imperiled by the occurrence of errors, especially program bugs, after cutover. The special character of real-time systems makes it difficult to fulfill these requirements of high reliability and error-free performance. Some of the factors contributing to this difficulty are these:

- Magnitude of the programming effort
- Ambiguity in specifications
- Inability to make errors repeat
- Multiprocessing
- Multiprogramming
- Inherent logical complexity
- Random access storage

As a consequence, real-time programs must pass through several well-defined levels of testing before it can be said with assurance that the system is ready for productive operation. These include:

- Testing in a simulated environment
- Testing with the Control Program
- Subsystem testing
- System testing

To conduct testing of this scope, considerable attention must be devoted to test planning and to development of testing standards. In addition, special programs must be written in support of the testing effort; these include:

- Control Program simulator
- Control Program exerciser
- Test data generators
- Input/output and file simulators
- Data logging programs
- Data reduction programs

The testing phase of system integration may terminate in an acceptance test, but even if this is not the case, stringent testing requirements must be imposed and fulfilled to assure a smoothly functioning operational system.

CONVERSION AND MAINTENANCE | 12

12.1 ROLE OF THE SYSTEM INTEGRATION TEAM

CONVERSION OF the real-time system and its maintenance in operational status may be only partly under the aegis of the System Integration Team. At some stage of system development the *raison d'être* of the System Integration Team can be considered as fulfilled and a more regularized organizational approach taken to system operation. Usually though, the responsibilities of the System Integration Team cannot be considered discharged until there exists a system-in-being that satisfies the functional requirements, the design parameters of technical planning, and the terms of the system contract. Because real-time systems are so novel and because their functions are so vital, the System Integration Team should be kept intact until the adequacy of the system can be proved in actual operation on substantial quantities of working data. Only in this way can management be finally assured that the system is capable of producing the results promised by simulation and the other projections of performance ability made during system design.

If the system design is defective, it is during the conversion phase that the evidence so indicating becomes irrefutably clear. For this reason, if for no other, the System Integration Team should be held together as an organization so that everything possible can be done to get the system into production, including revision of program and equipment specifications when serious trouble is encountered.

12.2 PROBLEMS IN PARALLEL OPERATION

Most file-oriented systems, in making the transition from the final stages of system testing to the initial stages of productive operation, go through a period of parallel operation during which the application processing is performed not only by the computer system but by manual methods as well. In a demand deposit accounting application, for example, ledger accounts might be posted by the computer and in the conventional manner by bookkeepers using their key-driven posting machines, with the results compared on a summary-total and spot-check basis by a conversion team familiar with both posting methods. Usually, such a review of the parallel operation reveals far more deficiencies in the manual system than in the computer system because of the bookkeepers' failure to adhere uniformly to manual standards and procedures. Occasionally, however (and the frequency depends upon the thoroughness of prior system testing), an error is found in the computer programs as the result of parallel operation.

The purpose of parallel operation in any data processing system is twofold: (1) to help discover errors in the computer system by checking its results against manually derived results; (2) to provide a backup means of processing when the computer results are unavailable or unacceptable. These are the goals in a real-time system as well as in other systems, but because of the immediacy of the processing they are more difficult to realize in the real-time system.

When program errors are discovered as a result of operating in parallel, it is normal to "rewrite history" by rerunning work produced by the defective program. If customer statements were turned out by a ledger run that calculated service charges incorrectly because of a mistake in the subroutine for computing account earning percentage, then the input tapes to this run (yesterday's master ledger and today's journal) would be remounted on the tape drives and the ledger run performed anew with the defective service-charge formula corrected. Statements produced by the faulty run would be destroyed and the new set printed and (after another audit by the conversion specialists) sent out to customers.

In a real-time system, there is no such procedure as parallel operation in the conventional sense of the term. Some of the reasons for this follow.

1) The operators of the system, based at their terminals, cannot tolerate the delay inherent in doing everything twice, once by making use of the computer system via the terminal and then by the method normally used. This can perhaps be done on an experimental basis in a small office or at a few positions in a larger office, but as a rule the public cannot be queued up while the terminal operator performs a duplicate set of operations.

2) In a typical batch processing system with several master files on magnetic tape—say a main ledger, condensed ledger, and a name and address file—the source of an error can rapidly be narrowed down to one program or set of programs written to operate on a particular file. In a multifile real-time system, however, the same conclusion does not follow. The Passenger Name Record Program in an airline system may, in error, update a record from the Seat Inventory File and vice versa. This dangerous aura of "togetherness" in the real-time system has been brought up before. When unrelated programs have to coexist in main memory and unrelated records cohabit random access storage, there is sure to be difficulty in isolating errors during system testing as well as during productive operation.

3) One of the chief virtues of parallel operation, the ability to make corrections and rerun when an error is discovered, is not realizable in a system which does not utilize magnetic tape files in such a way that the output of one processing cycle becomes the input to the next. A real-time system has no predecessor or grandfather tape reel from which the current file can be reconstructed when an error is encountered. Once the copy of a file record in random access storage has been altered by an error in the real-time system, it is difficult to restore it to its earlier state without doing the following things:

- Elaborate backing up of records and programs
- Shutting down of the system while restoration is accomplished

These limitations should not prompt the System Integration Team to abandon all attempts at parallel operation. Instead they should serve as a reminder that parallel operation is more difficult under real-time conditions. In some real-time systems, parallel operation may be little more than a state of mind, an awareness on the part of the terminal operators that the system may be taken from them at any instant, at which time they will be forced to revert to manual procedures. Where the application is such that it is relatively easy to fall back to manual procedures and restart from them later, it may be best not to try to perform any sort of parallel operation in real time but to take the system away from the operators periodically in order to check results.

This kind of procedure is often inadmissible, however, and then a special mode of parallel operation must be programmed. Under such a mode the program filing records created or modified as a result of terminal action may also be required either to produce a hard copy of the results at an on-line printer or to write the results to magnetic tape for subsequent analysis. Then, if the input data has also been logged, a reasonably complete trail of records concerning each action may be preserved for human audit and subsequent reuse when errors are discovered. Unfortunately, if the error affects a customer who has, let us say, already departed from a teller's window in a savings bank, it is inevitably rather embarrassing to try to rectify the error after it occurs. The real-time processing situation, being more immediate, is significantly different from non-real-time creation and issuance of documents such as customer statements, which can be held up from mailing until an audit of their accuracy is completed.

12.3 MODULARITY IN CONVERSION

The advent of real-time systems has underscored a maxim well known to anyone who has ever sought to convert a large-scale business system: *Don't try to convert everything at once.* The transition from system testing to a fully operational system must be gradual. There are compelling reasons for this restraint. First, when trouble with either equipment or programs is encountered, its impact on operating departments will be minimal if conversion has proceeded slowly. Second, a slower pace permits the System Integration Team to purge the program bugs not discovered during testing in a more systematic way, first eliminating those associated with cutover but not dependent upon volume, then attacking those caused by a buildup in the volume of transactions or in the number of system functions performed as conversion continues. Third, the work load of the System Integration Team and personnel from the departments involved in preparing data for conversion can be better controlled and equalized if there is not a huge requirement at the beginning of the project to shovel manually created file records into the system.

The larger real-time systems, by virtue of their size and complexity, typically provide better opportunities for a modular approach to conversion than do smaller systems in which the choice of conversion methods is more limited. Offsetting this, greater pressure is usually exerted in large-scale system integration to proceed rapidly with conversion because of the heavy investment in equipment and software, an investment that cannot be economically justified until the system approaches its planned processing volumes.

Unless serious trouble forces the System Integration Team to depart from the conversion schedule or even to start all over after necessary fixes are made, conversion can be carried out at a rapidly accelerating rate once the initial steps are taken. This is because the software subsystem tends to become more solid the more it is exercised and because the clerical personnel responsible for preparing the input data for conversion gain in skill and experience.

Some possibilities that suggest themselves for a modular approach to conversion are discussed below. All these approaches will probably necessitate additional programming to modify tables and directories, insert new Operational Programs into the system library, and reflect the addition of new equipment.

Convert by Location

When the terminal locations are in offices geographically remote and relatively self-sufficient with respect to the manual maintenance of records, there is a ready-made pattern for converting. A multibranch bank may wish to convert its smallest office first, or perhaps its head office, as a pilot operation to make certain that the system is functionally adequate. An airline might do likewise by converting one of its smaller boarding cities. The main disadvantage of this approach is that, during the conversion period, the company has to live procedurally with two systems—the existing manual system and the real-time computer system—with an excellent probability that the two will be incompatible in a number of major respects.

If an airline, prior to conversion, routes teletype requests for space received from other airlines to each boarding location for manual processing, with a manually prepared teletype confirmation message sent by the boarding location back to the other airline in reply, then three alternatives present themselves during the transitional period of conversion: (1) let the computer take over this function entirely from the beginning, processing *all* requests centrally even though only one boarding location has been converted; (2) do not permit the computer to process any requests automatically until the system is entirely converted, in the meantime routing the requests to each local office for appropriate action (either manual or manual with the aid of computer inquiry capability if the location has been converted); (3) route all messages to a central point where a decision can be made (perhaps by the computer) whether they should be processed automatically, depending upon whether the boarding location is part of the computer system. There are many such transitional procedures requiring decision, with the result that the interim conversion period causes operating personnel to undergo annoying and confusing dislocations in their work habits. It is these dislocations which conversion planning must strive to minimize.

Convert by Equipment Module

Conversion by equipment module should hold great appeal for companies that have already attained some degree of automation of the applications to be placed on the real-time system. A company engaged in punched card or magnetic tape processing may, as a transitional phase, convert its files to a random access storage medium, but use this device to continue sequential processing instead of going immediately to true random access processing. When this interim stage of batch processing from random access storage has been accomplished, on-line features can be more readily added to the system. In this way, the step forward of obtaining random access ability is taken, even though the random access storage is used in a similar fashion to the card or tape system which preceded it.

When this conversion approach is adopted, programs presently in existence may be rewritten to abide by real-time constraints concerning program length, processing time, and relationship to the Control Program, but allowed to continue processing transactions against the files in a sorted and batched mode. Then when the point is reached at which terminals are to be placed on line, system testing and conversion problems can be largely isolated to the addition of remote terminals and an input/output multiplexor to replace the punched cards or other media used previously to introduce data into the system.

Convert by Application

Conversion by application is particularly appropriate to a management information system in which multiple use is made of system records. In such systems all *files* may be set up at the beginning but with the programs that will use them added gradually. In an airline system, the General Schedule Records, once stored in the system files for use in the reservation application, become available for use by other departments of the airline, notably these:

- Dispatch
- Aircraft Routing

- Aircraft Maintenance
- Crew Scheduling
- Flight Planning

There is no reason—except perhaps an economic one and even this may be specious when one considers the cost of false starts and conversion failures—why the reservation application alone cannot be programmed, tested, and placed into operation, then gradually augmented by the other applications. This approach is an appealing one in that it spreads the developmental costs of writing the programs and the operational hazards of getting the system going over a sufficiently long period that conversion problems can be cut down to manageable size.

Even within the airline reservation application itself, conversion may be scheduled by subapplication with, let us say, the programs for maintaining passenger records converted but with seat inventory control maintained outside the computer. Or possibly the automatic processing of requests from other airlines could be defined as lower priority and the programming deferred. In a banking system such a subapplication as on-line calculation of savings account interest is not really essential to an operational system at the start, nor are the automatic insertion and deletion of hold and stop payment orders for a checking account. In the latter case, there need be in the record only a flag that causes the program to advise the teller to check a manually maintained file of holds on the funds in particular accounts.

The System Integration Team should select the most workable method of phasing in the system, cooperating closely with the using departments in evaluating the costs and personnel dislocations expected during the period in which business must be done in a hybrid manner, with the real-time data processing coexisting with the portion of the system not yet converted. These must be weighed against the operational risks and the morale problems engendered by an overambitious approach to conversion.

12.4 CONVERSION PROGRAMS

Conversion programs to cut the system over from manual to automatic operation may be both real time and off line. Off-line programs include such routines as data editors and input conditioners, which accept and edit information about system records. Names and addresses must be checked, account numbers computed and verified, current balance information cross-footed and accumulated to summary totals. In planning the conversion programs, one must consider how much of the file information can be captured by relatively static off-line routines involving card-to-tape conversion and thorough data conditioning as compared with the amount of application data that has to be obtained for the computer files through use of real-time programs.

Upon analysis, some systems are found to be largely self-converting, with a boot-strap procedure readily obvious as the best means of accomplishing conversion. An airline reservation system conversion might revolve around two dates, a T date representing the time when the agents can begin to use the terminals at a given boarding location and a C date, some weeks later, representing the time when the computer system actually assumes responsibility for maintaining the records of passengers booked at that location. After T date, the agents would begin using their terminals to enter passenger data. The real-time programs, operating in a special conversion mode, would make a test on the date for which a reservation was requested. If the date of the request is beyond C date, the record would be sent out to system storage in the normal way, and that would be the end of it. If, however, the date of the reservation fell somewhere between T date and C date, the computer would not only file the copy of the record in system storage but would also cause a hard copy of the record to be printed out for insertion in a manual file system (which the computer system will replace completely after C date). In this fashion the computer system effectively "sneaks up" on the conversion date so that by the time C date is reached, all the manually maintained records will have served their purpose, the flights to which they pertain having already been flown and all future bookings already recorded in the system. The only special conversion requirement is the entry at T date of those records previously created for flights so far in the future that they are beyond C date. The period between T and C dates can be established to suit the particular booking pattern that an airline has been known to experience.

This conversion is relatively inexpensive from a programming standpoint, requiring only the modification of real-time routines that would be needed anyway rather than the writing of special conversion programs. Where this self-converting approach is not feasible, it is sometimes possible to combine the conversion programs with the programs needed to enable the system, once converted, to recover after a period of down time. In either case, such dual usage of programs must be preplanned. It must be anticipated by the technical planning staff and written into the program specifications so that the requirements of the conversion mode will be programmed as part of the real-time routines.

12.5 ENGINEERING AND PROGRAMMING FIXES

Design flaws, miscalculations of the execution time of programs, errors in inquiry and file access volumes, and below-standard equipment performance may be discovered for the first time during conversion. If these are sufficiently serious, conversion will have to be halted until remedies can be found and applied.

It may be learned, for example, that a disk file access arm cannot produce a sufficiently error-free performance in satisfying file record requests made by the Operational Programs. Why was this not discovered during system testing? The testing of the file subsystem operating in conjunction with the appropriate Operational Programs did, in fact, achieve the desired level of file event volume; the percentage of seeks to a certain area of the file modules, however, was not properly simulated by the test input data. As a consequence, one set of file records is actually accounting for 68 percent of the file arm movement rather than its anticipated share of 38 percent, and the file arm mechanism cannot perform reliably under this load.

The solution to a problem of this kind may lie in equipment modification, in program revision, or both. The most straightforward solution might be an engineering fix on the file access mechanism to improve its reliability under the operating conditions encountered. Alternatively, the system's records might be reorganized so that the access work load is more evenly distributed among the various portions of the file. The latter solution could be extremely deleterious in its effect on data already converted and stored in the files and on the programs that depend on the existing organization of the file records. In other circumstances, neither the engineering modification of the access mechanism nor the software change may, by itself, provide an adequate solution but must be combined to produce a workable system.

Only one situation is worse than that in which combined engineering and programming corrections are called for. This is when the best efforts of the engineers and programmers are not good enough to repair the design inadequacy. It can result in interminable delay while the functional requirements of the application are reworked to bring them into line with the state of the art in engineering and programming.

12.6 MAINTAINING THE OPERATIONAL SYSTEM

One of the major elements of system complexity cited in Chapter 2 has to do with system variability, that is, the susceptibility of an application to change. This encompasses not merely change in the form of increasing volume but substantive change in the application itself as the result of these factors:

1) External influences, including laws and government regulations, industry standards and practices, and competitive pressures

2) Increased desire by management to exploit the full potential of the system by transforming it from a record-keeping system into a management information system

In addition to these influences for change, is the necessity of introducing any changes that were deferred by the Controller during system integration as "desirable" rather than "essential."

Consequently, provision must be made for introducing changes of both major and minor scope into the system after it becomes operational. This consideration should be recognized during system design, so that sufficient capacity and program flexibility are specified to provide for any changes that can reasonably be anticipated.

If the equipment selected by the system designer is barely adequate in processing speed and throughput capacity to handle the application as currently defined, then future system changes and expansions may have to be inhibited to the detriment of the organization's growth pattern. Otherwise, the equipment, and conceivably the entire software subsystem as well, may have to be scrapped and, in effect, a virtually new system integration project started to achieve the necessary expansion.

Similarly, as regards programming, future events should be anticipated during technical planning. If a bank is merger-minded, it would be prudent to adhere to Federal Reserve System standards for classifying and numbering accounts so that, should a merger come about, there is a greater probability that its software subsystem will be compatible with that of the other party to the merger.

Of great importance to system maintenance, especially in the software area, is the dictum of modularity. It is imperative that the programming be divided into subsystems in place of one massive collection of instructions. This is not only for ease in making programming assignments or for a more logical approach to system testing. Modularity is also required to permit one part of the program to be changed without unduly disturbing the other parts. The rule of modularity is, unfortunately, easy to promulgate but difficult to execute.

It often appears that the strictures in favor of modularity run contrary to those stressing *integrated* system development. We are on the one hand admonished to keep applications separated so that a change, let us say, in savings account regulations for reporting interest accumulation to the Internal Revenue Service will not affect the demand deposit accounting application that is part of the same system. And on the other hand, we are urged to integrate the depositor records so that if a customer has both a savings and a demand deposit account, a common record can be established and programs developed to bring this combined customer account information under management scrutiny in one unified piece. This is one of the many unresolved contradictions in data processing today—conflict between the concept of modularity and that of integrated processing.

Even though the System Integration Team is unable to achieve much modularity in the software subsystem design because of the nature of the application or because of pressures to get one application on the air without thoroughly investigating its relationship with others, modularity is at least an ideal for the guidance of the System Integration Team. As with basic precepts of ethics and morality, one is probably better off for having been made aware of sound data processing principles, even if the exigencies of a situation impel him to violate them.

No matter how much forethought is given to system design and technical planning, unanticipated changes will nevertheless take place and ability must be provided to amalgamate these changes into the operating system with minimum disruption. The goal of the system planner here is well expressed by the French proverb *plus ça change, plus ce la meme chose,* for in real-time system maintenance, the more the system configuration changes, the more important it is that the system continue to present the same stable countenance to its users.

The idea of accommodating change according to a *model* concept is one that has proved useful in many real-time systems, most notably in the SAGE system. Rather than introduce changes into the system at the time they are proposed and agreed upon, the objective of a model approach is to accumulate changes until there is a sufficient number of them to warrant their introduction en masse into the operating system. In this way, the risks associated with introducing change into the system are minimized because the system is not being continually bombarded with changes. True, when a new model is installed the impact on the system in the form of error potential and other disruptions may be great, but at least changes are not being introduced every day or every week with a constant vulnerability to disaster.

There are many reasons why a new model must be developed; among them are these :

1) New equipment additions to handle increased volumes or entirely new applications.

2) Accumulation of modifications due to the various environmental changes that occur in the course of the system operation

3) Introduction of desirable but not essential features previously deferred by the Controller in the interest of configuration control

4) Reprogramming caused by the discovery that the initial programs were suboptimum and did not fully exploit the equipment capability

5) New application development

Before a new model is added to the system either as a complete or partial replacement for the existing programs, it should be subjected to testing at least as rigorous as that to which the original programs in the system were exposed. In a duplex system the standby computer can be used for testing; it can be exploited in an especially advantageous manner if the communication lines are able to provide test input to the standby computer by tapping off the inquiries being routed to the on-line computer for processing. If the system is nonduplex, hopefully the real-time operation will not extend beyond one working shift, leaving time available for testing during the off-line period. In any event the new model should not be placed in a productive operational environment until extensive testing has taken place. The choice of a time to introduce the new model into the system should be at a nonpeak period and, if possible, under conditions that will not disable the entire system if introduction of the new model causes processing difficulties. A savings bank would be injudicious to introduce a program change during a noon-hour peak near the first of the month, just as an airline with a north-south winter tourist peak should introduce its new models in June rather than in December. When the effect of the model change can be restricted to one office or one location on an experimental basis, that much more protection against the errors wrought by change can be achieved.

The SAGE system was able to introduce new program models at any one of its geographic processing sectors while keeping the other sectors operating under the old model. When the new model was being tested, the sector involved in the test was considered down, and fallback procedures were adhered to. These involved the assumption by computers in adjoining sectors of the work load of the sector under test. In this way, any failure resulting from conversion to the new model had no impact on the operational environment.

12.7 FALLBACK AND RECOVERY

The question of fallback and restart procedures is intimately related to system conversion and maintenance because of the likelihood that such procedures will have to be invoked frequently during conversion and initial operation. Fallback is here defined as covering those procedures and programs involved in taking the system down gracefully, either to an entirely manual system in place of the computer system or to some operational mode in which a degraded level of service is provided by the computer system until repairs are made on the equipment or programs and full service is restored. Recovery extends to the processes, both manual and computer, of making the real-time system operational again after fallback procedures have been invoked.

Although a wide variety of fallback and recovery modes may prove efficacious for particular applications and system configurations, at least two salient points merit consideration in the development of any real-time file-oriented system.

Generation of Special Records

Where random access files are being updated by terminal operators in real time, as they are in savings bank and airline reservation systems, there must be some method of data protection for the dual purpose of avoiding the loss of vital records in the event of an equipment of programming disaster that might, in error, destroy or damage the contents of these records, and of providing a back-up copy of the system records for use when the central files are unavailable.

The approach of duplicating records, possibly in another module of disk storage or on magnetic tape, for protection against loss of data has been mentioned before. In most systems there is need for back-up records that are either visible or capable of being made visible, as typified by magnetic tape records which can, when necessary, be transformed into hard copy by a high-speed printer.

To illustrate, most savings bank systems are planned to provide, at the end of each day's business, a hard-copy record called variously a Trial Balance, Condensed Ledger, or Customer Deposit Summary Record. This record contains current balance and account status information as of the close of the banking day. It is placed in the tellers' working area at the beginning of the next business day, where it can be consulted in the event the computer-stored depositor records become unavailable during working hours and a fallback period ensues. Similarly, in an airline reservation system a Fallback Recap Report may be generated nightly and transmitted to each reservation office as a precautionary measure. This report might contain the status of each Seat Inventory Record for the forthcoming week, showing the number of seats available for sale, with flights beyond seven days reported on an exception basis only.

This type of information facilitates smooth fallback, although even under the best of circumstances, operation in the fallback mode is inefficient and cumbersome. In a banking system, tellers not having access to the computer records may not be able to handle interbranch transactions or no-book withdrawals because of the limitations of the hard-copy information available to them as compared with the data normally provided by the computer system. Airline reservation supervisors may have to perform "seat-of-the-pants" approximations in shifting over to their manual fallback system. (The latest

Fallback Recap Report was issued for all flights as of their status at 6:oo A.M. today. The computer went down at 2:30 P.M. How many sales were made between 6:oo A.M. and 2:30 P.M. for which the hard-copy recap seat counts should be reduced before they are used by the agents?)

Development of a fallback plan typically involves the specification and production of special fallback programs. At minimum, programs are needed to scan through the system files and obtain information for the hard-copy reports to be used when the system goes down, or to transform the magnetic tape back-up copies of records into a human sensible document if a tape back-up approach is adopted.

Special-purpose procedures and programs are also needed to reintegrate the system into its operational environment following a period of down time. Suppose that a system fails because of the need for unscheduled maintenance somewhere in the central processing unit. Once the malfunctioning component has been repaired, it may not be a simple matter to get the system started once again. The equipment may be ready but often the system records are not, having fallen out of date because of the manual processing that has had to take place externally. In a savings bank application, it may be necessary to insert the records of all transactions—deposits, withdrawals, placement, and deletions of holds, for example—made during the period of down time. The airline reservation system will have to adjust the computer-stored seat counts by the amount of space sold by agents when they did not have access to the computer records.

These requirements usually lead to special recovery programs as companions to the programs that are associated with fallback. A savings bank recovery program may update records based on information contained in punched paper tape prepared for all transactions that took place during the period of down time, instead of processing the entries directly from the teller terminals, as would normally be the case. The airline system may require a special set of special inventory update action codes and programs to make certain that the computer-maintained seat inventory is reduced by high-priority entries reflecting space already committed to customers during the period of down time.

Thus there are anticipatory requirements to be planned and programmed to assure that sufficient information is available to operate the business in a fallback mode without benefit of some or all of the automatic system capability. And there are special updating and reinitializing routines that must be programmed to permit the system to recover from a down situation and restore full service to its users.

Timetable for Fallback and Recovery

The planning staff should map out in advance the fallback tactics to be adhered to according to a timetable of system availability and make this known to the system operators. It is especially desirable to have a preplanned timetable for fallback and recovery when there are locations remote from the computer center which may tend to panic when they discover that they are isolated from their source of information and which consequently need to be provided with special operating instructions to facilitate graceful degradation.

The steps to be taken during the first few minutes of operational trouble are usually devoted to the ascertainment by supervision at the terminal location of the full extent of the damage. Are all the terminals at the remote location malfunctioning? If there are high- and low-speed communication links to the center, are these both out? Are other offices in adjacent cities or geographic areas also isolated from the system?

When it has been determined to what extent the location is, in fact, isolated from the system, supervision should have a standing plan to make ready for fallback operations. In an airline reservation system, the agents might be instructed to revert temporarily to "free sale" (sell on the assumption that space is available) for up to an hour, under the theory that it is better to risk the consequent overbooking than to go over completely to cumbersome manual space control procedures when it is highly probable that the failure is temporary and that service will be restored momentarily. It may be believed, furthermore, that an hour of free sale with its risk of overbooking can be tolerated, as most overbookings can be compensated for by subsequent cancellations. During the first hour, when such initial fallback conditions prevail, local supervision is busily engaged in organizing its latest Fallback Recap Report so that it may be used by all the reservation agents at the isolated location. This may include (1) updating it by the estimated amount of space already sold on each flight since the report was received, (2) preparing it for reproduction and distribution in a form usable by each agent, and (3) setting up any visual displays such as flight status information on blackboards within view of the sales agents.

These are typical happenings during the initial phase of a system failure. This initial phase is followed, according to the fallback timetable, by an intermediate phase that occurs if service is not restored before time runs out on the initial phase. In this intermediate phase the system is operating on a completely manual basis, making use of the fallback records previously received from the data processing center. Usually the customers of the system, who are in touch with the terminal operators, experience a notable diminution in the quality of service when this phase is entered.

The third phase, hopefully very rare, is a somewhat institutionalized version of the second phase. The difference is that now, with the system down, not for a period of several hours but conceivably for days, local supervision and terminal operators enter a period in which they become better adapted to working without the computer. Temporary staff may be added to help maintain records, and alternative means of communicating data from one point in the system to another instituted, to compensate for the missing central files. One characteristic that often distinguishes this third phase in the fallback and recovery timetable from the second is that it may no longer be possible to update the computer records when service is restored. Consequently, any constraint that this requirement for eventual updating of the computer files has imposed on the manual fallback system is now removed. If terminal operators or clerical personnel have been preparing paper tape or punched cards for subsequent updating of the computer files, this work may be discontinued when the third phase is reached. This means, of course, that when service is restored, a procedure much like initial conversion will have to be adopted. The real-time system has here deteriorated to the point where reconversion is easier and more rapid than attempting to update hopelessly obsolete records.

The final phase of system failure encompasses those tasks precedent to the restoration of service. Here the terminals may once again be placed on-line, but perhaps only for the purpose of accepting transactions that accrued during the system-down period. This final phase should be covered in any fallback and recovery timetable, since the computer system, though once again capable of operation, is not yet able to provide full processing service.

Any standard practices manual for local supervision should contain complete fallback instructions, supplemented with illustrations explaining what the timetable for system failure is and what individual responsibilities are during each period. Fallback and recovery, to be efficient, must combine well-planned procedural steps with special programs to anticipate the manual procedure needs and to restore service after they are employed.

12.8 SUMMARY

It is usually necessary in commercial system development to go through a period of parallel operation during which the computer system and the manual system it is destined to replace both perform the work of the application. This is done to aid in detection of program errors in the computer system and to protect the application against failure of the computer system during the initial period of productive operation. It is, however, difficult to conduct this kind of parallel operation in a real-time system because:

- Terminal operators usually cannot afford the time to execute two sets of operations.
- It is not easy to detect the sources of error.
- It is not easy to correct the results of error.

Despite these handicaps, some means should be sought of introducing a form of parallel operation into the real-time system during conversion.

Modularity is a cardinal principle of conversion. A step-by-step approach to full-scale operation should be planned, with conversion phased to permit controlled expansion through gradual addition of:

- Locations served
- Equipment modules
- Applications

The System Integration Team must determine the best way of phasing in the system, working closely with the using departments.

Special programs are needed to achieve conversion or, alternatively, special conversion modes in the regular Operational Programs if a "bootstrap" approach is adopted.

The conversion phase may reveal the need for engineering and programming fixes to enable the system to adhere to the functional requirements. In a well-designed and soundly implemented system, these fixes will not cause serious deviation from the original system design or the conversion schedule.

The concept of modularity, employed during conversion, should be retained once the system is in full operation, as a guideline to introduction of the changes that are certain to be forthcoming. Accumulation of both hardware and software changes for inclusion in a new system model is the least disruptive approach to system maintenance.

Fallback and recovery procedures and programs are needed from the beginning of conversion throughout the useful life of the system. The following are two essentials of a fallback and recovery scheme in most systems:

- Generation of back-up file records for use when the system is down
- Establishment of a preplanned timetable to guide the users of the system in making the transition from automatic to manual operation and back again

GLOSSARY

GLOSSARY

THE ENGINEERING AND PROGRAMMING of real-time digital computer systems has given currency to many new technical words and expressions and has caused redefinition of many others already in wide use among computer specialists. Some of the definitions in this glossary have been adapted from the Glossary for Information Processing, IBM Form C20-8089, 1962. The remainder of the definitions, totaling almost half the entries, were especially written for this glossary. Full responsibility is assumed by the author for all definitions, however, as many of those drawn from the IBM source have been freely recast to heighten their meaning in the context of real-time processing. In the interest of completeness, a few generic computing terms have also been included to aid those whose interest in real-time systems represents their first acquaintance with automatic data processing.

ACCESS TIME
> The time required to condition a storage unit or device to receive or transmit data after the command to do so is given.

ACTION
> One item or piece of information communicated by a remote terminal to the computer. An action is normally completed by depressing an Enter key or Action button on the terminal set and is acknowledged by a computer response, such as carriage return.

ACTION CODE
> One or more characters at the beginning of a message to the computer that identify the processing action to be performed on the data contained in the message.

ADDRESS
> A label, name, or number identifying a register, location, or unit where information is stored.
> The operand part of an instruction.

In communications, the coded representation of the destination of a message.

ALLOCATION

The allotment or apportionment of available main memory and file storage to accommodate programs and data.

ALTERNATE ROUTING

A secondary communications path assigned to a destination if the primary path is unavailable.

ANALOG DATA

A physical representation of information such that the representation bears an exact relationship to the original information. The electrical signals on a telephone channel are an analog data representation of the original voice.

ANALOG-TO-DIGITAL CONVERTER

A device that changes analog signals to digital values for computer use.

ASSEMBLE

To convert a program written in nonmachine language into actual machine instructions and to assign memory storage for those instructions.

To accumulate in main or auxiliary memory portions of an incoming long message.

ASYNCHRONOUS INPUT

Input having no dependable pattern or cycle of origination. Input from a savings bank teller's terminal would be of this kind, since its origination is based on the random time of arrival of depositors at the teller's window.

AUTOMATION

Production by machines that are self-acting with respect to predetermined processes; for example, making automatic the process of moving work from one machine to the next.

BACKGROUND PROCESSING

Low-priority processing permitted to take place when no higher priority real-time entries are being handled by a system. A batch processing job such as payroll might be treated as background processing subject to interruption on receipt of an inquiry from a terminal.

BAUD

A unit of signaling speed in data transmission. The speed in bauds equals the number of bits per second.

BAUDOT CODE

A code for transmission of data in which five bits represent one character.

BIT

Contraction of "binary digit," the smallest unit of information. A bit has two possible states, one or zero.

BLAST

To release certain areas or blocks of main or auxiliary memory no longer required by an Operational Program. Such a program will execute a Blast macro instruction causing the control program to return the address of the area blasted to its list of storage available for use by subsequent Operational Programs.

BLOCK

A group of records, words, or characters handled as one unit. Used in real-time systems to describe input/output or working storage areas in main memory and units of record storage in auxiliary memory. A file storage block is sometimes referred to as a "physical record."

BUFFER

A storage device used to compensate for a difference in the rate of flow of information or the time of occurrence of events.

CHAINED RECORD

Physical records, in random locations in main or auxiliary storage, that are chained or linked together by means of a control field in each record, containing the address of the next record in the chain. Entire files or waiting lists may be chained in this manner.

CHAINING

A method of storing records in which each record belongs to a list or group of records and has a linking field for tracing the chain.

CHANNEL

A device that connects input/output units to the main memory of a computer or to each other.

A path for electrical transmission between two or more stations.

CHARACTER

The actual or coded representation of a digit, letter, or special symbol.

CHECKOUT

The testing or debugging of a program, subsystem, or system.

CIRCUIT

A physical, conducting connection between two points.

CIRCUIT SWITCHING

A technique in which connection is made prior to the start of a communication.

CLOSED-LOOP SYSTEM

A system in which the computer directly controls an external process without human intervention. In a closed-loop process control system, for example, the computer may be connected directly to instrumentation through a digital-to-analog converter to complete the feedback loop. The computer can then apply control action directly to the process by actuating the valves, setting the controllers, and so forth.

CODE

A system of symbols and rules for use in representing information.

To write computer instructions in accordance with a program specification or flow chart.

CODE DIRECTING CHARACTER

One or more routing indicators at the beginning of a message that establish message destination.

COMMON CARRIER

A company recognized by an appropriate regulatory agency as having a vested interest in furnishing communication services.

COMMUNICATION

The process of transferring information from one point, person, or device to another.

COMPILE

To produce a sequentially ordered machine-language program from a series of symbolic operation codes or statements. A special compiling program is used to perform this transformation from nonmachine to machine language.

COMPUTER

A device capable of accepting, processing, and reporting information. Used here to denote a stored program digital computer.

CONTENTION

A condition on a multipoint communication channel when two or more locations try to transmit at the same time.

CONTROL PROGRAM

The program responsible for handling input/output for both terminals and file storage, establishing processing priorities, maintaining waiting lists of work in process, activating operational programs, and performing other supervisory functions in a real-time system. Words sometimes used synonymously to designate such a program include driver, executive, monitor, supervisor.

CONTROL SYSTEM

A system in which a computer is employed to govern an external process. Closed-loop systems are often referred to as control systems.

CONTROL WORD

A computer word used to transmit processing information from the Control Program to the Operational Programs or between Operational Programs. System records normally contain one or more control words to describe the content and status of various significant fields within the record.

CONVERSATIONAL MODE

A procedure for communication between a terminal and the computer in which each entry from the terminal elicits a response from the computer, with the terminal "locked out" or inhibited while the response is being prepared.

CPU LOOP

See LOOP, CENTRAL PROCESSING UNIT.

CYCLE

An interval of time in which one of a recurring set of actions is completed. An instruction cycle, therefore, represents the amount of time required to execute one of a series of instructions, and a memory cycle represents the amount of time to obtain a character or word from memory storage.

CYCLING

Deletion, creation, or modification of system file records based on periodic external occurrences, for example, the posting of quarterly interest to savings account records.

DATA

A collection of facts, numbers, letters, symbols, that can be processed or produced by a computer, that is, a representation of information.

DATA COLLECTION

The act of bringing data from one or more points to a central point. May be in-plant or out-plant.

DATA ORIGINATION

The translation of information from its original form into a machine-sensible form.

DATA-PHONE

A term used by A. T. and T. to describe any of a family of devices used to permit data communication over telephone channels.

DATA PROCESSING

A generic term including all business applications.

DATA REDUCTION

The process of transforming raw data into intelligible form by adjusting, combining, scaling, ordering, and so on.

DEBUG

To examine or test a procedure, program, or piece of equipment for the purpose of detecting and correcting errors.

DEFERRED PROCESSING

Low-priority processing jobs that have been postponed until computer time is available during nonpeak periods.

DEGRADATION

A condition in which the system continues to operate but at a reduced level of service. Unavailability of major equipment subsystems or components is the usual cause.

DEMODULATION

The process of retrieving an original signal from a modulated carrier wave. This technique is used to make communication signals compatible with business machine signals.

DIAGNOSTIC ROUTINE

A routine designed to locate and identify errors in a computer routine or hardware component.

DIAL-UP

A service whereby a dial telephone can be used to initiate and effect a station-to-station telephone call for purposes of data transmission.

DISK STORAGE

A storage device that uses magnetic recording on flat rotating disks.

DRUM STORAGE

A storage device that uses magnetic recording on a rotating cylinder.

DUAL SYSTEM

A system configuration in which two computers receive identical inputs and execute the same routines with the results of such parallel processing subject to comparison. This approach is taken to obtain very high reliability.

DUPLEX CHANNEL

A communication channel providing simultaneous transmission in both directions.

DUPLEX CONSOLE

A switchover console connecting two or more computers and used to govern which computer is to be on-line.

DUPLEX SYSTEM

A system configuration employing two computers, one being on-line and the other standing by in case of malfunction of the on-line computer. Sometimes the standby computer may be executing an off-line program.

Duplicate Record

An image, or "carbon copy," of a file record, located in a file module or frame separate from the primary copy. Duplicate records are set up to guard against loss of critical files and data.

End of Message

A character or set of characters indicating the termination of a message.

Entry

An input received from a terminal device. On receipt, an entry is placed by the Control Program in an "entry block" whose address is inserted in a list of entries awaiting processing. Words sometime used synonymously: action, input, inquiry, message, transaction.

Entry Block

A block of main memory storage assigned on receipt of each entry into a system and associated with that entry throughout its life in the system.

Execute

To carry out an instruction or to perform a routine.

Executive Routine

That portion of a program which controls the execution of other routines.

Fallback

A processing condition in which special computer or manual procedures must be employed as a complete or partial substitute for a malfunctioning system. Fallback procedures may be invoked anywhere between complete system availability and total system failure.

Feedback

That part of the output of a machine, process, or system used as input for another phase, especially for self-correcting purposes. A feedback system is continually comparing its output with its input and making corrections. If closed loop, the feedback system is self-correcting.

FIELD

A set of one or more bits or characters treated as a unit of information.

FIFO

First-in, first-out. Sometimes used to describe one method of taking items from a list.

FILE

An organized collection of information directed toward some purpose, for example, a file of savings accounts or airline passenger names.

FILE EVENT

A single-file access, either reading or writing. The processing of an action usually requires one or more file events.

FILE MAINTENANCE

The processing of a file to effect changes in the file, for example, updating a master file. Cycling of a file is a form of file maintenance.

FILE-ORIENTED SYSTEM

A system in which references to file storage are of prime importance. Such auxiliary storage is essential in most commercial systems and incidental in most scientific systems.

FINE INDEX

The lower level index of a pair of indexes used to locate a particular file record, the higher level index being designated the "gross" index.

FLOW CHART

A chart to represent, for a program, the flow of data and the sequence of arithmetic and logical operations that must be included in the program.

FOREGROUND PROCESSING

High-priority processing, usually resulting from real-time entries, given precedence by means of interrupts over lower priority "background" processing.

FUNCTIONAL REQUIREMENT

A document, prepared by application analysts, detailing one of the functions to be performed by a system and, when appropriate, the manner in which the function will be accomplished. Functional requirements provide a basis for:

- Obtaining management approval of policy and procedure changes to facilitate system integration
- Guiding and assisting individuals preparing program specifications
- Preparing instruction manuals for personnel who will use and operate the system

Go Ahead

A polling signal sent from the computer to a terminal, or from one terminal down-line to another, directing the terminal to begin transmission to the computer.

Gross Index

The first of a pair of indexes consulted to locate a particular record, the secondary index being a "fine" index.

Half-Duplex Channel

A channel capable of transmitting and receiving signals, but in only one direction at a time.

Hard Copy

A printed copy of machine output in readable form for human beings, for example, reports, listings, documents, summaries.

Header

A file record containing common, constant, or identifying information for a group of records that follow.

The first part of a message, containing all necessary information for directing the message to its destination.

Host Computer

A computer to which a stored-program multiplexor is connected and upon which the multiplexor is dependent for certain vital functions such as program read-in. In such a configuration, the multiplexor may or may not have stand-alone capability in the event the host computer is unavailable.

Housekeeping

Operations that do not contribute directly to the solution of the problem but are necessary to the operation of the system.

INDEX
> A table of computer words or fields containing addresses of records located in file storage. There may, for example, be inventory indexes used to obtain inventory master records.

INFORMATION
> The meaning given to data by the conventions used in its representation.

INFORMATION RETRIEVAL
> That branch of computer technology concerned with techniques for storing and searching large quantities of information. An information retrieval system may or may not be a real-time system.

IN-LINE PROCESSING
> A method of processing in which each individual input action is completely processed and all pertinent records updated without previously having been batched or grouped. In this sense, a real-time system may or may not be an in-line system.

IN-PLANT SYSTEM
> A data handling system confined to one building or a number of buildings in one locality.

INPUT
> Information transferred from terminals or auxiliary storage into main memory storage.

INQUIRY
> A request for information from storage, for example, a request for a display of the number of available airline seats or for the initiation of a search of library records.

INSTRUCTION
> A set of identifying characters designed to cause a computer to perform a certain operation.

INTEGRATED DATA PROCESSING
> Information processing organized, directed, and carried out according to a system approach that gives recognition to the interrelated aspects of various applications.

INTERFACE
> A common boundary, for example, the boundary between two subsystems or two devices.

INTERRUPT

A break in the normal flow of a system or routine such that the flow can be resumed from that point at a later time. An interrupt is usually caused by a signal from an external source.

INTERVAL TIMER

A counting device operating in a computer system in such a way that should it fail to be reset by the computer program within a prescribed period, an audible alarm will be sounded.

ITEM

A small unit of related data.

JOB-ORIENTED TERMINAL

A terminal designed for a particular application.

LINKAGE

A technique for providing interconnections between two real-time programs or program segments.

LIST

See WAITING LIST and QUEUEING ANALYSIS.

LOCATION

A place in main memory or auxiliary storage where a unit of data may be stored or retrieved.

LOGICAL RECORD

A record whose length is governed by the nature of the information that it contains rather than by some feature or limitation of the storage device that holds it. Logical records usually differ in size from the "physical" records in which they are contained. In an airline system, a 500-character physical record size might be established as standard for each passenger's record, although most logical records for an individual passenger would require more or fewer than 500 characters.

LOOP

A coding technique in which a group of instructions is repeated, usually with modification of some instructions or data values.

A communication channel connecting a subscriber to a central exchange.

LOOP, CENTRAL PROCESSING UNIT (CPU)

The main routine of a Control Program and that which concerns itself with control of the internal status of the processing unit, in contrast to those control program routines concerned with terminals and file storage input/output.

MACRO INSTRUCTION

A machine-like symbolic language statement that can produce a variable number of machine instructions.

MASTER FILE

A main reference file, for example, a set of flight/date seat inventory records.

MASTER/SLAVE SYSTEM

A system configuration for scientific usage in which one computer, usually of medium size, exercises complete control over all input/output and schedules and transmits jobs to the slave computer, usually one with great capability, which performs the computations as directed by the master.

MEMORY

An organization of storage elements, primarily for the retrieval of information; examples are magnetic core memory, drum memory, relay memory. The rapid-access storage elements from which instructions are executed and data operated on are referred to as main memory.

MEMORY PROTECTION

A means of assuring, with special hardware, that the contents of main memory within certain specified but variable bounds will not be destroyed or altered. Memory-protection devices help guard a real-time system against the effects of equipment malfunctions and program bugs.

MESSAGE

A transmitted series of words or symbols intended to convey information. As used in message switching, a message consists of header, text, and an end of message symbol.

MESSAGE ROUTING

The function of selecting the route, or alternate route if required, by which a message will proceed to its destination.

MESSAGE SWITCHING

The technique of receiving a message, storing it until the proper outgoing circuit is available, and then retransmitting it to its destination.

MICROWAVE

An electromagnetic wave in the super-high-frequency radio spectrum ranging from 1000 to 300,000 megacycles per second.

MODEL, MATHEMATICAL

A collection of equations that represent mathematically what goes on in a process, that is, a mathematical description of the process.

MODEM

Contraction of modulator-demodulator.

MODE OF OPERATION

A method of operation, for example, fallback mode, training mode, off-line mode.

MODULARITY

A consideration in the design of equipment and programming subsystems. A system has modularity when its hardware and software components can be readily identified, altered, or augmented.

MODULATION

The process by which some characteristic of one wave is varied in accordance with another wave. This technique is used to make business-machine signals compatible with communication facilities.

MONITOR

A program to schedule and control the operation of several unrelated routines and machine runs so that the computer and computer time are used advantageously. A monitor program may or may not be designed to operate in real time.

MULTIPLE ADDRESS MESSAGE

A message to be delivered to more than one destination.

MULTIPLEXING

The division of a transmission facility into two or more channels.

MULTIPLEXOR

A specialized computer, with stored program capability, for handling the input/output functions of a real-time system.

MULTIPOINT CIRCUIT

A circuit interconnecting several stations that must communicate on a time-shared basis.

MULTIPROCESSING SYSTEM

A system configuration containing two or more interconnected computers but which perform functionally or geographically specialized processing tasks.

MULTIPROCESSOR

A computer with multiple arithmetic and logic units for simultaneous use.

MULTIPROGRAMMING

A technique for handling several programs simultaneously by overlapping or interleaving their execution. Many real-time systems are multiprogrammed.

NETWORK

A series of points interconnected by telephone or telegraph channels.

NETWORK AWARENESS

A condition in which the central processor is cognizant of the status of the network.

NOISE

Meaningless extra bits or words that must be ignored or removed from data.

OFF-LINE PROCESSING

Processing not directly associated with or required for real-time communication and control. In an off-line mode of operation, human intervention is required between data origination and ultimate data processing.

On-Line Processing

Operation of terminals, files, or other auxiliary devices under direct control of the central processor. An on-line processing system eliminates the need for human intervention between input origination and computer processing.

Open-Loop System

A system in which the computer does not directly control a process but instead displays or prints out information for the operator to assist him in determining and taking appropriate action. Most real-time commercial systems are, therefore, open-loop systems.

Operational Program

A program responsible for accomplishing substantive data processing tasks within a real-time environment. An Operational Program is activated and supervised by the Control Program to perform application-oriented processing such as selling airline space and updating deposit balances.

Out-Plant System

A data transmission system consisting of one or more terminals located at some distance from the processing center.

Perforated Paper Tape

A strip of paper on which characters are represented by combinations of punched holes.

Physical Record

A storage record of a standard and predetermined length. Records comprising logical files in the system, such as the records that form an inventory file, do not necessarily correspond in size to these physical records. Nevertheless, such logical records must be fitted into standard-sized physical records for ease of storage control and for processing convenience.

Pilot System

A collection of file records and supporting data, obtained from the actual operations of a business over an extended period and used to conduct a realistic system test by closely simulating the operational environment.

POLL
> A flexible, systematic method, centrally controlled, for permitting stations on a multipoint circuit to transmit without contending for the line.

PRIORITY
> The sequence in which various entries and jobs will be processed by the real-time system, as determined by program analysis of action codes and other priority-level indicators.

PRIVATE LINE
> A channel or circuit furnished a subscriber for his exclusive use.

PROCESS
> A generic computational term that may include computing, assembly, compilation, generation, editing, updating, and so forth.

PROCESS CONTROL SYSTEM
> A system whose purpose is to provide automation of continuous operations.

PROGRAM
> A group of related instructions fulfilling the requirements stated in a program specification.
>
> To plan the method of attack for a specified problem.

PROGRAM PACKAGE
> A collection of logically related Operational Program segments, for example, all those having to do with the processing of a certain type of inquiry.

PROGRAM READ-IN
> A means of procuring, by means of either hardware or software, programs that do not normally reside in main memory and that must, therefore, be read in from auxiliary storage when needed for current processing. Program read-in techniques are required in any system that cannot retain all computer instructions in main memory at the same time.

PROGRAM SEGMENT
> Computer instructions blocked into groups of an arbitrarily fixed size. Programs are segmented to fit into standard-sized areas of main or auxiliary memory in order to facilitate memory allocation and program read-in.

Program Specification

A precise definition of the logic and scope of the processing functions to be performed by a particular program. Program specifications may be based on less-detailed information contained in preliminary technical planning documents and functional requirements.

Push-Down List

A list of items where the last item entered becomes the first item of the list, and the relative position of the other items is pushed back one.

Push-Up List

A list of items where each item is entered at the end of the list, and the other items maintain their same relative position in the list.

Queueing Analysis

A study of the patterns involved and time required for discrete units to move through channels, for example, the elapsed time for auto traffic at a toll booth or for employees in a cafeteria line. Queueing analysis is employed to estimate the lengths of waiting lists of entries awaiting processing in those real-time systems that experience work-load peaks.

Random Access Storage

A storage medium in which the time required to obtain information is independent of the location of the information most recently obtained. This definition should be qualified by the observation that what is usually meant is *relatively* random. Thus, magnetic disks are relatively nonrandom access devices when compared to magnetic core or drum, but random when compared to magnetic tape.

Randomizing Scheme

A method of planning the distribution of file records among several file storage modules so that the accesses to these records will be evenly distributed and the waiting times for file information equalized.

READ
> To transfer information from any input device to main memory or auxiliary storage.

REAL-TIME CHANNEL
> Equipment that provides the interface between the termination of communication lines and the computer memory. A real-time channel performs the same basic function as a multiplexor but has more limited storage capacity and does not have stored program capability.

REAL-TIME CLOCK
> A real-time clock furnishes the computer with readable digits or periodic signals to permit computation of elapsed time between events and to trigger the performance of time-initiated processing.

REAL-TIME OPERATION
> Paralleling data processing with a physical process in such a fashion that the results of the data processing are immediately useful to the physical operation.

RECORD
> A group of related facts or fields of information treated as a unit. *See also* LOGICAL RECORD and PHYSICAL RECORD.

RECORD BLOCK
> A storage area of fixed size in main memory or file storage. Storage is organized into such standard blocks to permit more flexible storage allocation and control. Sometimes called a "physical" record.

RECORD READY
> A signal from a file access mechanism to the computer that a record whose address was previously provided by a Seek command has now been located and may be read into memory.

RECURSION
> The continued repetition of the same operation or group of operations.

RELOCATABLE PROGRAM
> A routine whose instructions are written in such a way that it can be located and executed in various areas of memory. This may involve modification, before execution, of instructions originally coded relative to a fixed starting place in

memory. Relocatable programs permit highly flexible real-time utilization of main memory.

REMOTE DEBUGGING

Use of remote terminals in a mode suitable for testing of programs, most frequently found in systems devoted to scientific or engineering computation.

REPEATER

A device used to amplify or reshape communication signals.

REPERFORATOR

A device that automatically punches a paper tape from received signals.

RESPONSE

Central processor acknowledgment of a terminal entry. Such a response might consist of a light display, a printout, or merely a carriage return.

RESPONSE TIME

The amount of time elapsed between generation of an inquiry at a terminal and receipt of a response at the terminal. Response time, thus defined, includes:

- Transmission time to the computer
- Processing time at the computer
- Access time to obtain any file records needed to answer the inquiry
- Transmission time back to the terminal

RETRIEVE

To find and select specific information, especially a record from file storage.

ROUTINE

A sequence of machine instructions that carry out a well-defined function; a program or part of a program.

ROUTING

Assignment of the communication path by which a message or response will reach its destination.

ROUTING INDICATOR

An address, or a group of directing characters in the header of a message, defining the circuit or terminal to which a message has to be delivered.

SAMPLING

A technique of systems analysis whereby traffic volumes, file activity, and so forth, are estimated based on a representative sample.

A method of communication line control whereby messages on a circuit are sampled by a computer that selects only those for which computer processing is required.

SCAN

To examine stored information for a specific purpose—for content, for arrangement.

To examine the status of communication lines or other input/output channels to determine whether data is being received or transmitted.

SCIENTIFIC SYSTEM

A system devoted primarily to computation, in contrast to a commercial or data processing system where the main emphasis is on file updating rather than the performance of calculations.

SELECTIVE CALLING

The ability of a transmitting station to specify which of several stations is to receive a message.

SENSOR

A device that permits a computer to obtain analog information concerning temperatures, flows, pressures, and so forth.

SEQUENCER

A device or program in a process control system that establishes the order in which input is obtained and operated upon.

SHARED-FILE SYSTEM

A system configuration in which two computers have access to the same file storage device, though not necessarily at the same time.

SIGNATURE

The portion of a message that identifies the originator.

SIMPLEX CHANNEL

A channel that permits transmission in one direction only.

SIMPLEX SYSTEM

> A system configuration that does not include standby equipment.

SIMULATOR

> A program or routine corresponding to a mathematical model or representing a physical model.
>
> A routine that runs on one computer and imitates the operations of some other computer system or subsystem.

SINGLE-ADDRESS MESSAGE

> A message to be delivered to only one destination.

SNAPSHOT

> A dynamic printout of selected data in storage at various break points and check points during a computing operation.

SPECIFICATION

> In an equipment sense, a technical or engineering description of the hardware. In programming, a precise definition of the records and programs needed to carry out a particular processing function.

STAND-ALONE CAPABILITY

> A multiplexor designed to function independent of a host computer, either all of the time or some of the time.

STANDARD

> An approved criterion or established requirement for controlling the technical performance and practices of programmers and others responsible for system integration. Such standards must be carefully written, thoughtfully reviewed, and widely distributed in order to be of maximum effectiveness.

STANDBY COMPUTER

> The computer in a dual or duplex system that is waiting to take over the real-time processing burden whenever the need arises.

STORAGE

> A general term for any device capable of retaining information.

STORE-AND-FORWARD

A type of message-switching system.

STUNT BOX

A device to control nonprinting functions of a teletype terminal.

SUBROUTINE

See ROUTINE.

SUBSET

A modulation/demodulation device designed to make business-machine signals compatible with communication facilities and vice versa.

SUPERVISOR ROUTINE

An executive routine.

SWITCH

A device that can alter flow. Switches may be activated manually or under program control.

SWITCHING CENTER

A location where an incoming message is automatically or manually directed to one or more outgoing circuits according to intelligence contained in the message.

SWITCHOVER

The act of transferring the real-time processing work load from one computer or multiplexor to another in a duplex system. In some systems, switchover must be initiated manually; in others, it is automatic.

SYSTEM

A collection of operations and procedures united to accomplish a specific objective. A real-time data processing system consists of equipment and program subsystems.

TANDEM SYSTEM

A system configuration in which data proceeds through one processor into another. Systems with multiplexors and master/slave systems are examples of tandem processing.

TAPE

A medium for storing information that can be used as computer input/output, that is, perforated paper tape or magnetic tape. Use of magnetic tape as the primary storage medium is less common in real-time systems than in others, because of the relatively slow access time for any particular record stored on magnetic tape.

TARIFF

The published rate for a specific unit of equipment, facility, or type of service provided by a communication common carrier.

TELECOMMUNICATION

Any transmission or reception of signals, writing, sounds, or intelligence of any nature by wire, radio, or visual or other electromagnetic means. Often used interchangeably with communication.

TELEMETER

To transmit digital or analog data by radio waves; for example, data can be telemetered from a missile and recorded at a ground station.

TELEPRINTER

Trade name used by Western Union to refer specifically to telegraph page printers.

TELE-PROCESSING ®

An IBM registered term denoting systems that transmit data from one point to another in the course of processing.

TELETYPE

Trademark of the Teletype Corporation. Usually refers to a series of different types of equipment such as transmitters, tape punches, reperforators, page printers, utilized for communication systems.

TELETYPEWRITER

Trade name used by A. T. & T. to refer specifically to telegraph page printers.

TELETYPEWRITER EXCHANGE SERVICE (TWX)

A semiautomatic switching service provided by A. T. & T. for interconnecting public Teletypewriter subscribers.

TELEX

An automatic-switching service provided by Western Union for interconnecting public Teleprinter subscribers.

TELPAK
> A tariff offered by A. T. & T. for the leasing of wide band channels.

TERMINAL
> A point at which information can enter or leave a communication network.
>
> An input/output device designed to receive source data in an environment associated with the job to be performed, and capable of transmitting entries to and obtaining output from the system of which it is a part.

TERMINAL INTERCHANGE
> A buffering device at a location remote from the processing center. Such a device provides temporary storage for messages originating at the terminals that it serves and at the processing center.

TEXT
> That part of the message which contains the substantive information to be conveyed.

THROUGHPUT CAPACITY
> The rate at which data can be transmitted by a computer to a terminal or auxiliary storage device through a connecting channel.

TIE LINE
> A leased communication channel or circuit.

TIME-ORIENTED PROGRAM
> A program whose execution is initiated not because of external demand but because either extra processing time is available or the system design requires that the program be initiated at a particular time.

TIME-SHARED SYSTEM
> A system in which available central computer time is shared among several jobs as dictated by a scheduling formula or algorithm.

TORN-TAPE SWITCHING CENTER
> A location where operators tear off incoming printed and punched paper tape and transfer it manually to the proper outgoing circuit.

TOTAL SYSTEM

An approach to system design with the objective of placing all significant operational components of an organization under total or partial control by computers. Real-time system configurations, with their immediacy of data collection, processing, and generation, are well adapted to this total system concept. *See also* INTEGRATED SYSTEM.

TRACK

That portion of a moving-type storage medium—film, drum, tape, or disk—which is accessible to a given reading station.

TRANSACTION

A grouping of several related actions entered by a terminal operator. In an airline reservation system, the sale of a seat on one flight would be an action, and the sale of an itinerary including several different flights for the same passenger would be a transaction.

TRANSMIT

To communicate information from one terminal or storage medium to another.

TRAP

See INTERRUPT.

TRUNK

A channel connecting two switching centers or a switching center with a single terminal.

TURNAROUND TIME

The amount of time required for a computation job to get from the programmer to the computing center, onto the machine for a test or production run, and back to the programmer in the form of results. Slow turnaround time is a severe problem in many scientific installations where a large number of "one-shot" programs must be tested and run.

TWX

See TELETYPEWRITER EXCHANGE SERVICE.

VOICE GRADE CHANNEL

A channel suitable for transmission of speech, digital or analog data, or facsimile.

WAIT

The condition a real-time program will encounter whenever it requires information from file storage. The program must experience a wait while the required file record is accessed and brought into main memory. It is this characteristic of file-oriented systems that leads to a multiprogrammed approach in order to attain greater efficiency by overlapping wait time for one program with process time for another that is not waiting.

WAITING LIST

A means of organizing and controlling data awaiting processing by various Operational Programs. Waiting lists are normally maintained by the Control Program.

WATS

See WIDE AREA TELEPHONE SERVICE.

WIDE AREA TELEPHONE SERVICE

A service provided by A. T. & T. which provides a special tie line allowing the subscriber to make unlimited calls to any location in a specific zone on a direct-distance dialing basis for a flat monthly charge.

INDEX

INDEX